P9-DMM-004

Teach Yourself C

Teach Yourself C

Herbert Schildt

Osborne McGraw-Hill

Berkeley New York St. Louis San Francisco
Auckland Bogatá Hamburg London Madrid
Mexico City Milan Montreal New Delhi Panama City
Paris São Paulo Singapore Sydney
Tokyo Toronto

Osborne **McGraw-Hill**
2600 Tenth Street
Berkeley, California 94710
U.S.A.

For information on translations and book distributors outside of the U.S.A., please write to Osborne **McGraw-Hill** at the above address.

FORTH is a registered trademark of FORTH, Inc. IBM is a registered trademark of International Business Machines Corp. DEC is a trademark of Digital Equipment Corp. QuickC is a trademark of Microsoft Corp. Turbo C is a registered trademark of Borland International, Inc. UNIX and UNIX C are registered trademarks of AT&T.

Teach Yourself C

Copyright © 1990 by McGraw-Hill, Inc. All rights reserved. Printed in the United States of America. Except as permitted under the Copyright Act of 1976, no part of this publication may be reproduced or distributed in any form or by any means, or stored in a database or retrieval system, without the prior written permission of the publisher, with the exception that the program listings may be entered, stored, and executed in a computer system, but they may not be reproduced for publication.

5 6 7 8 9 0   DOC/DOC   9 9 8 7 6 5 4 3 2 1 0

ISBN 881596-7

Acquisitions Editor: Steve Hom
Technical Editor: Eric Geyer
Copy Editor: Paul Medoff
Word Processors: Bonnie Bozorg, Judy Koplan
Proofreader: Barbara Conway
Technical Illustration: Judy Wohlfrom
Production Supervisor: Kevin Shafer

This book was produced using Ventura Version 2.

Information has been obtained by Osborne McGraw-Hill from sources believed to be reliable. However, because of the possibility of human or mechanical error by our sources, Osborne McGraw-Hill, or others, Osborne McGraw-Hill does not guarantee the accuracy, adequacy, or completeness of any information and is not responsible for any errors or omissions or the results obtained from the use of such information.

•Contents at a Glance•

•Contents•

2

Introducing C's Program Control Statements

42

3

More C Program Control Statements

74

A Closer Look at Data Types, Variables, and Expressions   114

4

Exploring Arrays and Strings   148

5

6

7

Console I/O 8

File I/O 9

10 Structures and Unions 330

11 Advanced Data Types and Operators 372

•Introduction•

C is one of the most sought after computer programming languages. The reason for this is simple: Programmers like it. Once a person learns to program in C, it is very uncommon for him or her to switch to another language. C combines subtlety and elegance with raw power and flexibility. It is a structured language that does not confine. C also is a language that puts you, the programmer, firmly in charge. C was created by a programmer for programmers. It is not the contrived product of a committee, but rather the outcome of programmers looking for a better language.

C was invented and first implemented by Dennis Ritchie on a DEC PDP-11 using the UNIX operating system. C is the result of a development process that started with an older language called BCPL, developed by Martin Richards. BCPL influenced a language called B, which was invented by Ken Thompson, and which led to the development of C in the 1970s.

For many years, the de facto standard for C was the one described in *The C Programming Language* by Brian Kernighan and Dennis Ritchie (Englewood Cliffs, NJ: Prentice-Hall, 1978). However, as C grew in popularity, a committee was organized in 1983 to create an ANSI standard for C. At the time of this writing, the standard is complete and awaiting final approval. Virtually all C compilers already comply with the standard and the version of C you will learn in this book is based on that standard.

C is often referred to as a *middle-level language*. Before C there were basically two types of languages used to program computers. One is called *assembly language*, which is the symbolic representation of the actual machine instructions executed by the computer. Assembly language is a *low-level language* because the programmer is working (in symbolic form) with the actual instructions that the computer will execute. Also, assembly language provides no control structures. By contrast, a *high-level language* buffers the programmer from the computer. A high-level language typically supplies various control structures, input and output commands, and the like, which make programming easier and faster. The elements of a high-level language may not relate very directly to the way the computer ultimately carries out the program. This separation often causes programs written using a high-level language to be less efficient than those written in assembly language. Because many people find assembly language programming to be an arduous task, there was a need for a language that could be used more easily and at the same time provide nearly the same efficiency as assembly language. This is one reason that C was initially designed. It successfully combines the structure of a high-level language with the power and efficiency of assembly language.

Initially, C was used primarily for creating *systems software*. Systems software consists of those programs that help run the computer. This includes such programs as operating systems, compilers, and editors. However, as C gained in popularity, it began to be used for general-purpose programming. Today C is used by programmers for virtually any programming task. It is a language that has survived the test of time and proven itself to be as versatile as it is powerful.

About This Book

This book is unique because it teaches you the C language by applying *Mastery Learning Theory*. Mastery Learning presents one idea at a time. It uses numerous examples and exercises to help you master each topic before moving on.

The material is presented sequentially. Therefore, work carefully through the chapters; each one assumes that you know the material presented in all preceding chapters.

This book teaches ANSI standard C. This ensures that your knowledge will be applicable to the widest range of C environments. The book also uses contemporary syntax and structure, which means that you will be learning the right way to write C programs from the very beginning.

How This Book Is Organized

This book is made up of 12 chapters and 3 appendixes. Each chapter (except Chapter 1) begins with a *Skills Check*, which consists of questions and exercises covering the previous chapter's material. The chapters are divided into sections. Each section covers one topic. At the end of each section are examples followed by exercises that test your mastery of the topic. At the end of each chapter, you will find a *Mastery Skills Check*, which checks your knowledge of the material in the chapter. Finally, each chapter presents an *Integrating New Skills Check*, which tests how well you are integrating new material with that presented in earlier chapters.

Conventions Used in This Book

Whenever a part of a program (such as a variable name) is referenced in text, it is indicated by boldface type. Whenever a general form is referenced in text, it is indicated by italic type.

Additional Help from Osborne/McGraw-Hill

Osborne/McGraw-Hill provides top-quality books for computer users at every level of computing experience. To help you build your skills, we suggest that you look for the books in the following Osborne series that best address your needs.

The "Teach Yourself" series is perfect for people who have never used a computer before or who want to gain confidence in using program basics. These books provide a simple, slow-paced introduction to the fundamental uses of popular software packages and programming languages. The "Mastery Skills Check" format ensures you understand concepts thoroughly before you progress to new material. Plenty of examples and exercises (with answers at the back of the book) are used throughout the text.

The "Made Easy" series is also for beginners or users who may need a refresher on the new features of an upgraded product. These in-depth introductions guide users step-by-step from the program basics to intermediate-level usage. Plenty of "hands-on" exercises and examples are used in every chapter.

The "Using" series presents fast-paced guides that cover beginning concepts quickly and move on to intermediate-level techniques and some advanced topics. These books are written for users already familiar with computers and software and who want to get up to speed fast with a certain product.

The "Advanced" series assumes that the reader is a user with at least an intermediate skill level and is ready to learn more sophisticated techqniques and refinements.

"The Complete Reference" series provides handy desktop references for popular software and programming languages that list every command, feature, and function of the product along with brief but detailed descriptions of how they are used. These books are fully indexed and often include tear-out command cards. "The Complete Reference" series is ideal for both beginners and pros.

"The Pocket Reference" series is a pocket-sized, shorter version of "The Complete Reference" series. It provides the essential commands, features, and functions of software and programming languages for users of every level who need a quick reminder.

The "Secrets, Solutions, Shortcuts" series is written for beginning users who are already somewhat familiar with the software and for experienced users at intermediate and advanced levels. This series provides clever tips and points out shortcuts for using the software to greater advantage and indicates traps to avoid.

Osborne/McGraw-Hill also publishes many fine books that are not included in the series described here. If you have questions about which Osborne books are right for you, ask the salesperson at your local book or computer store, or call us toll-free at 1-800-262-4729.

Other Osborne/McGraw-Hill Books Of Interest to You

We hope that *Teach Yourself C* will assist you in mastering this popular programming langauge and will also encourage you to learn more about other ways to better use your computer.

If you're interested in expanding your skills so you can be even more computer efficient, be sure to take advantage of Osborne/M-H's large selection of top-quality computer books covering all varieties of popular hardware, software, programming languages, and operating systems. While we cannot list every title here that may relate to C and to your special computing needs, here are just a few related books that complement *Teach Yourself C.*

UNIX Made Easy is a step-by-step, in-depth introduction to UNIX that guides beginners to intermediate-level skills with the operating system developed by AT&T.

If you're looking for an intermediate-level book, see *Using UNIX System V Release 3,* a fast-paced, hands-on guide that quickly covers basics and then discusses intermediate techniques and some advanced topics. If you're using UNIX System V Release 2, see *A User Guide to the UNIX System, Second Edition.*

For all UNIX users of System V Release 3.1 (from beginners who are somewhat familiar with the operating system to veteran users), see *UNIX: The Complete Reference,* the ideal desktop resource that discusses every command, as well as text processing, editing, programming, communications, the Shell, and the UNIX file system.

Disk Offer

There are many useful and interesting functions and programs contained in this book. If you're like me, you probably would like to use them but hate typing them into the computer. When I key in routines from a book it always seems that I type something wrong and spend hours trying to get the program to work. For this reason, I am offering the source code on disk for all the functions and programs contained in this book for $24.95. Just fill in the order blank on the next page and mail it, along with your payment, to the address shown. Or, if you're in a hurry, just call (217) 586-4021 (the number of my consulting office) and place your order by telephone (VISA and MasterCard accepted).

Please send me _____ copies, at $24.95 each, of the source code to the programs in *Teach Yourself C*. Foreign orders, please add $5 shipping and handling.

_____
Name

_____
Address

_____ _____ _____
City   State   ZIP

_____
Telephone

Disk size (check one): 5 1/4" _____ 3 1/2"_____
Method of payment: check_____ VISA_____ MC_____
Credit card number:

_____
Expiration date:

_____
Signature:

_____

Send to:
Herbert Schildt
RR 1, Box 130
Mahomet, Il 61853

or phone: (217) 586-4021

This offer subject to change or cancellation at any time.

This is solely the offering of the author. Osborne McGraw-Hill takes no responsibility for the fulfillment of this offer. Please allow four to six weeks for delivery.

•Why This Book Is for You•

If you want to learn to program in C, this book is for you. It assumes that you have no previous programming experience. However, if you can already program in another language, you will be able to move along more quickly.

This book teaches you to program in ANSI Standard C. This means that you will be able to use this book with virtually any C compiler. This book focuses on style and structure from the start; by the time you finish, you will be writing professional-looking programs.

Computer programming is learned best by doing. Towards this end, this book contains numerous examples and exercises that you can work through. When you complete the book, you can definitely call yourself a C programmer.

Learn More About C

Here is an excellent selection of other Osborne/McGraw-Hill books on C that will help you build your skills and maximize the power of the programming language you have selected.

ANSI C Made Easy is a thorough, step-by-step introduction to the ANSI standard of the C programming language. Plenty of clear examples and hands-on exercises that facilitate both quick and lasting comprehension are included. This book guides you from beginning to intermediate-level programming.

Using C++ covers beginning concepts to intermediate-level techniques, as well as some advanced programming topics. You'll find out all about the object-oriented version of C that's the talk of programmers everywhere.

C: The Complete Reference, now available in a second edition that covers ANSI C, is for all C programmers, from beginners who are somewhat familiar with the language to veteran C programmers. This comprehensive reference discusses C basics as well as C library functions by category, algorithms, C applications, the programming environment, and C's latest direction—C++.

If you're an experienced C programmer, *Advanced C, Second Edition* explores more sophisticated ANSI C topics such as dynamic allocation and interfacing to assembly language routines and the operating system.

CHAPTER OBJECTIVES

1.1 Understand the components of a C program

1.2 Create and compile a program

1.3 Declare variables and assign values

1.4 Input numbers from the keyboard

1.5 Perform calculations using arithmetic expressions

1.6 Add comments to a program

1.7 Write your own functions

1.8 Use functions to return values

1.9 Use function arguments

1.10 Remember the C keywords

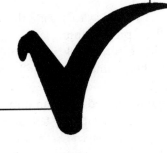

·1·
C Fundamentals

The individual elements of a computer language such as C do not stand alone, but rather in conjunction with one another. Therefore, it is necessary to understand several key aspects of C before examining each element of the language in detail. To this end, this chapter presents a quick overview of the C language. Its goal is to give you sufficient working knowledge of C so that you can understand the examples in later chapters.

As you work through this chapter, don't worry if a few points are not entirely clear. The main thing you need to understand is how and why the example programs execute as they do. Keep in mind that most of the topics introduced in this chapter will be discussed in greater detail later in this book. In this chapter, you will learn about the basic structure of a C program; what a C statement is; and what variables, constants, and functions are. You will learn how to display text on the screen and input information from the keyboard.

To use this book completely, you must have a computer, a C compiler, and a text editor. Your compiler may include its own text editor, in which case you won't need a separate one. For the best results, you should work along with the examples and try the exercises.

1.1 UNDERSTAND THE COMPONENTS OF A C PROGRAM

All C programs share certain essential components and traits. All C programs consist of one or more *functions*, each of which contains one or more *statements*. In C, a function is a named subroutine that can be called by other parts of the program. Functions are the building blocks of C. A statement specifies an action to be performed by the program. In other words, statements are the parts of your program that actually perform operations. Statements are contained within functions.

All C statements end with a semicolon. C does not recognize the end of the line as a terminator. This means there are no constraints on the position of statements within a line. Also, you may place two or more statements on one line.

The simplest form of a C function is shown here.

```
function-name( )
{
    statement sequence
}
```

where *function-name* is the name of the function and the *statement sequence* may be one or more statements. (Technically, a function can contain no statements, but since this means that the function performs no action, it is a degenerative case.) With few exceptions, you can call a function by any name you like. But, it must be comprised of only the upper- and lowercase letters of the alphabet, the digits 0-9, and the underscore. C is *case-sensitive*, which means that C recognizes the difference between upper- and lowercase letters. Thus, as far as C is concerned, **Myfunc** and **myfunc** are entirely different names.

Although a C program may contain several functions, the only function that it *must* have is **main ( )**. The **main( )** function is the function at which execution of your program begins. That is, when your program begins running, it starts executing the statements inside the **main( )** function, beginning with the first statement after the opening curly brace. Execution of your program terminates when (conceptually) the closing curly brace is reached. (The actual curly brace does not exist in the compiled version of your program, but it is helpful to think of it in this way.)

Throughout this book, when a function is referred to in text, it will be printed in bold and followed by parentheses. This way, you can see immediately that the name refers to a function, not some other part of the program.

Another important component of all C programs is *library functions*. The ANSI C standard specifies a minimal set of library functions to be supplied by all C compilers, which your program may use. This collection of functions is usually referred to as the *C standard library*. The standard library contains functions to perform disk I/O (input/output), string manipulations, mathematics, and much more. When your program is compiled, the code for library functions is automatically added to your program. In most other computer languages, like BASIC or Pascal, these functions are built into the language. The advantage of having them as library functions is increased flexibility. As you will see, virtually all C programs you create will use functions from the C standard library.

One of the most common library functions is called **printf( )**. This is C's general-purpose output function. Although **printf( )** is quite versatile, its simplest form is

printf("*string-to-output*");

The **printf( )** function outputs the characters that are contained between the beginning and ending double quotes to the screen. (The double quotes are not displayed on the screen.) In C, one or more characters enclosed between double quotes is called a *string*. The quoted string between **printf( )**'s parentheses is said to be an *argument* to **printf( )**. In general, information passed to a function is called an argument. In C, calling a library function is a statement; therefore, it must end with a semicolon.

To call a function, you specify its name followed by a parenthesized list of arguments that you will be passing to it. If the function does not require any arguments, no arguments will be specified—and the parenthesized list will be empty. If there is more than one argument, the arguments must be separated by commas.

Another component common to most C programs is the *header file*. In C, information about the standard library functions is found in various files supplied with your compiler. The files all end with a .H extension. The C compiler uses the information in these files to handle the library functions properly. You add these files to your program using the **#include** compiler *preprocessor directive*. All C compilers use as their first phase of compilation a *preprocessor*, which performs various manipulations on your source file before it is actually compiled. Preprocessor directives are not actually part of the C language, but rather instructions from you to the compiler. The **#include** directive tells the preprocessor to read in another file and include it with your program. You will learn more about the preprocessor later in this book. The most commonly required header file is called STDIO.H. This directive includes this file.

```
#include "stdio.h"
```

You can specify the file name in either upper- or lowercase, but lowercase is the traditional method. The STDIO.H header file contains, among other things, information related to the **printf( )** library function. Notice that the **#include** directive does not end with a semicolon. The reason for this is that **#include** is not a C keyword that can define a statement. Instead, it is an instruction to the C compiler itself.

One last point: With few exceptions, C ignores spaces. That is, it doesn't care where on a line a statement, curly brace, or function name occurs. If you like, you can even put two or more of these items on the same line. The examples you will see in this book reflect the way C code is normally written; it is a form you should follow. The actual positioning of statements, functions, and braces, however, is a stylistic, not a programming, decision.

Examples

1. Since all C programs share certain common traits, understanding one program will help you understand many others. One of the simplest C programs is shown here.

```
#include "stdio.h"
main( )
{
   printf("This is a short C program.");
}
```

When compiled and executed, this program displays the message **This is a short C program** on the screen of your computer.

Even though this program is only five lines long, it illustrates those aspects common to all C programs. Let's examine it line by line.

The first line of the program is

```
#include "stdio.h"
```

It causes the file STDIO.H to be read by the C compiler and to be included with the program. This file contains information related to **printf( )**.

The second line,

```
main( )
```

begins the **main( )** function. As stated earlier, all C programs must have a **main( )** function. This is where program execution begins.

After **main( )** is an opening curly brace. This marks the beginning of statements that make up the function.

The next line in the program is

```
printf("This is a short C program.");
```

This is a C statement. It calls the standard library function, **printf( )**, which causes the string to be displayed. Finally, the program ends when the closing curly brace is encountered.

2. Here is another simple C program.

```
#include "stdio.h"

main( )
{
  printf("This is ");
  printf("another C ");
  printf("program.");
}
```

This program displays **This is another C program** on the screen. The key point to this program is that statements are executed sequentially, beginning with the opening curly brace and ending with the closing curly brace.

1.2 CREATE AND COMPILE A PROGRAM

How you will create and compile a program is determined to a very large extent by the compiler you are using and the operating system under which it is running. If you are using an IBM PC or compatible, you have your choice of a number of excellent compilers, such as Turbo C and Quick C, that contain integrated program-development environments. If you are using such an environment, you can edit, compile, and run your programs directly inside this environment. This is an excellent option for beginners—just follow the instructions supplied with your compiler.

If you are using a traditional command-line compiler, such as the UNIX C compiler, then you need to follow these steps to create and compile a program.

1. Create your program using an editor.

2. Compile the program.

3. Execute your program.

The exact method to accomplish these steps will be explained in the user's manual for your compiler.

When naming your program's file, you should give it a .C extension. This will help you recognize those files that contain C programs. Also, some compilers automatically assume that a file containing a C program will use the .C extension.

The file that contains the C program that you create is called the *source file*. The file that contains the compiled form of your program that the computer executes is called the *object file* or, sometimes, the *executable file*.

If you enter something into your program incorrectly, the compiler will report syntax error messages when it attempts to compile your entry. Most C compilers attempt to make sense out of your source code no matter what you have written. For this reason, the error that gets reported may not always reflect the actual cause of the error. For example, accidentally forgetting the opening curly brace to the **main( )** function in the preceding sample programs will cause some compilers to report the **printf( )** statement as an incorrect identifier. So, when you receive a syntax error message, be prepared to look at the last few lines of code in your program before the point at which the error is reported to find its cause.

Many C compilers report not only actual errors but also warning errors. The C language was designed to be very forgiving and to allow virtually anything that is syntactically correct to be compiled. However, some things, even though syntactically correct, are highly suspicious. When the compiler encounters one of these situations it prints a warning. You, as the programmer, then decide whether its suspicions are justified or not. Frankly, some compilers are a bit too helpful and flag warnings on perfectly correct C statements. More important, some compilers allow you to enable various options that simply report information about your program that you might like to know. Sometimes this type of information is reported in the form of a warning message, even though there is nothing to be "warned" about. The programs in this book are in compliance with the ANSI standard for C and will not generate any warning messages about which you need be concerned. Generally speaking, if you use your compiler's default error checking, you will not see any warning messages.

Examples

1. If you are using Turbo C, you can create and compile your program using the integrated environment. If you are using the command-line interface, you will use a command line such as this (assuming that the name of your program is called TEST.C) to compile the program once you have used a text editor to create it.

```
TCC TEST.C
```

2. If you are using Microsoft C, this command line will compile your program after using a text file to create it. (Again, assume that the program is called TEST.C.)

```
CL TEST.C
```

3. If you are using QuickC, you can edit, compile, and run your program from within its integrated environment.

Exercises

1. Enter into your computer the example programs from Section 1.1. Compile them and run them.

1.3 DECLARE VARIABLES AND ASSIGN VALUES

A *variable* is a named memory location that can hold various values. Only the most trivial C programs do not include variables. In C, unlike some computer languages, all variables must be declared before they can be used. A variable's declaration serves one important purpose: It tells the C compiler *what type of variable* is being used. C supports five different basic data types, as shown in Table 1-1 along with the C keywords that represent them. Don't be confused by **void**. This is a special-purpose data type, which we will examine closely in later chapters.

A variable of type **char** is generally 8 bits long and is most commonly used to hold a single character. Because C is very flexible, a variable of type **char** can also be used as a "little integer" if desired.

TABLE 1-1.   C's Five Basic Data Types

Type	Meaning	Keyword
character	character data	char
integer	signed whole numbers	int
float	floating-point numbers	float
double	double precision floating-point numbers	double
void	valueless	void

Integer variables (**int**) may hold signed whole numbers (numbers with no fractional part). Typically, an integer variable may hold values in the range − 32,768 to 32,767 (although on some computers, the range will be greater).

Variables of type **float** and **double** hold signed floating-point values, which may have fractional components. The difference between **float** and **double** is that **double** provides about twice the precision (number of significant digits) as does **float**. Variables of types **float** and **double** can hold very large values.

To declare a variable, use this general form.

type var-name;

where *type* is a C data type and *var-name* is the name of the variable. For example, this declares **counter** to be of type **int**.

```
int counter;
```

In C, a variable declaration is a statement and it must end in a semicolon.

There are two places where variables are declared: inside a function or outside all functions. Variables declared outside all functions are called *global variables* and they may be accessed by any function in your program. Global variables exist the entire time your program is executing.

Variables declared inside a function are called *local variables*. A local variable is known to and may be accessed by only the function in which it is declared. It is common practice to declare all local variables used by a function at the start of the function, after the opening curly brace. There are two important points you need to know about local varables at this time. First, the local variables in one function have no relationship to the local variables in another function. That is, if a variable called **count** is declared in one function, another variable called **count** may also be declared in a second function—the two variables are completely separate from and unrelated to each other. The second thing you need to know is that local variables are created when a function is called, and they are destroyed when the function is exited. Therefore local variables do not maintain their values between function calls. The examples in this and the next few chapters will use only local variables. Chapter 4 discusses more thoroughly the issues and implications of global and local variables.

You can declare more than one variable of the same type by using a comma-separated list. For example, this declares three floating-point variables, **x**, **y**, and **z**.

```
float x, y, z;
```

Like function names, variable names in C can consist of the letters of the alphabet, the digits 0 through 9, and the underscore. C is case-sensitive. This means that the upper- and lowercase letters are treated as entirely different letters. As far as C is concerned, for example, **count** and **COUNT** are two completely different variable names.

To assign a value to a variable, put its name to the left of an equal sign. Put the value you want to give the variable to the right of the equal sign. In C, an assignment operation is a statement; therefore, it must be terminated by a semicolon. The general form of an assignment statement is

variable-name = value;

For example, to assign an integer variable named **num** the value 100, you can use this statement:

```
num = 100;
```

Just as there are different types of variables, there are different types of constants. A *constant* is a fixed value used in your program. Constants are often used to initialize variables at the beginning of a program's execution.

A character constant is specified by placing the character between single quotes. For example, to specify the letter "A," you would use **'A'**. Integers are specified as whole numbers. Floating-point values must include a decimal point. For example, to specify 100.1, you would use **100.1**. If the floating-point value you wish to specify does not have any digits to the right of the decimal point, then you must use 0. For example, to tell the C compiler that 100 is a floating-point number, use **100.0**.

You can use **printf( )** to display values of characters, integers, and floating-point values. To do so, however, requires that you know more about the **printf( )** function. To see how this is done, let's look first at an example. This statement

```
printf("this prints the number %d", 99);
```

displays **this prints the number 99** on the screen. As you can see, this call to **printf( )** contains not one, but two arguments. The first is the quoted string and the other is the constant 99. Notice that the arguments are separated from each other by a comma. In general, when there is more than one argument to a function, the arguments are separated from each other by commas. The operation of the **printf( )** function is as follows. The first argument is a quoted string that may contain either normal characters or format specifiers that begin with the percent sign. Normal characters are simply displayed as is on the screen in the order in which they are encountered in the string (reading left to right). A format specifier, on the other hand, informs **printf( )** that a different type item is to be displayed. In this case, the %**d** means that an integer is to be output in decimal format. The value to be displayed is found in the second argument. This value is then output to the screen at the point at which the format specifier is found in the string. To understand the relationship between the normal characters and the format codes, examine this statement.

```
printf("This displays %d, too", 99);
```

Now the call to **printf( )** displays **This displays 99, too**. The key point is that the value associated with a format code is displayed at the point where that format code is encountered in the string.

If you want to specify a character value, the format specifier is %c. To specify a floating-point value, use %f. The %f works for both **float** and **double**. As you will see, **printf( )** has many more capabilities.

Keep in mind that the values matched with the format specifier need not be constants; they may be variables, too.

Examples

1. The program shown here illustrates the three new concepts introduced in this section. First, it declares a variable named **num**. Second, it assigns this variable the value 100. Finally, it uses **printf( )** to display **the value is 100** on the screen. Examine this program closely.

```
#include "stdio.h"
main( )
{
   int num;
   num = 100;
   printf("the value is %d", num);
}
```

The statement

```
int num;
```

declares **num** to be an integer variable.

To display the value of **num**, the program uses this statement.

```
printf("the value is %d", num);
```

2. This program creates variables of types **char**, **float**, and **double**; assigns each a value; and outputs these values to the screen.

```
#include "stdio.h"

main( )
{
   char ch;
   float f;
   double d;

   ch = 'X';
   f = 100.123;
   d = 123.009;

   printf("ch is %c, ", ch);
   printf("f is %f, ", f);
   printf("d is %f", d);
}
```

Exercises

1. Enter, compile, and run the example programs in this section.

2. Write a program that declares one integer variable called **num**. Give this variable the value 1000 and then, using one **printf( )** statement, display the value on the screen like this:

```
1000 is the value of num
```

1.4 INPUT NUMBERS FROM THE KEYBOARD

Although there are actually several ways to input numeric values from the keyboard, one of the easiest is to use another of C's standard library functions called

scanf( ). Although it possesses considerable versatility, we will use it in this chapter to read only integers and floating-point numbers entered from the keyboard.

To use **scanf( )** to read an integer value from the keyboard, call it using the general form

scanf("%d", &*int-var-name*);

where *int-var-name* is the name of the integer variable you wish to receive the value. The first argument to **scanf( )** is a string that determines how the second argument will be treated. In this case, the **%d** specifies that the second argument will be receiving an integer value entered in decimal format. This fragment, for example, reads an integer entered from the keyboard.

```
int num;
scanf("%d", &num);
```

The **&** preceding the variable name is essential to the operation of **scanf( )**. Although a detailed explanation will have to wait until later, loosely, the **&** allows a function to place a value into one of its arguments.

It is important to understand one key point: When you enter a number at the keyboard, you are simply typing a string of digits. The **scanf( )** function waits until you have pressed ENTER before it converts the string into the internal binary format used by the computer.

To read a floating-point number from the keyboard, call **scanf( )** using the general form

scanf("%f", &*float-var-name*);

where *float-var-name* is the name of a variable that is declared as being of type **float**. If you want to input to a **double** variable, use the %lf specifier.

Notice that the format specifiers for **scanf( )** are similar to those used for **printf( )** for the corresponding data types except that %lf is used to read a **double**. This is no coincidence—**printf( )** and **scanf( )** are complementary functions.

Examples

1. This program asks you to input an integer and a floating-point number and displays the values.

```
#include "stdio.h"

main( )
{
  int num;
  float f;

  printf("Enter an integer: ");
  scanf("%d", &num);

  printf("Enter a floating point number: ");
  scanf("%f", &f);
  printf("%d ", num);
  printf("%f", f);
}
```

Exercises

1. Enter, compile, and run the example program.

2. Write a program that inputs two floating-point numbers (use type **float**) and then displays their sum.

1.5 PERFORM CALCULATIONS USING ARITHMETIC EXPRESSIONS

In C, the expression plays a much more important role than it does in most other programming languages. Part of the reason for this is that C defines many more operators than do most other langauges. An *expression* is a combination of operators and operands. C expressions follow the rules of algebra, so, for the most part, they will be familiar. In this section we will look only at arithmetic expressions.

C defines these five arithmetic operators:

Operator	Meaning
+	addition
−	subtraction
*	multiplication
/	division
%	modulus

The +, −, / and * operators may be used with any of the basic data types. However, the % may be used with integer types only. The modulus operator produces the remainder of an integer division. This has no meaning when applied to floating-point types.

The − has two meanings. First, it is the subtraction operator. Second, it can be used as a unary minus to reverse the sign of a number. A unary operator uses only one operand.

An expression may appear on the right side of an assignment statement. For example, this program fragment assigns the integer variable **answer** the value of 100*31.

```
int answer;
answer = 100*31;
```

The *, /, and % are higher in precedence than the + and the −. However, you can use parentheses to alter the order of evaluation. For example, this expression produces the value 0,

10 − 2 * 5

but this one produces the value 40.

(10 − 2) * 5

A C expression may contain variables, constants, or both. For example, assuming that **answer** and **count** are variables, this expression is perfectly valid.

```
answer = count - 100;
```

Finally, you may use spaces liberally within an expression.

Examples

1. As stated earlier, the modulus operator returns the remainder of an integer division. The remainder of 10 % 3 equals 1, for example. This program shows the outcome of some integer divisions and their remainders.

```
#include "stdio.h"

main( )
{
  printf("%d", 5/2);
  printf(" %d", 5%2);
  printf(" %d", 4/2);
  printf(" %d", 4%2);
}
```

This program displays **2 1 2 0** on the screen.

2. In long expressions, the use of parentheses and spaces can add clarity, even if they are not necessary. For example, examine this expression.

```
count*num+88/val-19%count
```

This expression produces the same result, but is much easier to read.

```
(count * num) + (88 / val) - (19 % count)
```

3. This program computes the area of a rectangle, given its dimensions. It first prompts the user for the length and width of the rectangle and then displays the area.

```
#include "stdio.h"

main( )
{
  int len, width;

  printf("Enter length: ");
  scanf("%d", &len);
  printf("Enter width: ");
  scanf("%d", &width);

  printf("area is %d", len * width);
}
```

4. As stated earlier, the – can be used as a unary operator to reverse the sign of its operand. To see how this works, try this program.

```
#include "stdio.h"

main( )
{
  int i;

  i = 10;
  i = -i;
  printf("this is i: %d", i);
}
```

Exercises

1. Write a program that computes the volume of a cube. Have the program prompt the user for each dimension.

2. Write a program that computes the number of seconds in a year.

1.6 ADD COMMENTS TO A PROGRAM

A *comment* is a note to yourself (or others) that you put into your source code. All comments are ignored by the compiler. They exist solely for your benefit. Comments are used primarily to document the meaning and purpose of your source code, so that you can remember later how it functions and how to use it.

In C, the start of a comment is signaled by the /* character pair. A comment is ended by */. For example, this is a syntactically correct C comment:

```
/* This is a comment. */
```

Comments can extend over several lines. For example, this is completely valid in C.

```
/*
  This is a longer comment
  that extends over
  five lines.
*/
```

In C, a comment can go anywhere except in the middle of any C keyword, function name, or variable name.

You can use a comment to temporarily remove a line of code. Simply surround the line with the comment symbols.

One final point: In C, you can't have one comment within another comment. That is, comments may not be nested. For example, C will not accept this:

```
/* this is a comment /* this is another comment
   nested inside the first - which will cause
   a syntax error */ with a nested comment
*/
```

Examples

1. A year on Jupiter (the time it takes for Jupiter to make one full circuit around the Sun) takes about 12 Earth years. The following program allows you to convert Earth days to Jovian years. Simply specify the number of Earth days, and it computes the equivalent number of Jovian years. Notice the use of comments throughout the program.

```
/* This program converts earth days into Jovian years. */

#include "stdio.h"

main( )
{
  float e_days; /* number of earth days */
  float j_years; /* equivalent number of Jovian years */

  /* get number of earth days */
  printf("Enter number of earth days: ");
  scanf("%f", &e_days);

  /* now, compute Jovian years */
  j_years = e_days / (365.0 * 12.0);

  /* display the answer */
  printf("Equivalent Jovian years: %f", j_years);
}
```

Notice that comments can appear on the same line as do other C program statements.

Comments are often used to help describe what the program is doing. Although this program is easy to understand even without the comments, many programs are very difficult to understand even with the liberal use of comments. For more complex programs, the general approach is the same as used here: simply describe what the program is doing. Also, notice the comment at the start of the program. In general, it is a good idea to identify the purpose of a program at the top of its source file.

2. You cannot place a comment inside the name of a function or variable name. For example, this is an incorrect statement.

```
pri/* wrong */ntf("this won't work");
```

Exercises

1. Go back and add comments to the programs developed in previous sections.

2. Is this comment correct?

   ```
   /**/
   ```

3. Is this comment correct?

   ```
   /* printf("this is a test"); */
   ```

1.7 WRITE YOUR OWN FUNCTIONS

Functions are the building blocks of C. So far, the programs that you have seen have included only one function: **main( )**. Most real-world programs that you will write, however, will contain many functions. In this section you will see some examples of programs that contain multiple functions.

The general form of a C program that has multitple functions is shown here:

```
/* include header files here */

main( )
{
   .
   .
   .
}

f1( )
```

```
{
    .
    .
    .
}

f2( )
{
    .
    .
    .
}

    .
    .
    .

fN( )
{
    .
    .
    .
}
```

Of course, you will call your functions by different names.

When a function (except **main( )**) encounters its closing curly brace, it returns to the line after the point it was called. Also, any function inside the program may call any other function at any time. (Traditionally, **main( )** is not called by any other function, however, even though there is no technical restriction to this effect.)

Examples

1. The following program contains two functions: **main( )** and **func1( )**. Try to determine what it displays on the screen before reading the description that follows it.

```
/* A program with two functions */

#include "stdio.h"

main( )
{
  printf("I ");
  func1( );
  printf("C.");
}

func1( )
{
  printf("like ");
}
```

This program displays **I like C** on the screen. Here is how it works. In **main( )**, the first call to **printf( )** executes, printing the I. Next, **func1( )** is called. This causes the **printf( )** inside **func1( )** to execute, displaying **like**. Since this is the only statement inside **func1( )**, the function returns. This causes execution to resume inside **main( )** and the C. is printed. Notice that the statement that calls **func1( )** ends with a semicolon. (Remember a function call is a statement.)

The key point to understand about writing your own functions is that, except for **main( )**, when the closing curly brace is reached the function will return, and execution resumes one line after the point at which the function was called.

2. This program prints **1 2 3** on the screen.

```
/* This program has three functions. */

#include "stdio.h"

main( )
{
  func2( )
  printf("3");
}

func2( )
{
  func1( );
  printf("2 ");
}

func1( )
{
  printf("1 ");
}
```

In this program, **main( )** first calls **func2( )**, which then calls **func1( )**. Next, **func1( )** displays **1** and then returns to **func2( )**, which prints **2** and then returns to **main( )**, which prints **3**.

Exercises

1. Enter, compile, and run the two example programs in this section.

2. Write a program that contains at least two functions and prints the message **The summer soldier, the sunshine patriot.**

1.8 USE FUNCTIONS TO RETURN VALUES

In C, a function may return a value to the calling routine. For example, another of C's standard library functions is **sqrt( )**, which returns the square root of its argument. For your program to obtain the return value, you must put the function on the right side of an assignment statement. For example, this program prints the square root of 10.

```c
#include "stdio.h"
#include "math.h"  /* needed by sqrt( ) */

main( )
{
  double answer;

  answer = sqrt(10.0);
  printf("%f", answer);
}
```

This program calls **sqrt( )** and assigns its return value to **answer**. Notice that **sqrt( )** uses the MATH.H header file.

Actually, the assignment statement in the preceding program is not technically necessary because **sqrt( )** could simply be used as an argument to **printf( )**, as shown here.

```c
#include "stdio.h"
#include "math.h"  /* needed by sqrt( ) */

main( )
{
  printf("%f", sqrt(10.0));
}
```

The reason this works is that C will automatically call **sqrt( )** and obtain its return value before calling **printf( )**. The return value then becomes the second argument to **printf( )**. If this seems strange, don't worry; you will understand this sort of situation better as you learn more about C.

The **sqrt( )** function requires a floating-point value for its argument, and the value it returns is of type **double**. It is important that you match the type of value a function returns with the variable that it will be assigned to. As you learn more about C, you will see why this is so important. It is also important that you match the types of a function's arguments to the types it requires.

When writing your own functions, you can return a value to the calling routine using the **return** statement. The return statement takes the general form

return *value;*

where *value* is the value to be returned. For example, this program prints **10** on the screen.

```
#include "stdio.h"

main( )
{
   int num;

   num = func( );
   printf("%d", num);
}

func( )
{
   return 10;
}
```

In this example, **func( )** returns an integer value. Although you can create functions that return any type of data, functions return values of type **int** by default. Later in this book, you will learn how to return other types.

One important point: When the **return** statement is encountered, the function returns immediately. No statements after it will be executed.

The value associated with the **return** statement need not be a constant. It can be any valid C expression.

It is possible to cause a function to return by using the **return** statement without any value attached to it, making the returned value undefined. Also, there can be more than one **return** in a function. You will see examples of these uses for **return** later in this book.

Even though a function returns a value, you don't necessarily have to assign that value to anything. If the return value of a function is not used, it is lost, but no harm is done.

Examples

1. This program displays the square of a number entered from the keyboard. The square is computed using the **get_sqr( )** function. Its operation should be clear.

```
#include "stdio.h"

main( )
{
  int sqr;

  sqr = get_sqr( );
  printf("square: %d", sqr);
}
```

```
get_sqr( )
{
  int num;

  printf("enter a number: ");
  scanf("%d", &num);
  return num*num;  /* square the number */
}
```

2. As mentioned earlier, you can use **return** without specifying a value. This allows a function to return before its closing curly brace is reached. For example, in the following program, the line **this is never printed** will not be dislayed.

```
#include "stdio.h"

main( )
{
  func1( );
}

func1( )
{
  printf("this is printed");
  return;
  printf("this is never printed");
}
```

Exercises

1. Enter, compile, and run the example program, in this section.

2. Write a program that uses a function called **convert( )**, which prompts the user for an amount in dollars and returns this value converted into pounds. (Use an exchange rate of $2.00 per pound.) Display the conversion.

3. What is wrong with this program?

```
#include "stdio.h"

main( )
{
  double answer;

  answer = f1( );
  printf("%f", answer);
}
f1( )
{
  return 100;
}
```

1.9 USE FUNCTION ARGUMENTS

As stated earlier, a function's argument is a value that is passed to the function when the function is called. A function in C can have from zero to several arguments. (The upper limit is determined by the compiler you are using, but the ANSI standard specifies that a function must be able to take at least 31 arguments.) For a function to be able to take arguments, special variables to receive argument values must be declared. These are called the *formal parameters* of the function. The parameters are declared between the parentheses that follow the function's name. For example, the function listed below prints the sum of the two integer arguments used to call it.

```
sum(int x, int y)
{
  printf("%d", x + y);
}
```

Each time **sum( )** is called, it will sum the value passed
to **x** with the value passed to **y**. Remember, however,
that **x** and **y** are simply the function's operational variables, which receive the values you use when calling the
function. Consider the following short program, which
illustrates how to call **sum( )**.

```
/* A simple program that demonstrates sum( ). */

#include "stdio.h"

main( )
{
  sum(1, 20);
  sum(9, 6);
  sum(81, 9);
}

sum(int x, int y)
{
  printf("%d ", x + y);
}
```

This program will print **21**, **15**, and **90** on the screen.
When **sum( )** is called, the C compiler copies the value
of each argument into the matching parameter. That is,
in the first call to **sum( )**, 1 is copied into **x** and 20 is
copied into **y**. In the second call, 9 is copied into **x** and
6 into **y**. In the third call, 81 is copied into **x** and 9 into
y.

Important note: If you try this program (or when
you work through the example that follows), you might
see a compiler warning message about a missing prototype for **sum( )**. Don't worry about this. Prototypes are
an important feature of C, but they are not necessary. It
is not an error not to use a prototype; in fact, the original
version of C did not even support them. You will need

to know more about C before you begin using prototypes.

If you have never worked with a language that allows parameterized functions, the preceding process may seem strange. Don't worry—as you see more examples of C programs, the concept of arguments, parameters, and functions will become clear.

It is important to keep two terms straight. First, *argument* refers to the value that is passed to a function. The variable that receives the values of the arguments used in the function call is called a *formal parameter* of the function. Functions that take arguments are called *parameterized functions*. Remember, if a variable is used as an argument to a function, it has nothing to do with the formal parameter that receives its value.

In C functions, arguments are always separated by commas. In this book, the term *argument list* will refer to comma-separated arguments. For example, the argument list for **sum( )** is **x,y**.

All function arguments are declared in a fashion similar to that used by **sum( )**. You must specify the type and name of each parameter and, if there is more than one parameter, you must use a comma to separate them.

Example

1. This program uses the **outchar( )** function to output characters to the screen. The program prints **ABC**.

    ```c
    #include "stdio.h"

    main( )
    {
      outchar('A');
      outchar('B');
      outchar('C');
    }
    ```

```
outchar(char ch)
{
  printf("%c", ch);
}
```

Exercises

1. Write a program that uses a function called **outnum( )** that takes one integer argument and displays it on the screen.

2. What is wrong with this program?

```
#include "stdio.h"

main( )
{
  sqr_it(10.0);
}

sqr_it(int num)
{
  printf("%d", num * num);
}
```

1.10 REMEMBER THE C KEYWORDS

Before concluding this chapter, you should familiarize yourself with the keywords that make up the C language. ANSI standard C has 32 *keywords* that may not be used as variable or function names. These words, combined with the formal C syntax, form the C programming language. They are listed in Table 1-2.

TABLE 1-2. The 32 Keywords as Defined by the Proposed ANSI Standard

auto	double	int	struct
break	else	long	switch
case	enum	register	typedef
char	extern	return	union
const	float	short	unsigned
continue	for	signed	void
default	goto	sizeof	volatile
do	if	static	while

Many C compilers have added several additional keywords that are used to take better advantage of the 8088/8086 family of processors' memory organization, and that give support for interlanguage programming and interrupts. The most commonly used extended keywords are shown in Table 1-3.

The lowercase lettering of the keywords is significant. C requires that all keywords be in lowercase form. For example, **RETURN** will *not* be recognized as the keyword **return**. Also, no keyword may be used as a variable or function name.

TABLE 1-3. Some Common C Extended Keywords

asm	_cs	_ds	_es
_ss	cdecl	far	huge
interrupt	near	pascal	

EXERCISES

1. The moon's gravity is about 17 percent that of earth's. Write a program that allows you to enter your weight and computes your effective weight on the moon.

2. What is wrong with this program fragment?

```
/* this inputs a number
scanf("%d", &num);
```

3. There are 8 ounces in a cup. Write a program that converts ounces to cups. Use a function called **o_to_c( )** to perform the conversion. Call it with the number of ounces and have it return the number of cups.

4. What are the five basic data types in C?

5. What is wrong with each of these variable names?

   a. short-fall

   b. $balance

   c. last+name

CHAPTER OBJECTIVES

2.1 Become familiar with the **if**

2.2 Add the **else**

2.3 Create blocks of code

2.4 Use the **for** loop

2.5 Substitute C's increment and decrement operators

2.6 Expand **printf( )**'s capabilities

2.7 Program with C's relational
   and logical operators

·2·
Introducing C's Program Control Statements

In this chapter you will learn about two of C's most important program control statements: **if** and **for**. In general, program control statements control your program's flow of execution. As such, they form the backbone of your programs. In addition to these, you will also learn about blocks of code and the relational and logical operators. You will also learn more about the **printf( )** function.

EXERCISES

Before proceeding, you should be able to correctly answer these questions and do these exercises.

SKILLS CHECK

√

1. All C programs are composed of one or more functions. What is the name of the function that all programs must have? Further, what special purpose does it perform?

2. The **printf( )** function is used to output information to the screen. Write a program that displays **This is the number 100**. (Output the **100** as a number, not as a string.)

3. Header files contain information used by the standard library functions. How do you tell the compiler to include one in your program? Give an example.

4. C supports five basic types of data. Name them.

5. Which of these variable names are invalid in C?

   a. _count

   b. 123count

   c. $test

   d. This_is_a_long_name

   e. new-word

6. What is **scanf( )** used for?

7. Write a program that inputs an integer from the keyboard and displays its square.

8. How are comments entered into a C program? Give an example.

9. How does a function return a value to the routine that called it?

10. A function called **Myfunc( )** has these three parameters: an **int** called **count**, a **float** called **balance**, and a **char** called **ch**. Show how this function is declared.

2.1 BECOME FAMILIAR WITH THE if

The **if** statement is one of C's *selection statements* (sometimes called *conditional statements*). Its operation is governed by the outcome of a conditional test that evaluates to either true or false. Simply put, selection statements make decisions based upon the outcome of a condition.

In its simplest form, the **if** statement allows your program to conditionally execute a statement. This form of the **if** is shown here.

if(*expression*) *statement*;

The expression may be any valid C expression. If the expression evaluates as true, the statement will be executed. If it does not, the statement is bypassed, and the line of code following the **if** is executed. In C, an expression is true if it evaluates to any non-0 value. If it evaluates to 0, it is false. The statement that follows an **if** is commonly referred to as the *target* of the **if** statement.

Commonly, the expression inside the **if** compares one value with another using a *relational operator*. Although you will learn about all the relational operators later in this chapter, three are introduced here so that we can create some example programs. A relational operator tests how one value relates to another. For example, to see if one value is greater than another, C uses the > relational operator. The outcome of this comparison is either true or false. For example, **10 > 9** is true, but **9 > 10** is false. Therefore, this **if** will cause the message **true** to be displayed.

```
if(10 > 9) printf("true");
```

However, because the expression in the following statement is false, the **if** does not execute its target statement.

```
if(1 > 2) printf("this will not print");
```

C uses < as its *less than operator*. For example, **10 < 11** is true. To test for equality, C provides the == operator. There may be no space between the two equal signs. Therefore, **10 == 10** is true, but **10 == 11** is not.

Of course, the expression inside the **if** may involve variables. For example, the following program tells whether a number entered from the keyboard is positive or negative.

```
#include "stdio.h"

main( )
{
  int num;

  printf("enter a number: ");
  scanf("%d", &num);

  if(num > 0) printf("number is positive");
  if(num < 0) printf("number is negative");
}
```

Remember, in C, true is any non-0 value and false is 0. Therefore, it is pefectly valid to have an **if** statement such as the one shown here.

```
if(count+1) printf("not zero");
```

Examples

1. This program forms the basis for an addition drill. It displays two numbers and asks the user what the answer is. The program then tells the user if the answer is right or wrong.

```
#include "stdio.h"

main( )
{
  int answer;

  printf("What is 10 + 14? ");
  scanf("%d", &answer);
  if(answer == 10+14) printf("Right!");
}
```

2. This program either converts feet to meters or meters to feet, depending upon what the user requests.

```
#include "stdio.h"

main( )
{
  float num;
  int choice;

  printf("enter value: ");
  scanf("%f", &num);
```

```
    printf("1: feet to meters, 2: meters to feet ");
    printf("enter choice: ");
    scanf("%d", &choice);

    if(choice == 1) printf("%f", num / 3.28);
    if(choice == 2) printf("%f", num * 3.28);
}
```

Exercises

1. Which of these expressions are true?

    a. 0

    b. 1

    c. 10*9 < 90

    d. 1 == 1

    e. -1

2. Write a program that asks the user for an integer and then tells the user if that number is even or odd. (Hint, use C's modulus operator %.)

2.2 ADD THE else

You can add an **else** statement to the **if**. When this is done, the **if** statement looks like this:

if(*expression*) *statement1*;
else *statement2*;

If the expression is true, then the target of the **if** will execute, and the **else** portion will be skipped. However, if the expression is false, then the target of the **if** is bypassed, and the target of the **else** will execute. Under no circumstances will both statements execute. Thus, the addition of the **else** provides a two-way decision path.

Examples

1. You can use the **else** to create more efficient code in some cases. For example, here the **else** is used in place of a second **if** in the program from the preceding section, which determines whether a number is positive or negative.

```
#include "stdio.h"

main( )
{
    int num;

    printf("enter a number: ");
    scanf("%d", &num);

    if(num < 0) printf("number is negative");
    else printf("number is positive");
}
```

Since there are only two possibilities, there is no reason to test **num** again to see if it is 0 or greater. The original version of this program explicitly tested for **num** to be greater than 0 using a second **if** statement. Because of the way a C compiler generates code, the **else** requires far fewer machine instructions than an additional **if**.

2. This program prompts the user for two numbers, divides the first by the second, and displays the result. However, division by 0 is undefined, so the

program uses an **if** and an **else** statement to prevent division by 0 from occurring.

```c
#include "stdio.h"

main( )
{
  int num1, num2;

  printf("enter first number: ");
  scanf("%d", &num1);

  printf("enter second number: ");
  scanf("%d", &num2);

  if(num2==0) printf("cannot divide by zero");
  else printf("answer is: %d", num1 / num2);
}
```

Exercises

1. Write a program that requests two numbers and then displays either their sum or product, depending upon what the user selects.

2. Rewrite Exercise 2 from Section 2.1 so that it uses an **else** statement.

2.3 CREATE BLOCKS OF CODE

In C, you can link two or more statements together. This is called a *block of code* or a *code block*. To create a block of code, you surround the statements in the block with opening and closing curly braces. Once this is done, the statements form one logical unit, which may be used anywhere that a single statement may.

For example, the general form of the **if** using blocks of code is

```
if(expression) {
    statement1;
    statement2;
      .

      .

      .
    statementN;
}
else {
    statement1;
    statement2;
      .

      .

      .
    statementN;
}
```

If the expression evaluates to true, then all the statements in the block of code associated with the **if** will be executed. If the expression is false, then all the statements in the **else** block will be executed. (Remember, the **else** is optional and need not be present.) For example, this fragment prints the message **This is an example of a code block** if the user enters any positive number.

```
scanf("%d", &num);

if(num > 0 ) {
  printf("This is ");
  printf("an example of ");
  printf("a code block");
}
```

Keep in mind that a block of code represents one indivisible logical unit. This means that under no circumstances could one of the **printf( )** statements in this fragment execute without the others also executing.

In the example shown, the statements that appear within the block of code are indented. Although C does not care where a statement appears on a line, it is common practice to indent one level at the start of a block. Indenting makes the structure of a program easier to understand. Also, the placement of the curly braces is arbitrary. However, the way they are shown in the example is a common method and will be used by the examples in this book.

In C, as you will see, you can use a block of code anywhere you can use a single statement.

Examples

1. This program is an improved version of the feet-to-meters, meters-to-feet conversion program. Notice how the use of code blocks allow the program to prompt specifically for each unit.

```
#include "stdio.h"

main( )
{
  float num;
  int choice;

  printf("1: feet to meters, 2: meters to feet ");
  printf("enter choice: ");
  scanf("%d", &choice);

  if(choice == 1) {
    printf("enter number of feet: ");
    scanf("%f", &num);
    printf("meters: %f", num / 3.28);
```

```
  }
  else {
    printf("enter number of meters: ");
    scanf("%f", &num);
    printf("feet: %f", num * 3.28);
  }
}
```

2. Using code blocks, we can improve the addition
    drill program so that it also prints the correct answer
    when the user makes a mistake.

```
#include "stdio.h"

main( )
{
  int answer;

  printf("What is 10 + 14? ");
  scanf("%d", &answer);
  if(answer == 10+14) printf("Right!");
  else {
    printf("Sorry, you're wrong, ");
    printf("the answer is 24");
  }
}
```

This example illustrates an important point: it is not
necessary for targets of both the **if** and the **else**
statements to be blocks of code. In this case, the
target of **if** is a single statement, while the target of
else is a block. Remember, you are free to use either
a single statement or a code block at either place.

Exercises

1. Write a program that either adds or subtracts two
    integers. First, prompt the user to choose an opera-
    tion; then prompt for the two numbers and display
    the result.

2. Is this fragment correct?

```
if(count < 100)
  printf("number is less than 100");
  printf("its square is %d", count * count);
}
```

2.4 USE THE for LOOP

The **for** loop is one of C's three loop statements. It allows one or more statements to be repeated. If you have programmed in any other computer language, such as BASIC or Pascal, you will be pleased to learn that the **for** behaves much like its equivalant in other languages.

The **for** loop is considered by many C programmers to be its most flexible loop. Although the **for** loop allows a large number of variations, we will examine only its most common form in this section.

In its most common form, the **for** loop is used to repeat a statement or block of statements a specified number of times. Its general form for repeating a single statement is shown here.

for(*initialization*; *conditional test*; *increment*) statement;

The *initialization* section is used to give an initial value to the variable that controls the loop. This variable is usually referred to as the *loop-control variable*. The initialization section is executed only once, before the loop begins. The *conditional-test portion* of the loop tests the loop-control variable against a target value each time the loop repeats. If the conditional test evaluates true, the loop repeats. If it is false, the loop stops, and program execution picks up with the next line of code that follows the loop. The conditional test is performed at the start or *top* of the loop each time the loop is repeated. The *increment portion* of the **for** is executed at the bottom of each loop. That is, the increment portion is executed after the statement or block has been executed, but before the conditional test. The purpose of the increment portion is to increase (or decrease) the loop-control value by a certain amount.

    As a simple first example, this program uses a **for** loop to print the numbers **1** through **10** on the screen.

```
#include "stdio.h"

main( )
{
   int num;

   for(num=1; num<11; num=num+1) printf("%d ", num);
   printf("terminating");
}
```

    This program produces the following output:

1 2 3 4 5 6 7 8 9 10 terminating

The program works like this. First, the loop control variable **num** is initialized to 1. Next, the expression **num < 11** is evaluated. Since it is true, the **for** loop begins running. After the number is printed, **num** is incremented by one and the conditional test is evaluated again. This process continues until **num** equals 11. When this happens, the **for** loop stops, and **terminating** is displayed. Keep in mind that the initialization portion of the **for** loop is only executed once, when the loop is first entered.

As stated earlier, the conditional test is performed at the start of each iteration. This means that if the test is false to begin with, the loop will not execute even once. For example, this program only displays **terminating** because **num** is initialized to 11, causing the conditional test to fail.

```
#include "stdio.h"

main( )
{
   int num;

   /* this loop will not execute */
   for(num=11; num<11; num=num+1) printf("%d ", num);

   printf("terminating");
}
```

To repeat several statements, use a block of code as the target of the **for** loop. For example, this program computes the product and sum of the numbers from 1 to 10.

```
#include "stdio.h"

main( )
{
   int num, sum, prod;

   sum = 0;
   prod = 1;

   for(num=1; num<11; num=num+1) {
     sum = sum + num;
     prod = prod * num;
```

```
    }
    printf("product and sum: %d %d", prod, sum);
}
```

A **for** loop can run negatively. For example, this fragment decrements the loop-control variable.

```
for(num=20; num>0; num=num-1) . . .
```

Further, the loop-control variable may be incremented or decremented by more than one. For example, this program counts to 100 by fives.

```
#include "stdio.h"

main( )
{
    int i;

    for(i=0; i<101; i=i+5) printf("%d ", i);
}
```

Examples

1. The addition-drill program created earlier can be enhanced using a **for** loop. The version shown here asks for the sums of the numbers between 1 and 10. That is, it asks for 1 + 1, then 2 + 2, and so on. This program would be useful to a first grader who is learning addition.

    ```
    #include "stdio.h"

    main( )
    {
        int answer, count;
    ```

```
for(count=1; count < 11; count=count+1) {
  printf("What is %d + %d? ", count, count);
  scanf("%d", &answer);
  if(answer == count+count) printf("Right!  ");
  else {
    printf("Sorry, you're wrong ");
    printf("the answer is %d. ", count+count);
  }
 }
}
```

Notice that this program has an **if** statement as part of the **for** block. Notice further that the target of **else** is a block of code. This is perfectly valid. In C, a code block may contain statements that create other code blocks. Notice how the indentation adds clarity to the structure of the program.

2. We can use a **for** loop to create a program that determines if a number is prime. The following program asks the user to enter a number and then checks to see if it has any factors.

```
/* Prime number tester. */

#include "stdio.h"

main( )
{
  int num, i, is_prime;
  printf("Enter the number to test: ");
  scanf("%d", &num);

  /* now test for factors */
  is_prime = 1;
  for(i=2; i<num/2; i=i+1)
  if((num%i)==0) is_prime = 0;

  if(is_prime==1) printf("The number is prime.");
  else printf("The number is not prime.");
}
```

Exercises

1. Create a program that prints the numbers from **1** to **100**.

2. Write a program that prints the numbers between **17** and **100** that can be evenly divided by 17.

3. Write a program similar to the prime-number tester, except that it displays all the factors of a number entered by the user. For example, if the user entered **8**, it would respond with **2** and **4**.

2.5 SUBSTITUTE C's INCREMENT AND DECREMENT OPERATORS

When you learned about the **for** in the preceding section, the increment portion of the loop looked more or less like the one shown here.

```
for(num=0; num<some_value; num=num+1) . . .
```

Although not incorrect, you will almost never see a statement like **num = num+1** in professionally written C programs because C provides a special operator that increments a variable by one. The *increment operator* is **++** (two pluses with no intervening space). Using the increment operator, you can change this line of code

```
i = i + 1;
```

into

```
i++;
```

Therefore, the **for** shown earlier will normally be written like this:

```
for(num=0; num<some_value; num++) . . .
```

In a similar fashion, to decrease a variable by one, you can use C's *decrement operator*: --. (There must be no space between the two minus signs.) Therefore,

```
count = count - 1;
```

can be rewritten as

```
count--;
```

Aside from saving you a little typing effort, the reason you will want to use the increment and decrement operators is that, for most C compilers, they will be faster than the equivalent assignment statements. The reason for this difference is that the C compiler can often avoid separate load-and-store machine-language instructions and substitute a single increment or decrement instruction in the executable version of a program.

The increment and decrement operators do not need to follow the variable; they can precede it. Although the effect on the variable is the same, the position of the operator does affect when the operation is performed. To see how, examine this program.

```
#include "stdio.h"
main( )
{
  int i, j;

  i = 10;
```

```
  j = i++;

  /* this will print 11 10 */
  printf("i and j: %d %d", i, j);
}
```

Don't let the **j** = **i++** statement trouble you. The increment operator may be used as part of any valid C expression. This statement works like this. First, the current value of **i** is assigned to **j**. Then **i** is incremented. This is why **j** has the value 10, not 11. When the increment or decrement operator follows the variable, the operation is performed *after* its value has been obtained for use in the expression. Therefore, assuming that **max** has the value 1, an expression such as this

```
count = 10 * max++;
```

assigns the value 10 to **count** and increases **max** by one.

   If the variable is preceded by the increment or decrement operator, the operation is performed first, and then the value of the variable is obtained for use in the expression. For example, rewriting the previous program as follows causes **j** to be 11.

```
#include "stdio.h"

main( )
{
   int i, j;

   i = 10;
   j = ++i;

   /* this will print 11 11 */
   printf("i and j: %d %d", i, j);
}
```

If you are simply using the increment or decrement operators to replace equivalent assignment statements, it doesn't matter if the operator precedes or follows the variable. This is a matter of your own personal style.

Examples

1. Here is the addition drill program developed in Section 2 rewritten using the increment operator.

```
#include "stdio.h"

main( )
{
  int answer, count;

  for(count=1; count<11; count++) {
    printf("What is %d + %d? ", count, count);
    scanf("%d", &answer);
    if(answer == count+count) printf("Right!  ");
    else {
      printf("Sorry, you're wrong ");
      printf("the answer is %d. ", count+count);
    }
  }
}
```

2. This program illustrates the use of the increment and decrement operators.

```
#include "stdio.h"

main( )
{
  int i;

  i = 0;

  i++;
  printf("%d ", i); /* prints 1 */
```

```
    i--;
    printf("%d ", i); /* prints 0 */
}
```

Exercises

1. Rewrite the answers to the **for** loop exercises in the previous section so that they use the increment or decrement operators.

2. Change all assignment statements in this program to increment or decrement statements.

```
#include "stdio.h"

main( )
{
   int a, b;

   a = 1;

   a = a + 1;

   b = a;

   b = b - 1;

   printf("%d %d", a, b);
}
```

2.6 EXPAND printf( )'s CAPABILITIES

So far, we have used **printf( )** to output strings and numbers. However, you might have been wondering how to tell **printf( )** that you want the output to advance to the next line. The way to accomplish this and other actions is to use C's *backslash-character constants*. The C

TABLE 2-1.   C's Backslash Codes

Code	Meaning
\b	backspace
\f	form feed
\n	newline
\r	carriage return
\t	horizontal tab
\"	double quote
\'	single quote
\0	null
\\	backslash
\v	vertical tab
\a	bell
\N	octal constant (where N is an octal constant)
\xN	hexadecimal constant (where N is a hexadecimal constant)

language defines 13 special codes, shown in Table 2-1, which are used to output characters that cannot be entered from the keyboard. You can use the backslash codes anywhere you can use a normal character.

Perhaps the single most important backslash code is \n, which is often referred to as a *newline character*. When the C compiler encounters \n, it translates it into a carriage return/linefeed combination. For example, this program

```
#include "stdio.h"

main( )
{
  printf("this is line one\n");
  printf("this is line two\n");
  printf("this is line three");
}
```

displays

this is line one
this is line two
this is line three

on the screen.

Remember, the backslash codes are character constants. Therefore, to assign one to a character variable, you must enclose the backslash code with single quotes, as shown in this fragment.

```
char ch;

ch = '\t';   /* assign ch the tab character */
```

Examples

1. This program sounds the bell.

    ```
    #include "stdio.h"

    main( )
    {
      printf("\a");
    }
    ```

2. You can enter any special character by specifying it as an octal or hexadecimal value following the backslash. The octal number system is based on 8 and uses the digits 0 through 7. In octal, the number 10 is the same as 8 in decimal. The hexadecimal number system is based on 16 and uses the digits 0 through 9 plus the letters 'A' through 'F,' which stand for 10, 11, 12, 13, 14, and 15. For example, the hexadecimal

number 10 is 16 in decimal. When specifying a character in hexadecimal, you must follow the backslash
with an 'x', followed by the number.

    The ASCII character set is defined from 0 to 127.
However, many computers, including most PCs,
use the values 128 to 255 for special characters and
graphics characters. If your computer supports
these extra characters, the following program will
display a few on the screen.

```c
#include "stdio.h"

main( )
{
  printf("\xA0 \xA1 \xA2 \xA3");
}
```

3. The \n newline character does not have to go at the
    end of the string that is being output by **printf( )**; it
    can go anywhere in the string. Further, there can be
    as many newline characters in a string as you desire.
    The point is that there is no connection between a
    newline and the end of string. For example, this
    program

    ```c
    #include "stdio.h"

    main( )
    {
      printf("one\ntwo\nthree\nfour");
    }
    ```

    displays

    one
    two
    three
    four

    on the screen.

Exercises

1. Write a program that outputs a table of numbers. Each line in the table contains three entries: the number, its square, and its cube. Begin with **1** and end with **10**. Also, use a **for** loop to generate the numbers.

2. Write a program that prompts the user for an integer value. Next, using a **for** loop, make it count down from this value to 0, displaying each number on its own line. When it reaches 0, have it sound the bell.

3. Experiment on your own with the backslash codes.

2.7 PROGRAM WITH C's RELATIONAL AND LOGICAL OPERATORS

The C language contains a rich set of operators. In this section you will learn about C's relational and logical operators. As you learned earlier, the relational operators compare two values and return a true or false result based upon that comparison. The logical operators connect together true/false results. These operators are shown in Table 2-2.

The logical operators are used to support the basic logical operations of AND, OR, and NOT according to this truth table. The table uses 1 for true and 0 for false.

p	q	p && q	p || q	! p
0	0	0	0	1
0	1	0	1	1
1	1	1	1	0
1	0	0	1	0

TABLE 2-2.   Relational and Logical Operators

Relational Operators

Operator	Relationship
>	greater than
>=	greater than or equal
<	less than
<=	less than or equal
==	equal
!=	not equal

Logical Operators

Operator	Operation
&&	AND
||	OR
!	NOT

The relational and logical operators are both lower in precedence than the arithmetic operators. This means that an expression like **10 + count > a + 12** is evaluated as if it were written **(10 + count) > (a + 12)**.

You may link any number of relational operations together using logical operators. For example, this expression joins three relational operations.

```
var>max || !(max==100) && 0<=item
```

The table below shows the relative precedence of the relational and logical operators.

Highest	!
	> >= < <=
	== !=
	&&
Lowest	||

There is one important fact to remember about the values produced by the relational and logical operators:

the result is either 0 or 1. Even though C defines true as any non-0 value, the relational and logical operators always produce the value 1 for true. Your programs may make use of this fact.

You can use the relational and logical operators in both the **if** and **for** statements. For example, the following statement reports when both **i** and **j** are positive.

```
if(a>0 && b>0) printf("both are positive");
```

Examples

1. In professionally written C code, it is uncommon to find a statement like this:

    ```
    if(count!=0) ...
    ```

    The reason is that in C, true is any non-0 value and false is 0. Therefore, the preceding statement is generally written as

    ```
    if(count) ...
    ```

    Further, statements like

    ```
    if(count==0) ...
    ```

    are generally written as

    ```
    if(!count) ...
    ```

    The expression **!count** is true only if **count** is zero.

2. It is important to remember that the outcome of a relational or logical operation is 0 when false and 1 when true. For example, the following program requests two integers, then displays the outcome of each relational and logical operation when applied to them.

```
#include "stdio.h"

main( )
{
  int i, j;

  printf("enter first number: ");
  scanf("%d\n", &i);
  printf("enter second number: ");
  scanf("%d\n", &j);

  /* relational operations */
  printf("i < j %d\n", i < j);
  printf("i <= j %d\n", i <= j);
  printf("i == j %d\n", i == j);
  printf("i > j %d\n", i > j);
  printf("i >= j %d\n", i >= j);

  /* logical operations */
  printf("i && j %d\n", i && j);
  printf("i || j %d\n", i || j);
  printf("!i !j %d %d\n", !i, !j);
}
```

3. C does not define an exclusive-**OR (XOR)** logical operator. However, it is easy to create a function that performs the operation. The **XOR** operation uses this truth table.

p	q	XOR
0	0	0
0	1	1
1	0	1
1	1	0

That is, the XOR operation produces a true result when one and only one operand is true. The following function uses the **&&** and **||** operators to construct an XOR operation. It compares the values of its two arguments and returns the outcome of an XOR operation.

```
xor(int a, int b)
{
  return (a || b) && !(a && b);
}
```

The following program uses this function. It displays the results of an AND, OR, and XOR on the values you enter.

```
/* This program demonstrates the xor( ) function. */
#include "stdio.h"

main( )
{
  int p, q;

  printf("enter P (0 or 1): ");
  scanf("%d", &p);
  printf("enter Q (0 or 1): ");
  scanf("%d", &q);
  printf("P AND Q: %d\n", p && q);
  printf("P OR Q: %d\n", p || q);
  printf("P XOR Q: %d\n", xor(p, q));
}

xor(int a, int b)
{
  return (a || b) && !(a && b);
}
```

Exercises

1. What does this loop do?

   ```
   for(x=0; x<100; x++) printf("%d ", x);
   ```

2. Is this expression true?

   ```
   !(10==9)
   ```

3. Do these two expressions evaluate to the same outcome?

   a. 0 && 1 || 1

   b. 0 && (1 || 1)

EXERCISES

MASTERY
SKILLS CHECK

√

1. Write a program that plays a computerized form of
   the "guess the magic number" game. It works like
   this. The player has ten tries to guess the magic
   number. If the number entered is the value you have
   selected for your magic number, have the program
   print the message "RIGHT!" and then terminate.
   Otherwise, have the program report whether the
   guess was high or low and then let the player enter
   another number. This process goes on until the
   player guesses the number. For fun, you might want
   to report the number of tries.

2. Write a program that computes the square footage
   of a house given the dimensions of each room. Have
   the program ask the user how many rooms are in
   the house and then request the dimensions of each
   room. Display the resulting total square footage.

3. What are the increment and decrement operators
   and what do they do?

4. Create an improved addition-drill program that
   keeps track of the number of right and wrong answers and displays them when the program ends.

5. Write a program that prints the numbers **1** to **100**
   using 5 columns. Have each number separated from
   the next by a tab.

CHAPTER OBJECTIVES

3.1 Input characters

3.2 Nest **if** statements

3.3 Examine **for** loop variations

3.4 Understand C's **while** loop

3.5 Use the **do** loop

3.6 Create nested loops

3.7 Use **break** to exit a loop

3.8 Know when to use the **continue** statement

3.9 Select paths with the **switch** statement

3.10 Understand the **goto** statement

·3·
More C Program Control Statements

This chapter continues the discussion of C's program control statements. Before doing so, however, the chapter begins by explaining how to enter characters from the keyboard. Although you know how to enter numbers, it is now time for you to know how to enter characters because several examples in this chapter will make use of them. Next, the chapter finishes the dicussion of the **if** and **for** statements. Then it presents C's two other loop statements, the **while** and **do**. Next you will learn about nested loops and two more of C's control statements, the **break** and **continue**. It also covers C's other selection statement, the **switch**. The chapter ends with a short discussion of C's unconditional jump statement, **goto**.

EXERCISES

Before proceeding, you should be able to answer these questions and perform these exercises.

SKILLS CHECK

√

1. What are C's relational and logical operators?

2. What is a block of code? How do you make one?

3. How do you output a newline using **printf( )**?

4. Write a program that prints the numbers **−100** to **100**.

5. Write a program that prints 5 different proverbs. The program prompts the user for the number of the proverb to print and then displays it. (Use any proverbs you like.)

6. How can this statement be rewritten?

    ```
    count = count + 1;
    ```

7. What values are true in C? What values are false?

3.1 INPUT CHARACTERS

Although numbers are important, your programs will also need to read characters from the keyboard. In C you can do this in a variety of ways. Unfortunately, this conceptually simple task is complicated by some baggage left over from the origins of C. However, let's begin with the traditional way characters are read from the keyboard. Later you will learn some alternatives.

The original version of C defined a function called **getchar( )**, which returns a single character typed on the keyboard. When called, the function waits for a key to be pressed. Then **getchar( )** echoes the keystroke to the screen and returns the value of the key to the caller. The **getchar( )** function is defined by the ANSI C standard and requires the header file STDIO.H. This program illustrates its use by reading a character and then telling you what it received. (Remember, to display a character, use the **%c printf( )** format specifier.)

```
#include "stdio.h"

main( )
{
  char ch;

  ch = getchar( ); /* read a char */
  printf(" you typed: %c", ch);
}
```

If you try this program, it may behave differently than you expected. The trouble is this: in many C compilers, **getchar( )** is implemented in such a way that it *line buffers* input. This means that even though it will return one character to your program, it waits until you press ENTER before doing so. The reason for this is that the early version of UNIX, for which C was developed, line buffered input. When C compilers were created for other interactive environments, developers had to decide how to make **getchar( )** behave. Many C compiler developers have decided, for the sake of compatibility, to keep **getchar( )** line-buffered, even though there is no reason for it. (In fact, the ANSI standard states that **getchar( )** need not be line-buffered.) When **getchar( )** is implemented in a line-buffered fashion in a modern interactive environment, it is rendered nearly useless.

Because many implementations have implemented line-buffered versions of **getchar( )**, most C compilers supply another function to perform interactive console input. Although it is not defined by the ANSI C standard, most compilers call this function **getche( )**. You use it just like **getchar( )**, except that it will return its value immediately after a key is pressed; it does not line-buffer input. For most compilers, this function requires a header file called CONIO.H, but it might be called something different in your compiler.

The examples in this book will use the **getche( )** function. However, if your compiler does not include this function, substitute **getchar( )**.

Virtually all computers use the ASCII character codes when representing characters. Therefore, characters returned by either **getchar( )** or **getche( )** will be represented by their ASCII codes. This is useful because the ASCII characters codes are an ordered sequence; each letter's code is one greater than the one it precedes. In C, you may compare characters just like you compare numbers. This means that "a" is less than "b," and so on. For example,

```
ch = getche( );
if(ch < 'f') printf("character is less than f");
```

is a perfectly valid fragment that will display its message if the user enters any character that comes before **f**.

Examples

1. This program reads a character and displays its ASCII code. This illustrates an important feature of C: you can use a character as if it were a "little integer."

```
#include "conio.h"
#include "stdio.h"

main( )
{
  char ch;

  printf("enter a character: ");
  ch = getche( );
  printf("\nIts ASCII code is %d", ch);
}
```

2. One of the most common uses of **getche( )** is to return a menu selection. For example, this program allows the user to add, subtract, multiply, or divide two numbers.

```
#include "conio.h"
#include "stdio.h"

main( )
{
  int a, b;
  char ch;

  printf("Do you want to:\n");
  printf("Add, Subtract, Multiply, or Divide?\n");
  printf("Enter first letter: ");
  ch = getche( );
  printf("\n");

  printf("Enter first number: ");
  scanf("%d", &a);
  printf("Enter second number: ");
  scanf("%d", &b);

  if(ch=='A') printf("%d", a+b);
  if(ch=='S') printf("%d", a-b);
  if(ch=='M') printf("%d", a*b);
  if(ch=='D' && b!=0) printf("%d", a/b);
}
```

One point to keep in mind is that C makes a distinction between upper- and lowercase letters. So, if the user enters an **s**, the program will not recognize it as a request to subtract. (Later, you will learn how to convert the case of a character.)

3. Another common reason that your program will need to read a character from the keyboard is to obtain a yes/no response from the user. For example, this fragment determines if the user wants to proceed.

```
printf("Do you wish to continue? (Y/N): ");
ch = getche( );
if(ch=='Y') {
  /* continue with something */
  .
  .
  .

}
```

Exercise

1. Write a program that reads ten letters. After the letters have been read, display the one that comes earliest in the alphabet. (The one with the smallest value comes first.)

3.2 NEST if STATEMENTS

When an **if** statement is the target of another **if** or **else**, it is said to be *nested* within the outer **if**. Here is a simple example of a nested **if**.

```
if(count>max) /* outer if */
  if(error) printf("error, try again"); /* nested if */
```

Notice how the nested **if** is indented. This is common practice. It enables anyone reading your program to know quickly that the **if** is nested and what actions are nested. A nested **if** may appear inside a block of statements that are the target of the outer **if**.

An ANSI-standard compiler will allow you to nest **ifs** at least 15 levels deep. (However, it would be rare to find such deep nesting.)

One confusing aspect of nested **ifs** is illustrated by the following fragment.

```
if(p)
  if(q) printf("a and b are true");
else printf("To which statement does this else apply?");
```

The question, as suggested by the second **printf( )**, is: which **if** is associated with the **else**? Fortunately, the answer is quite easy: an **else** always associates with the nearest **if** within the same block. In this example, the **else** is associated with the second **if**.

Examples

1. It is possible to string together several **ifs** and **elses** into what is sometimes called an *if-else-if ladder* or *if-else staircase* because of its visual appearance. In this situation a nested **if** has as its target another **if**. The general form of the if-else-if ladder is shown here.

```
if (expression) statement;
else
   if (expression) statement;
   else
      if (expression) statement;

      .

      .

      .

            else statement;
```

The conditions are evaluated from the top downward. As soon as a true condition is found, the statement associated with it is executed, and the rest of the ladder is bypassed. If none of the conditions is true, the final **else** will be executed. That is, if all other conditional tests fail, the last **else** statement is performed. If the final **else** is not present, no action will take place if all other conditions are false.

Although the indentation of the general form of the if-else-if ladder is technically correct, it can lead to overly deep indentation. Because of this, the if-else-if ladder is generally indented like this:

```
if(expression)
   statement;
else if(expression)
   statement;
else if(expression)
   statement;

   .

   .

   .

else
   statement;
```

We can improve the arithmetic program developed in Section 3.1 by using an if-else-if ladder, as shown here.

```
#include "conio.h"
#include "stdio.h"

main( )
{
  int a, b;
  char ch;

  printf("Do you want to:\n");
  printf("Add, Subtract, Multiply, or Divide?\n");
  printf("Enter first letter: ");
  ch = getche( );
  printf("\n");

  printf("Enter first number: ");
  scanf("%d", &a);
  printf("Enter second number: ");
  scanf("%d", &b);

  if(ch=='A') printf("%d", a+b);
  else if(ch=='S') printf("%d", a-b);
  else if(ch=='M') printf("%d", a*b);
  else if(ch=='D' && b!=0) printf("%d", a/b);
}
```

This is an improvement over the original version because once a match is found, any remaining **if** statements are skipped. This means that the program isn't wasting time on needless operations. While this is not too important in this example, you will encounter situations where it will be.

2. Nested **if** statements are very common in programming. For example, here is a further improvement to the addition drill program developed in the pre-

ceding chapter. It lets the user have a second try at getting the right answer.

```c
#include "conio.h"
#include "stdio.h"

main( )
{
  int answer, count;
  char again;

  for(count=1; count<11; count++) {
    printf("What is %d + %d? ", count, count);
    scanf("%d", &answer);
    if(answer == count+count) printf("Right!\n");
    else {
      printf("Sorry, you're wrong\n");
      printf("Would you like to try again? (Y/N)");
      again = getche( );
      printf("\n");

      /* nested if */
      if(again=='Y') {
        printf("\nWhat is %d + %d? ", count, count);
        scanf("%d", &answer);
        if(answer == count+count) printf("Right!\n");
        else
          printf("Wrong, the answer is %d\n", count+count);
      }
      else
        printf("the answer is %d\n", count+count);
    }
  }
}
```

Exercises

1. To which **if** does the **else** relate to in this example?

```
if(ch=='S') {   /* first if */
  printf("Enter a number: ");
  scanf("%d", &y);

  /* second if */
  if(y) printf("its square is %d", y*y);
}
else printf("make next selection");
```

2. Write a program that computes the area of either a circle, rectangle, or triangle. Use an if-else-if ladder.

3.3 EXAMINE for LOOP VARIATIONS

The **for** loop in C is significantly more powerful and flexible than in most other computer languages. When you were introduced to the **for** loop in Chapter 2, you were only shown the form similar to that used by other languages. However, you will see that **for** is much more flexible.

The reason that **for** is so flexible is that the expressions we called the initialization, conditional test, and increment portions of the loop are not limited to these narrow roles. The C **for** loop places no limits on the types of expressions that occur inside it. For example, you do not have to use the initialization section to initialize a loop-control variable. Further, there does not need to be any loop-control variable because the conditional test expression may use some other means of stopping the loop. Finally, the increment portion is technically just an expression that is evaluated each time the loop iterates. It does not have to increment or decrement a variable.

Another important reason that the **for** is so flexible is that one or more of the expressions inside it may be empty. For example, if the loop control variable has already been initialized outside the **for**, there is no need for an initialization expression.

Examples

1. This program continues to loop until a **q** is entered at the keyboard. Instead of testing a loop control variable, the conditional test in this **for** checks the value of a character entered by the user.

```
#include "stdio.h"
#include "conio.h"

main( )
{
  int i;
  char ch;

  ch = 'a';  /* give ch an initial value */

  for(i=0; ch!='q'; i++) {
    printf("pass: %d\n", i);
    ch = getche( );
  }
}
```

Here, the condition that controls the loop has nothing to do with the loop-control variable. The reason **ch** is given an initial value is to prevent it from accidentally containing a **q** when the program begins.

2. As stated earlier, it is possible to leave an expression in a loop empty. For example, this program asks the user for a value and then counts down to 0 from this number. Here, the loop-control variable is initial-

ized by the user outside the loop, so the initialization portion of the loop is emtpy.

```
#include "stdio.h"

main( )
{
  int i;

  printf("Enter an integer: ");
  scanf("%d", &i);

  for( ; i; i--) printf("%d ", i);
}
```

3. Another variation to **for** is that its target may be empty. For example, this program simply keeps inputting characters until the user types **q**.

```
#include "stdio.h"
#include "conio.h"

main( )
{
  char ch;

  for(ch=getche( ); ch!='q'; ch=getche( ))   ;
  printf("found the q");
}
```

Notice that the statements assigning **ch** a value have been moved into the loop. This means that when the loop starts, **getche( )** is called. Then, the value of **ch** is tested against **q**. Next, conceptually, the nonexistent target of the **for** is executed, and the call to **getche( )** in the increment portion of the loop is executed. This process repeats until the user enters a **q**.

The reason the target of the **for** can be empty is because C allows null statements.

4. Using the **for**, it is possible to create a loop that never stops. This type of loop is usually called an *infinite loop*. Although accidentally creating an infinite loop is a bug, you will sometimes want to create one on purpose. (Later in this chapter, you will see that there are ways to exit even an infinite loop!) To create an infinite loop, use a **for** construct like this:

```
for( ; ; ) {
  .
  .
  .

}
```

As you can see, there are no expressions in the **for**. When there is no expression in the conditional portion, the compiler assumes that it is true. Therefore, the loop continues to run.

5. In C, unlike most other computer languages, it is perfectly valid for the loop-control variable to be altered outside the increment section. For example, the following program manually increments **i** at the bottom of the loop.

```
#include "stdio.h"

main( )
{
  int i;

  for(i=0; i<10; ) {
    printf("%d ", i);
    i++;
  }
}
```

Exercises

1. Write a program that computes driving time when given the distance and the average speed. Use a loop and prompt the user like this:

    ```
    Again? (Y/N)
    ```

    Repeat the process each time a **Y** is entered.

2. To create time-delay loops **for** loops with empty targets are often used. Create a program that asks the user for a number and then iterates until 0 is reached. Once the countdown is done, sound the bell, but don't display anything on the screen.

3. Even if a **for** loop uses a loop-control variable, it need not be incremented or decremented by a fixed amount. Instead, the amount added or subtracted may vary. Write a program that begins at 1 and runs to 1000. Have the program add the loop-control variable to itself inside the increment expression. This is an easy way to produce the arithmetic progression 1 2 4 8 16, and so on.

3.4   UNDERSTAND C's while LOOP

Another of C's loops is **while**. It has this general form:

while(*expression*) *statement*;

Of course, the target of **while** may also be a block of code. The **while** loop works by repeating its target as long as the expression is true. When it becomes false, the loop stops. The value of the expression is checked at the top of the loop. This means that if the expression is false to begin with, the loop will not execute even once.

Examples

1. Even though the **for** is flexible enough to allow itself to be controlled by factors not related to its traditional use, you should generally select the loop that best fits the needs of the situation. For example, a better way to wait for the letter 'q' to be typed is shown here using **while**. If you compare it to Example 3 in Section 3.3, you will see how much clearer this version is. (However, you will soon see that a better loop for this job exists.)

```c
#include "stdio.h"
#include "conio.h"

main( )
{
  char ch;

  ch = getche( );

  while(ch!='q') ch = getche( );

  printf("found the q");
}
```

2. The following program is a simple code machine. It translates the characters you type into a coded form by adding 1 to each letter. That is, 'A' becomes 'B,' and so forth. The program stops when you press ENTER. (The **getche( )** function returns \r when ENTER is pressed.)

```
#include "stdio.h"
#include "conio.h"

main( )
{
  char ch;

  printf("Enter your message.\n");

  ch = getche( );
  while(ch!='\r') {
    printf("%c", ch+1);
    ch = getche( );
  }
}
```

Exercises

1. In Exercise 1 of Section 3.3, you created a program that computed driving time, given distance, and average speed. You used a **for** loop to let the user compute several drive times. Rework that program so that it uses a **while** loop.

2. Write a program that will decode messages that have been encoded using the code machine program in the second example in this section.

3.5 USE THE do LOOP

C's final loop is **do**, which has this general form:

do {
    statements
} while(*expression*);

If only one statement is being repeated, the curly braces are not necessary. Most programmers include them, however, so that they can easily recognize that the **while** that ends the **do** is part of a **do** loop, not the beginning of a **while** loop.

The **do** loop repeats the statement or statements while the expression is true. It stops when the expression becomes false. The **do** loop is unique because it will always execute the code within the loop at least once, since the expression controlling the loop is tested at the bottom of the loop.

Examples

1. The fact that **do** will always execute the body of its loop at least once makes it perfect for checking menu input. For example, this version of the arithmetic program reprompts the user until a valid response is entered.

```c
#include "conio.h"
#include "stdio.h"

main( )
{
  int a, b;
  char ch;

  printf("Do you want to:\n");
  printf("Add, Subtract, Multiply, or Divide?\n");

  /* force user to enter a valid response */
  do {
    printf("Enter first letter: ");
    ch = getche( );
    printf("\n");
  } while(ch!='A' && ch!='S' && ch!='M' && ch!='D');
```

```
      printf("Enter first number: ");
      scanf("%d", &a);
      printf("Enter second number: ");
      scanf("%d", &b);

      if(ch=='A') printf("%d", a+b);
      else if(ch=='S') printf("%d", a-b);
      else if(ch=='M') printf("%d", a*b);
      else if(ch=='D' && b!=0) printf("%d", a/b);
    }
```

2. The **do** loop is especially useful when your program is waiting for some event to occur. For example, this program waits for the user to type a **q**. Notice that it contains one less call to **getche( )** than the equivalent program described in the section on the **while** loop.

```
#include "stdio.h"
#include "conio.h"

main( )
{
  char ch;

  do {
    ch = getche( );
  } while(ch!='q');

  printf("found the q");
}
```

Since the loop condition is tested at the bottom, it is not necessary to initialize **ch** prior to entering the loop.

Exercises

1. Write a program that converts gallons to liters. Using a **do** loop, allow the user to repeat the conversion. (One gallon is approximately 3.7854 liters.)

2. Write a program that displays the menu below and uses a **do** loop to check for valid responses. (Your program does not need to implement the actual functions shown in the menu.)

Mailing list menu:

1. Enter addresses

2. Delete address

3. Search the list

4. Print the list

5. Quit

Enter the number of your choice (1-5):

3.6 CREATE NESTED LOOPS

When the body of one loop contains another, the second is said to be nested inside the first. Any of C's loops may be nested within any other loop. The ANSI C standard specifies that loops may be nested at least 15 levels deep. However, most compilers allow nesting to virtually any level. As a simple example of nested **for**s, this fragment prints the numbers **1** to **10** on the screen ten times.

```
for(i=0; i<10; i++) {
  for(j=1; j<11; j++) printf("%d ", j);
  printf("\n");
}
```

Examples

1. You can use a nested **for** to make another improvement to the arithmetic drill. In the version shown below, the program will give the user three chances to get the right answer. Notice the use of the variable **right** to stop the loop early if the correct answer is given.

```c
#include "conio.h"
#include "stdio.h"

main( )
{
  int answer, count, chances, right;

  for(count=1; count<11; count++) {
    printf("What is %d + %d? ", count, count);
    scanf("%d", &answer);
    if(answer == count+count) printf("Right!\n");
    else {
      printf("Sorry, you're wrong\n");
      printf("Try again\n");

      right = 0;
      /* nested for */
      for(chances=0; chances<3 && !right; chances++) {
        printf("\nWhat is %d + %d? ", count, count);
        scanf("%d", &answer);
        if(answer == count+count) {
          printf("Right!\n");
          right = 1;
        }
      }
    }
```

```
      /* if answer still wrong, tell user */
      if (!right)
        printf("the answer is %d.\n", count+count);
    }
  }
}
```

2. This program uses three **for** loops to print the alphabet three times, each time printing each letter twice.

```
#include "stdio.h"

main ( )
{
  int i, j, k;
  for (i=0; i<3; i++)
    for (j=0; j<26; j++)
      for (k=0; k<2; k++) printf ("%c", 'A'+j);
}
```

The statement

```
printf ("%c", 'A'+j);
```

works because ASCII codes for the letters of the alphabet are strictly ascending, each one greater than the one that precedes it.

Exercises

1. Write a program that finds all the prime numbers between 2 and 1000.

2. Write a program that reads ten characters from the keyboard. Each time a character is read, use its ASCII code value to output a string of periods equal in number to this code. For example, given the letter 'A,' whose code is 65, your program would output 65 periods.

3.7 USE break TO EXIT A LOOP

The **break** statement allows you to exit a loop from any point within its body, bypassing its normal termination expression. When the **break** statement is encountered inside a loop, the loop is immediately terminated, and program control resumes at the next statement following the loop. For example, this loop prints only the numbers **1** to **10**

```
#include "stdio.h"

main( )
{
  int i;

  for(i=1; i<100; i++) {
    printf("%d ", i);
    if(i==10) break;  /* exit the loop */
  }
}
```

The **break** statement can be used with all three of C's loops.

You can have as many **break** statements within a loop as you desire. However, since too many exit points from a loop tend to destructure your code, it is generally best to use the **break** for special purposes, not as your normal loop exit.

Examples

1. The **break** statement is commonly used in loops in which a special condition can cause immediate termination. This is an example of such a situation,

where a keypress can stop the execution of the program.

```c
#include "stdio.h"
#include "conio.h"

main( )
{
  int i;
  char ch;

  /* display all numbers which are multiples of 6 */
  for(i=1; i<10000; i++) {
    if(!(i%6)) {
      printf("%d more? (Y/N)", i);
      ch = getche( );
      if(ch=='N') break;
      printf("\n");
    }
  }
}
```

2. A **break** will cause an exit from only the innermost loop. For example, this program prints the numbers **1** to **5** five times.

```c
#include "stdio.h"

main( )
{
  int i, j;

  for(i=0; i<5; i++) {
    for(j=0; j<100; j++) {
      printf("%d", j);
      if(j==5) break;
    }
    printf("\n");
  }
}
```

3. The reason that C includes the **break** statement is to allow your programs to be more efficient. For example, examine this fragment.

```
do {
  printf("Load, Save, Edit, Quit?\n");
  do {
    printf("Enter your selection: ");
    ch = getche( );
  } while(ch!='L' && ch!='S' && ch!='E' && ch!='Q');

  if(ch!='Q') {
    /* do something */
  }

  if(ch!='Q') {
    /* do something else */
  }
  /* etc. */
} while(ch!='Q')
```

In this situation, several additional tests are performed on **ch** to see if it is equal to **Q** to avoid executing irrelevant code when the **Quit** option is selected. Most C programmers will write a loop such as this, instead.

```
for( ; ; ) {  /* infinite for loop */
  printf("Load, Save, Edit, Quit?\n");
  do {
    printf("Enter your selection: ");
    ch = getche( );
  } while(ch!='L' && ch!='S' && ch!='E' && ch!='Q');

  if(ch=='Q') break;

  /* do something */
  /* do something else */
  /* etc. */
}
```

In this way, **ch** need only be tested once to see if it contains a **Q**.

Exercise

1. On your own, write several short programs that use **break** to exit a loop. Be sure to try all three loop statements.

2. Write a program that prints a table showing the proper amount of tip to leave. Start the table at $1 and stop at $100, using increments of $1. Compute three tip percentages: 10%, 15%, and 20%. After each line, ask the user if he or she wants to continue. If not, use **break** to stop the loop and end the program.

3.8 KNOW WHEN TO USE THE continue STATEMENT

The **continue** statement is somewhat the opposite of the **break** statement. It forces the next iteration of the loop to take place, skipping any code in between itself and the test condition of the loop. For example, this program never displays any output.

```
#include "stdio.h"

main( )
{
  int x;
```

```
for(x=0; x<100; x++) {
  continue;
  printf("%d ", x); /* this is never executed */
}
}
```

Each time the **continue** statement is reached, it causes the loop to repeat, skipping the **printf( )** statement.

In **while** and **do-while** loops, a **continue** statement will cause control to go directly to the test condition and then continue the looping process. In the case of **for**, the increment part of the loop is performed, the conditional test is executed, and the loop continues.

Frankly, **continue** is seldom used, not because it is poor practice to use it, but simply because good applications for it are not common.

Example

1. One good use for **continue** is to restart a statement sequence when an error occurs. For example, this program computes a running total of numbers entered by the user. Before adding a value to the running total, it verifies that the number was correctly entered. If it wasn't, it uses **continue** to restart the loop.

```
#include "stdio.h"
#include "conio.h"

main( )
{
```

```
int total, i;
char ch;

total = 0;
do {
  printf("Enter next number (0 to stop): ");
  scanf("%d", &i);
  printf("Is %d correct? (Y/N): ", i);
  ch = getche( );
  printf("\n");
  if(ch=='N') continue;
  total = total + i;
} while(i);

printf("Total is %d\n", total);
}
```

Exercise

1. Write a program that prints only the odd numbers
   between **1** and **100**. Use a **for** loop that looks like this:

   ```
   for(i=1; i<101; i++) . . .
   ```

   Use a **continue** statement to avoid printing even
   numbers.

3.9 SELECT PATHS WITH THE switch STATEMENT

While **if** is good for choosing between two alternatives,
it quickly becomes cumbersome when several alternatives are needed. C's solution to this problem is the
switch statement. The **switch** statement is C's multiple
selection statement. It is used to select one of several

alternative paths in program execution and works like this: A variable is successively tested against a list of integer or character constants. When a match is found, the statement sequence associated with that match is executed. The general form of the **switch** statement is

```
switch(variable) {
    case constant1:
        statement sequence
        break;
    case constant2:
        statement sequence
        break;
    case constant3:
        statement sequence
        break;
        .

        .

        .

    default:
        statement sequence
}
```

where the **default** statement sequence is performed if no matches are found. The **default** is optional. If all matches fail and **default** is absent, no action takes place. When a match is found, the statements associated with that **case** are executed until **break** is encountered or, in the case of **default** or the last **case**, the end of the **switch** is reached.

As a very simple example, this program recognizes the numbers 1, 2, 3, and 4 and prints the name of the one you enter. That is, if you enter **2**, the program displays **two**.

```
#include "stdio.h"

main( )
{
  int i;

  printf("Enter a number between 1 and 4: ");
  scanf("%d", &i);
  switch(i) {
    case 1:
      printf("one");
      break;
    case 2:
      printf("two");
      break;
    case 3:
      printf("three");
      break;
    case 4:
      printf("four");
      break;
    default:
      printf("unrecognized number");
  }
}
```

The **switch** statement differs from **if**, in that **switch** can only test for equality, whereas the **if** conditional expression can be of any type. Also, **switch** will work with only **int** or **char** types. You cannot, for example, use floating-point numbers.

The statement sequences associated with each **case** are *not* blocks; they are not enclosed by curly braces.

The ANSI standard states that at least 257 **case** statements will be allowed. In practice, you should limit the amount of **case** statements to a much smaller number for efficiency reasons. Also, no two **case** constants in the same **switch** can have identical values.

It is possible to have a **switch** as part of the statement sequence of an outer **switch**. This is called a *nested* *switch*. If the **case** constants of the inner and outer **switch** contain common values, no conflicts will arise. For example, the following code fragment is perfectly acceptable.

```
switch(a) {
  case 1:
    switch(b) {
      case 0: printf("b is false");
              break;
      case 1: printf("b is true");
    }
    break;
  case 2:

    .

    .

    .
```

An ANSI-standard compiler will allow at least 15 levels of nesting for **switch** statements.

Examples

1. The **switch** statement is often used to process menu commands. For example, the arithmetic program can be recoded as shown here. This version reflects the way professional C code is written.

   ```
   #include "conio.h"
   #include "stdio.h"

   main( )
   {
     int a, b;
     char ch;

     printf("Do you want to:\n");
     printf("Add, Subtract, Multiply, or Divide?\n");
   ```

```
/* force user to enter a valid response */
do {
  printf("Enter first letter: ");
  ch = getche( );
  printf("\n");
} while(ch!='A' && ch!='S' && ch!='M' && ch!='D');

printf("Enter first number: ");
scanf("%d", &a);
printf("Enter second number: ");
scanf("%d", &b);

switch(ch) {
  case 'A': printf("%d", a+b);
    break;
  case 'S': printf("%d", a-b);
    break;
  case 'M': printf("%d", a*b);
    break;
  case 'D': if(b!=0) printf("%d", a/b);
}
}
```

2. Technically, the **break** statement is optional. The **break** statement, when encountered within a **switch**, causes the program flow to exit from the entire **switch** statement and continue on to the next statement outside the **switch**. This is much the way it works when breaking out of a loop. However, if a **break** statement is omitted, the execution continues into the following **case** or **default** statement (if either exists). That is, when a **break** statement is missing, execution "falls through" into the next **case** and stops only when a **break** statement or the end of the **switch** is encountered. For example, study this program carefully.

```
#include "stdio.h"
#include "conio.h"

main( )
{
  char ch;

  do {
    printf("\nEnter a character, q to quit: ");
    ch = getche( );
    printf("\n");

    switch(ch) {
      case 'a':
        printf("Now is ");
      case 'b':
        printf("the time ");
      case 'c':
        printf("for all good men");
        break;
      case 'd':
        printf("The summer ");
      case 'e':
        printf("soldier ");
    }
  } while (ch!='q');
}
```

If the user types **a**, the entire phrase **Now is the time for all good men** is displayed. Typing **b** displays **the time for all good men**. As you can see, once execution begins inside a **case**, it continues until a **break** statement or the end of the **switch** is encountered.

3. The statement sequence associated with a **case** may be empty. This allows two or more **case**s to share a common statement sequence without duplication of

code. For example, here is a program that categorizes letters into vowels and consonants.

```c
#include "stdio.h"
#include "conio.h"

main( )
{
  char ch;

  printf("Enter the letter: ");
  ch = getche( );

  switch(ch) {
    case 'a':
    case 'e':
    case 'i':
    case 'o':
    case 'u':
    case 'y':
      printf(" is a vowel\n");
      break;
    default:
      printf(" is a consonant");
  }
}
```

Exercises

1. What is wrong with this fragment?

```c
float f;

scanf("%f", &f);

switch(f) {
  case 10.05:
    .
    .
    .
```

2. Write a program that counts the number of letters, digits, and common punctuation symbols entered by the user. Stop inputting when the user presses ENTER. Use a **switch** statement to categorize the characters into punctuation, digits, and letters. When the program ends, report the number of characters in each category. (If you like, simply assume that, if a character is not a digit or punctuation, it is a letter. Also, just use the most common punctuation symbols.)

3.10 UNDERSTAND THE goto STATEMENT

C supports a non-conditional jump statement, called the **goto**. Because C is a replacement for assembly code, the inclusion of **goto** is necessary because it can be used to create very fast routines. However, most programmers do not use **goto** because it destructures a program and, if frequently used, can render the program virtually impossible to understand later. Also, there is no routine that requires a **goto**. For these reasons, it is not used in this book outside of this section.

The **goto** statement can perform a jump within a function. It cannot jump between functions. It works with a label. In C, a *label* is a valid identifier name followed by a colon. For example, the following **goto** jumps around the **printf( )** statement.

```
goto mylabel;
printf("this will not print");
mylabel: printf("this will print");
```

About the only good use for **goto** is to jump out of a deeply nested routine when a catastrophic error occurs.

Example

1. This program uses **goto** to create the equivalent of a **for** loop running from 1 to 10. (This is just an example of **goto**. In actual practice, you should use a real **for** loop when one is needed.)

```
#include "stdio.h"

main( )
{
  int i;

  i = 1;
  again:
    printf("%d ", i);
    i++;
    if(i<10) goto again;
}
```

Exercise

1. Write a program that uses **goto** to emulate a **while** loop that counts from 1 to 10.

EXERCISES

At this point, you should be able to answer these questions and perform these exercises.

MASTERY
SKILLS CHECK

√

1. The ASCII codes for the lowercase letters are separated from the uppercase letters by a difference of 32. Therefore, to convert a lowercase letter to an uppercase one, simply subtract 32 from it. Write a program that reads characters from the keyboard and dis-

plays lowercase letters as uppercase ones. Stop when ENTER is pressed.

2. Using a nested **if** statement, write a program that prompts the user for a number and then reports if the number is positive, zero, or negative.

3. Is this a valid **for** loop?

```
char ch;

ch = 'x';
for( ; ch!=' '; ) ch = getche( );
```

4. Show the traditional way to create an infinite loop in C.

5. Using the three loop statements, show three different ways to count from 1 to 10.

6. What does the **break** statement do when used in a loop?

7. Is this switch statement correct?

```
switch(i) {
  case 1: printf("nickel");
    break;
  case 2: printf("dime");
    break;
  case 3: printf("quarter");
}
```

8. Is this **goto** fragment correct?

```
goto alldone;
 .
 .
 .
alldone
```

EXERCISES

This section checks how well you have integrated the material in this chapter with that from earlier chapters.

1. Using a **switch** statement, write a program that reads characters from the keyboard and watches for tabs, newlines, and backspaces. When one is recieved, display what it is in words. For example, when the user presses the TAB key, print **tab**. Have the user enter a **q** to stop the program.

2. While this program is not incorrect, show how it would look if written by an experienced C programmer.

```
#include "stdio.h"

main( )
{
  int i, j, k;

  for(k=0; k<10; k=k+1) {
    printf("Enter first number: ");
    scanf("%d", &i);

    printf("Enter second number: ");
    scanf("%d", &j);

    if(j!=0) printf("%d\n", i/j);
    if(j==0) printf("cannot divide by zero\n");
  }
}
```

CHAPTER OBJECTIVES

4-1. Use C's data-type modifiers

4-2. Learn where variables are declared

4-3. Take a closer look at constants

4-4. Initialize variables

4-5. Understand type conversion in expressions

4-6. Understand type conversions in assignments

4-7. Program with type casts

•4•

A Closer Look at
Data Types, Variables,
and Expressions

This chapter examines more fully several concepts presented in Chapter 1. It covers C's data-type modifiers, global and local variables, and constants. It also discusses how C handles various type conversions.

EXERCISES

Before proceeding you should be able to answer these questions and perform these exercises.

1. Using C's three loop statements, show three ways to write a loop that counts from 1 to 10.

2. Convert this series of **ifs** into an equivalent **switch**.

```
if(ch=='L') load( );
else if(ch=='S') save( );
else if(ch=='E') enter( );
else if(ch=='D') display( );
else if(ch=='Q') quit( );
```

3. Write a program that inputs characters until the user strikes the ENTER key.

4. What does **break** do?

5. What does **continue** do?

6. Write a program that displays this menu, performs the selected operation, and then repeats until the user selects **Quit**.

   Convert

   1. feet to meters

   2. meters to feet

   3. ounces to pounds

   4. pounds to ounces

   5. Quit

   Enter the number of your choice:

4.1 USE C'S DATA-TYPE MODIFIERS

In Chapter 1 you learned that C has five basic data types: **void**, **char**, **int**, **float**, and **double**. These basic types, except type **void**, can be modified using C's *type modifiers* to more precisely fit your specific need. The type modifiers are

signed
unsigned
long
short

The type modifier precedes the type name. For example, this declares a **long** integer.

```
long int i;
```

Although allowed, the use of **signed** on integers is redundant because the default integer declaration assumes a signed number. (A signed number means that it can be positive or negative.) The **signed** modifier is used with **char** to create a small signed integer. In some implementions, **char** is unsigned. This means that when it is used as an integer, it can hold the positive numbers between 0 and 255. Specified as **signed**, it can hold numbers in the range −128 to 127. Since most implementations use **signed chars**, this book assumes that characters are **signed**.

The **long** modifier may be applied to **int** or **double**. When applied to **int**, it essentially doubles the length, in bits, of the base type that it modifies. For example, an integer, in many environments, is 16 bits. Therefore, a long int is 32 bits in length. When long is applied to double it roughly doubles the precision.

In theory, the short modifier halves the size of an int. Therefore, if your compiler uses 32-bit integers, a short int will be 16 bits long. However, it may have no effect in your environment. Most PC-based C compilers use 16-bit integers because that is the word size of the 8086. The ANSI C standard states that the smallest acceptable size for an int is 16 bits. It also states that the smallest acceptable size for a short int is 16 bits. Therefore, in many environments there is no difference between an int and a short int.

The unsigned modifier can be applied to char and int. It may also be used in combination with long or short. It is used to create an unsigned integer. The difference between signed and unsigned integers is in the way the high-order bit of the integer is interpreted. If a signed integer is specified, then the C compiler will generate code that assumes that the high-order bit of an integer is used as a sign flag. If the sign flag is 0, the number is positive; if it is 1, the number is negative. Negative numbers are generally represented using the *two's complement* approach. In this method, all bits in the number (except the sign flag) are reversed, and 1 is added to this number. Finally, the sign flag is set to 1. (The reason for this method of representation is that it makes it easier for the CPU to perform arithmetic operations.)

Signed integers are important for a great many algorithms, but they only have half the absolute magnitude of their unsigned brothers. For example, here is 32,767 shown in binary.

01111111 11111111

TABLE 4-1.   All Possible Combinations of C's Basic Types and
             Modifiers with Common Bit Lengths and Ranges

Type	Bit Width	Range
char	8	−128 to 127
unsigned char	8	0 to 255
signed char	8	−128 to 127
int	16	−32768 to 32767
unsigned int	16	0 to 65535
short int	15	−32768 to 32767
unsigned short int	16	0 to 65535
long int	32	−2147483648 to 2147483647
unsigned long int	32	0 to 4294967295
float	32	3.4E−38 to 3.4E+38
double	64	1.7E−308 to 1.7E+308
long double	80	3.4E−4932 to 1.1E+4932

If the high-order bit were set to 1, the number would then be interpreted as −1 (assuming two's complement format). However, if this is declared as an **unsigned int**, then when the high order bit is set to 1, the number becomes 65,535.

Table 4-1 shows all allowed combinations of the basic types and the type modifiers. The table also shows the most common size and range for each type.

C allows a shorthand notation for declaring **unsigned, short,** or **long** integers. You may simply use the word **unsigned, short,** or **long** without the **int**. The **int** is implied. For example,

```
unsigned count;
unsigned int num;
```

both declare **unsigned int** variables.

It is very important to understand that variables of type **char** may be used to hold values other than just the ASCII character set. C makes little distinction between a character and an integer, except for the magnitudes of the values each may hold. Therefore, as mentioned earlier, a **char** variable can also be used as a "small" integer with the range –128 through 127 and can be used in place of an integer when the situation does not require larger numbers.

When outputting integers modified by **short** or **long** using **printf( )**, you cannot simply use the %d specifier. The reason is that **printf( )** needs to know what type of data it is receiving. To use **printf( )** to output a **short**, use %**hd**. To output a **long**, use %**ld**. Also, when outputting an **unsigned** value, use %**u**. Finally, to output a **long double** use %**Lf**. To output an **unsigned long int**, use %**uld**.

The **scanf( )** function operates in similar fashion to **printf( )**. When reading a **short** value using **scanf( )**, use %**hd**. When reading a **long**, use %**ld**. To read a **double**, use %**ld**. To read a **long double**, use %**Ld**. To read an **unsigned long int**, use %**uld**.

Examples

1. This program shows how to input and output **short**, **long**, and **unsigned** values.

```
#include "stdio.h"

main( )
{
```

```
    unsigned u;
    long l;
    short s;

    printf("Enter an unsigned: ");
    scanf("%d", &u);
    printf("Enter a long: ");
    scanf("%ld", &l);
    printf("Enter a short: ");
    scanf("%hd", &s);

    printf("%u %ld %hd\n", u, l, s);
}
```

2. To understand the difference between the way that signed and unsigned integers are interpreted by C, run the following short program.

```
#include "stdio.h"

main( )
{
  int i;    /* a signed integer */
  unsigned int u; /* an unsigned integer */

  u = 33000;
  i = u;
  printf("%d %u", i, u);
}
```

When this program is run, the output is **–32536 33000**. The reason for this is that the bit pattern that 33000 represents as an **unsigned int** is interpreted as –32536 by a **signed int**. As you know, the %d tells **printf( )** to display an integer in decimal form.

3. In C, you may use a **char** variable any place you would use an **int** variable (assuming the differences in their ranges is not a factor). For example, the following program uses a **char** variable to control the loop that is summing the numbers between 1 and 100. For many computers, it takes the computer

less time to access a single byte (one character) than it does to access two bytes. Therefore, many professional programs use a character variable rather than an **integer** one when the range permits.

```
#include "stdio.h"

main( )
{
   int i;
   char j;

   i = 0;
   for(j=1; j<101; j++) i = j + i;

   printf("Total is: %d", i);
}
```

Exercises

1. Show how to declare an **unsigned short int** called **loc_counter**.

2. Write a program that prompts the user for a distance and computes how long it takes light to travel that distance. Use an **unsigned long int** to hold the distance. (Light travels at approximately 186,000 miles per second.)

3. Write this statement another way.

    ```
    short int i;
    ```

4.2 LEARN WHERE VARIABLES ARE DECLARED

As you learned in Chapter 1, there are two basic places where a variable will be declared: inside a function and outside all functions. These variables are called local variables and global variables, respectively. It is now time to take a closer look at these two types of variables.

Local variables (declared *inside* a function) may be referenced only by statements that are inside that function. They are not known outside their own function. One of the most important things to understand about local variables is that they exist only while the function in which they are declared is executing. That is, a local variable is created upon entry into its function and destroyed upon exit.

Since local variables are not known outside their own function, it is perfectly acceptable for local variables in different functions to have the same name. Consider the following program.

```
#include "stdio.h"

main( )
{
   f1( );
}

f1( )
{
   int count;

   for(count=0; count<10; count++) f2( );
}

f2( )
{
   int count;

   for(count=0; count<10; count++) printf("%d ", count);
}
```

This program prints the numbers **0** through **9** on the screen ten times. The fact that both functions use a variable called **count** has no effect upon the operation of the code. Therefore, what happens to **count** inside **f2( )** has no effect upon **count** in **f1( )**.

The C language contains the keyword **auto**, which can be used to declare local variables. However, since all local variables are, by default, assumed to be **auto**, it is virtually never used. Hence, you will not see it in any of the examples in this book.

Remember one important point: You must declare all local variables at the start of the function in which they are defined, prior to any program statements. For example, the following is incorrect.

```
#include "stdio.h"

main( )
{
  printf("this program won't compile");
  int i; /* this should come first */
  i = 10;
  printf("%d", i);
}
```

When a function is called, its local variables are created, and upon its return, they are destroyed. This means that local variables cannot retain their values between calls.

The formal parameters to a function are also local variables. Even though these variables perform the special task of receiving the value of the arguments passed to the function, they can be used like any other local variable within that function.

Unlike local variables, global variables are known throughout the entire program and may be used by any piece of code in the program. Also, they will hold their value during the entire execution of the program.

Global variables are created by declaring them outside
any function. For example, consider this program.

```c
#include "stdio.h"

int max; /* this is a global variable */

main( )
{
  max = 10;
  f1( );
}

f1( )
{
  int i;

  for(i=0; i<max; i++) printf("%d ", i);
}
```

Here, both **main( )** and **f1( )** reference the global variable **max**. The **main( )** function sets the value of **max** to
10, and **f1( )** uses this value to control its **for** loop.

Examples

1. In C, a local variable and a global variable may have
    the same name. For example, this is a valid program.

    ```c
    #include "stdio.h"

    int count; /* global count */

    main( )
    {
      count = 10;
      f1( );
      printf("count in main( ): %d\n", count);
    }
    ```

```
f1( )
{
  int count; /* local count */

  count = 100;
  printf("count in f1( ): %d\n", count);
}
```

The program displays this output.

```
count in f1( ): 100
count in main( ): 10
```

In **main( )**, the reference to **count** is to the global variable. Inside **f1( )**, a local variable called **count** is also defined. When the assignment statement inside **f1( )** is encountered, the compiler first looks to see if there is a local variable called **count**. Since there is, the local variable is used, not the global one with the same name. That is, when local and global variables share the same name, the compiler will always use the local variable.

2. Global variables are very helpful when the same data is used in many functions in your program. However, you should always use local variables where you can because the excessive use of global variables has some negative consequences. First, global variables use memory the entire time your program is executing, not just when they are needed. In situations where memory is in short supply, this could be a problem. Second, using a global where a local variable will do makes a function less general, because it relies on something that must be defined outside itself. For example, here is a case where global values are being used for no reason.

```
#include "stdio.h"

int m, e;

main( )
{
  m = 2;
  e = 3;

printf("%d raised to the %d power is %d", m, e, power( ));
}

/* Non-general version of power. */
power( )
{
  int temp, temp2;

  temp = 1;
  temp2 = e;
  for( ; temp2>=0; temp2--) temp = temp * m;
  return temp;
}
```

Here, the function **power( )** is created to compute the value of **m** raised to the **e**th power. Since **m** and **e** are global, the function cannot be used to compute the power of other values. However, if the program is rewritten like this, **power( )** can be used with any two values.

```
#include "stdio.h"

main( )
{
  int m, e;
  m = 2;
  e = 3;

  printf("%d to the %d is %d\n", m, e, power(m, e));
```

```
  printf("4 to the 5 is %d", power(4, 5));
}

/* Parameterized version of power. */
power(int m, int e)
{
  int temp;

  temp = 1;
  for( ; e>=0; e--) temp = temp * m;
  return temp;
}
```

By parameterizing **power ( )**, you can now use it to return the result of any value raised to some power, as the program now shows.

The important point is that in the non-generalized version, any program that uses **power( )** must always declare **m** and **e** as global variables and then load them with the desired values each time **power( )** is used. In the parameterized form, the function is complete within itself—no extra baggage need be carried about when it is used.

Finally, using a large number of global variables can lead to program errors because of unknown and unwanted side effects. A major problem in developing large programs is the accidental modification of a variable's value because it was used elsewhere in the program. This can happen in C if you use too many global variables in your programs.

3. Remember, local variables do not maintain their values between function calls. For example, the following program will not work correctly.

```
#include "stdio.h"

main( )
{
  int i;

  for(i=0; i<10; i++) printf("%d", series( ));

}

/* This is incorrect. */
series( )
{
  int total;

  total = (total + 1423) % 1422;
  return total;
}
```

This program attempts to use **series( )** to generate a number series in which each number is based upon the value of the preceding one. However, the value **total** will not be maintained between function calls, and the function fails to carry out its intended task.

Exercises

1. What are key differences between local and global variables?

2. Write a program that contains a function called **soundspeed( )**, which computes the number of seconds it will take sound to travel a specified distance.

Make the program repeatedly request distances until the user enters **0**. Write the program two ways: first, with **soundspeed( )** as a nongeneral function and second, with **soundspeed( )** parameterized. (For the speed of sound, use 1129 feet per second).

4.3 TAKE A CLOSER LOOK AT CONSTANTS

Constants refer to fixed values that may not be altered by the program. For example, the number 100 is a constant. We have been using constants in the preceding sample programs without much fanfare because, in most cases, their use is intuitive. However, the time has come to cover them formally.

Integer constants are specified as numbers without fractional components. For example, 10 and −100 are integer constants. Floating-point constants require the use of the decimal point followed by the number's fractional component. For example, 11.123 is a floating-point constant. C also allows you to use scientific notation for floating-point numbers. Constants using scientific notation must follow this general form.

number E *sign exponent*

The *sign* is optional. Although the general form is shown with spaces between the component parts for clarity, there may be no spaces between the parts in an actual number. For example, the following defines the value 1234.56 using scientific notation.

```
123.456E1
```

Character constants are enclosed between single quotes. For example 'a' and '%' are both character constants. As some of the examples have shown, this means that if you wish to assign a character to a variable of type **char**, you will use a statement similar to

```
ch = 'Z';
```

However, there is nothing in C that prevents you from assigning a character variable a value using a numeric constant. For example, the ASCII code for 'A' is 65. Therefore, these two assignment statements are equivalent.

```
char ch;

ch = 'A';
ch = 65;
```

When you enter numeric constants into your program, the compiler must decide what type of constant they are. For example, is 1000 an **int**, an **unsigned**, or a **short**? The reason we haven't worried about this earlier is that C automatically converts the type of the right side of an assignment statement to that of the variable on the left. (We will examine this process more fully later in this chapter.) So, for many situations it doesn't matter what the compiler thinks 1000 is. However, this can be important when you use a constant as an argument to a function. In such a situation, the compiler must pass the correctly sized value to the function.

By default, the C compiler fits a numeric constant into the smallest compatible data type that will hold it. Therefore, 10 is an **int** by default, but 64000 is **unsigned** and 100001 is a **long**. Even though the value 10 could be fit into a **char**, the compiler will not do this because it means crossing type boundaries. The only exceptions to the smallest-type rule are floating-point constants, which are assumed to be **double**s. For virtually all progams you will write as a beginner, the compiler defaults are perfectly adequate. However, as you will see later in this book, there will come a point when you will need to specify precisely the type of constant you want.

In cases where the default assumption that C makes about a numeric constant is not what you want, C allows you to specify the exact type of numeric constant by using a suffix. For floating-point types, if you follow the number with an 'F,' the number is treated as a **float**. If you follow it with an 'L,' the number becomes a **long double**. For integer types, the 'U' suffix stands for **unsigned** and the 'L' for **long**.

As you may know, in programming it is sometimes easier to use a number system based on 8 or 16 instead of 10. As you learned in Chapter 2, the number system based on 8 is called *octal* and it uses the digits 0 through 7. The base-16 number system is called *hexadecimal* and uses the digits 0 through 9 plus the letters 'A' through 'F,' which stand for 10 through 15. C allows you to specify integer constants as hexadecimal or octal instead of decimal if you prefer. A hexadecimal constant must begin with '0x' (a zero followed by an 'x') then the constant in hexadecimal form. An octal constant begins with a zero. For example, **0xAB** is a hexadecimal constant, and **024** is an octal constant. You may use either upper- or lowercase letters when entering hexadecimal constants.

C supports one other type of constant in addition to those of the predefined data types: the string. A string is a set of characters enclosed by double quotes. You have been working with strings since Chapter 1 because both the **printf( )** and **scanf( )** functions use them. Keep in mind one important fact: although C allows you to define string constants, it does not formally have a string data type. Instead, as you will see a little later in this book, strings are supported in C as character arrays. (Arrays are discussed in Chapter 5.)

To display a string using **printf( )** you can either just make it part of the control string or you can use the **%s** format code. For example, this program prints the sentence **Once upon a time** on the screen.

```
#include "stdio.h"

main( )
{
  printf("%s %s %s", "Once ", "upon ", "a time");
}
```

Examples

1. To see why it is important to use the correct type specifier with **printf( )**, try this program. Instead of printing the number **42340**, it displays – **23196**, because it thinks that it is receiving a signed integer. To make it work properly, you must use the **%u** specifier.

    ```
    #include "stdio.h"

    main( )
    {
      printf("%d", 42340); /* this won't work right */
    }
    ```

2. To see why you may need to explicitly tell the compiler what type of constant you are using, try this program.

```
#include "stdio.h"

main( )
{
   printf("%ld", 2309);
}
```

This program is telling **printf( )** to expect a **long int**, but the compiler assumes that 2309 is simply an **int**. Hence, it does not output the correct value. To fix it, you must specify **2309** as **2309L**.

Exercises

1. How do you tell the C compiler that a floating-point constant should be represented as a **float** instead of a **double**?

2. Write a program that reads and writes a **long int** value.

3. Write a program that outputs **I like C** using three separate strings.

4.4 INITIALIZE VARIABLES

A variable may be given an initial value when it is declared. This is called *variable initialization*. The general form of variable initialization is shown here.

type var-name = constant;

For example, this statement declares **count** as an **int** and gives it an initial value of 100.

```
int count = 100;
```

The main advantage of using an initialization rather than separate assignment statement is that the compiler may be able to produce faster code. Also, this saves some typing effort on your part.

Remember, you can only use constants in initializations. You may not use a variable name.

Global variables are initialized only once, at the start of program execution. Local variables are initialized each time a function is entered.

Variables that are not initialized should be assumed to contain unknown values. Although some C compilers automatically initialize noninitialized variables to 0, you should not count on this.

Examples

1. This program gives **i** the initial value of −1 and then displays its value.

```
#include "stdio.h"

main( )
{
   int i = -1;

   printf("i is initialized to %d", i);
}
```

2. When you declare a list of variables, you may initialize one or more of them. For example, this fragment initializes **min** to 0 and **max** to 100. It does not initialize **count**.

```
int min=0, count, max=100;
```

3. As stated earlier, local variables are initialized each time the function is entered. For this reason, this program prints **10** three times.

```
#include "stdio.h"

main( )
{
  f( );
  f( );
  f( );
}

f( )
{
  int i = 10;

  printf("%d ", i);
}
```

Exercises

1. Write a program that gives an integer variable called **count** an initial value of 100 and then uses **count** to control a **for** loop that displays the numbers **100** down to **1**.

2. Is this line of code correct?

    ```
    int a=1, b=2, c=a;
    ```

4.5 UNDERSTAND TYPE CONVERSION IN EXPRESSIONS

Unlike many other computer languages, C lets you mix different types of data together in one expression. For example, this is a perfectly valid C code.

```
char ch;
int i;
float f;
double outcome;
```

```
ch = '0';
i = 10;
f = 10.2;

outcome = ch*i/f;
```

C allows the mixing of types within an expression because it has a strict set of conversion rules that dictate how type differences are resolved. Let's look closely at them in this section.

One portion of C's conversion rules is called *type promotions*. In C, whenever a **char** or a **short int** is used in an expression, its value is automatically elevated to **int** during the evaluation of that expression. This is why you can use **char** variables as "little integers" anywhere you can use an **int** variable. Keep in mind that the type promotion is only in effect during the evaluation of an expression. The variable does not become physically larger. (In essence, the compiler just uses a temporary copy of its value.)

After the automatic type promotions have been applied, the C compiler will convert all operands "up" to the type of the largest operand. This is done on an operation-by-operation basis, as described in the following type-conversion algorithm.

IF an operand is a **long double**
THEN the second is converted to **long double**
ELSE IF an operand is a **double**
THEN the second is converted to **double**
ELSE IF an operand is a **float**
THEN the second is converted to **float**
ELSE IF an operand is an **unsigned long**
THEN the second is converted to **unsigned long**
ELSE IF an operand is **long**
THEN the second is converted to **long**

ELSE IF an operand is **unsigned**

THEN the second is converted to **unsigned**

Once these conversion rules have been applied, each pair of operands will be of the same type and the result of each operation will be the same as the type of both operands.

Examples

1. In this program, **i** is elevated to a **float**. Thus, the program prints **232.3**.

```
#include "stdio.h"

main( )
{
  int i;
  float f;

  i = 10;
  f = 23.23;

  printf("%f", i*f);
}
```

2. This program illustrates how **short ints** are automatically promoted to **ints**. The **printf( )** statement works correctly even though the %**d** modifier is used.

```
#include "stdio.h"

main( )
{
  short int i;

  i = -10;
  printf("%d", i);
}
```

3. Even though the final outcome of an expression will be of the largest type, the type conversion rules are applied on an operation-by-operation basis. For example, in this expression

```
100.0/(10/3)
```

the division of 10 by 3 produces an integer result, since both are integers. Then this value is elevated to 3.0 to divide 100.0.

Exercises

1. Given these variables,

   char ch;
   short i;
   unsigned long ul;
   float f;

   what is the overall type of this expression:

   ```
   f/ch-(i*ul)
   ```

2. What is the type of the subexpression **i*ul**, above?

4.6 UNDERSTAND TYPE CONVERSIONS IN ASSIGNMENTS

In an assignment statement in which the type of the right side differs from that of the left, the type of the right side is converted into that of the left. When the type of the left side is larger than the type of the right side, this process causes no problems. However, when the type of the left side is smaller than the type of the right, data loss may occur. For example, this program displays –24.

```
#include "stdio.h"

main( )
{
   char ch;
   int i;

   i = 1000;
   ch = i;

   printf("%d", ch);
}
```

The reason for this is that only the low-order eight bits of **i** are copied into **ch**. Since this sort of assignment type conversion is not an error in C, you will receive no error message. Remember, one reason C was created is to replace assembly language, so it must allow all sorts of type conversions. For example, in some instances you may only want the low-order eight bits of **i**, and this sort of assignment is an easy way to obtain them.

When there is an integer-to-character or a longer-integer-to-shorter-integer type conversion across an assignment, the basic rule is that the appropriate number of high-order bits will be removed. For example, in many environments, this means 8 bits will be lost when going from an **int** to a **char**, and 16 bits will be lost when going from a **long** to an **int**.

When converting from a **long double** to a **double** or from a **double** to a **float**, precision is lost. When converting from a floating-point value to an integer value, the fractional part is lost, and if the number is too large to fit in the target type, a garbage value will result.

Remember two important points: First, the conversion of an **int** to a **float** or a **float** to **double**, and so on, will not add any precision or accuracy. These kinds of conversions will only change the form in which the value is represented. Second, some C compilers will always treat a **char** variable as an **unsigned** value. Others will treat it as a **signed** value. Thus, what will happen when a character variable holds a value greater than 127 is implementation-dependent. If this is important in a program that you write, it is best to declare the variable explicitly as either **signed** or **unsigned**.

Examples

1. As stated, when converting from a floating-point value to an integer value, the fractional portion of the number is lost. The following program illustrates this fact. It prints **1234.0098 1234**

```
#include "stdio.h"

main( )
{
  int i;
  float f;

  f = 1234.0098;
  i = f; /* convert to int */
  printf("%f %d", f, i);
}
```

2. When converting from a larger integer type to a smaller one, it is possible to generate a garbage value, as this program illustrates.

```
#include "stdio.h"

main( )
{
  int i;
```

```
    long int l;

    l = 100000;
    i = l; /* convert to int */

    printf("%d", i);
}
```

Since the largest value that an integer can hold is 32,767, it cannot hold 100,000. What the compiler does, however, is copy the lower order half of l into i. This produces the meaningless value of −31072 on the screen.

Exercises

1. What will this program display?

```
#include "stdio.h"

main( )
{
  int i;
  long double ld;

  ld = 10.0;
  i = ld;

  printf("%d", i);
}
```

2. What does this program display?

```
#include "stdio.h"

main( )
{
  float f;
```

```
    f = 10 / 3;

    printf("%f", f);
}
```

4.7 PROGRAM WITH TYPE CASTS

Sometimes you may want to transform the type of a variable temporarily. For example, you may want to use a floating-point value for one computation, but wish to apply the modulus operator to it elsewhere. Since the modulus operator can only be used on integer values, you have a problem. One solution is to create an integer variable for use in the modulus operation and assign the value of the floating-point variable to it when the time comes. This is a somewhat inelegant solution, however. The other way around this problem is to use a type cast, which causes a temporary type change.

A type cast takes this general form:

(type) value

where *type* is the name of a valid C data type. For example,

```
float f;
```

```
f = 100.2;
```

```
/* print f as an integer */
printf("%d", (int) f);
```

Here, the type cast causes the value of f to be converted to an **int**.

Examples

1. As you learned in Chapter 1, **sqrt( )**, one of C's library functions, returns the square root of its argument. It uses the MATH.H header file. Its single argument must be of type **double**. It also returns a **double** value. The following program prints the square roots of the numbers between 1 and 100. It uses a type cast to convert the **int** variable controlling the loop temporarily into a **double**.

```
#include "stdio.h"
#include "math.h"

main( )
{
   int i;

   for(i=1; i<101; i++)
     printf("%d %lf\n", i, sqrt((double) i));
}
```

Keep in mind that the loop could have been controlled using a **double** variable, but it would have been less efficient.

2. You cannot cast a variable that is on the left side of an assignment statement. For example, this is an invalid statement in C.

```
int num;

(float) num = 123.23; /* this is incorrect */
```

Exercise

1. Write a program that uses **for** to print the numbers **1** to **10** by tenths. Use a floating-point variable to control the loop. However, use a type cast so that the

conditional expression is evaluated as an integer expression in the interest of speed.

EXERCISES

At this point you should be able to answer these questions and perform these exercises.

MASTERY
SKILLS CHECK

√

1. What are C's data-type modifiers and what function do they perform?

2. How do you explicitly define an **unsigned** constant, a **long** constant, and a **long double** constant?

3. Show how to give a **float** variable called **balance** an initial value of 0.0.

4. What are C's automatic type promotions?

5. What is the difference between a **signed** and an **unsigned** integer?

6. Give one reason why you might want to use a global variable in your program.

7. Write a program that contains a function called **series( )**. Have this function generate a series of numbers, based upon this formula:

   *next number = (previous number * 1468) % 467*

   Give the number an initial value of 21. Use a global variable to hold the last value between function calls. In **main( )** demonstrate that the function works by calling it ten times and displaying the result.

8. What is a type cast? Give an example.

EXERCISES

This section checks how well you have integrated the material in this chapter with that from earlier chapters.

1. As you know from Chapter 3, no two **case**s with the same **switch** may use the same value. Therefore, is this **switch** valid or invalid? Why? (Hint, the ASCII code for 'A' is 65.)

```
switch(x) {
  case 'A': printf("is an A");
    break;
  case 65: printf("is the number 65");
    break;
}
```

2. Technically, for traditional reasons the **getchar( )** and **getche( )** functions are declared as returning integers, not character values. However, the character read from the keyboard is contained in the lower-order byte. Can you explain why this value can be assigned to **char** variables?

3. In this fragment, will the loop ever terminate? Why? (Assume integers are 16 bits long.)

```
int i
for(i=0; i<33000; i++) ;
```

CHAPTER OBJECTIVES

5.1 Declare one-dimensional arrays

5.2 Use strings

5.3 Create multidimensional arrays

5.4 Initialize arrays

5.5 Build arrays of strings

·5·
Exploring Arrays and Strings

In this chapter you will learn about arrays. An *array* is essentially a list of related variables and can be very useful in a variety of situations. Since in C strings are simply arrays of characters, you will also learn about strings and several of C's string functions.

EXERCISES

Before proceeding, you should be able to answer these   SKILLS CHECK
questions and perform these exercises.

√

1. What is the difference between a local and a global
    variable?

2. What data type will a C compiler assign to these
    numbers?

    a. 10

    b. 10000

    c. 123.45

    d. 123564

    e. – 45099

3. Write a program that inputs a **long**, a **short**, and a
    double and then writes these values to the screen.

4. What does a type cast do? Write a program that
    prints the square roots of the numbers 1 to 10. Cast
    the integer that controls the loop into a **double**, so
    that it can be used as an argument to **sqrt( )**.

5. To which **if** is the **else** in this fragment associated?
    What is the general rule?

    ```
    if(i)
       if(j)  printf("i and j are true");
    else printf("i is false");
    ```

6. Using the following fragment, what is the value of
    a when **i** is 1? What is **a**'s value when **i** is 4?

```
switch(i) {
  case 1: a = 1;
  case 2: a = 2;
    break;
  case 3: a = 3;
    break;
  case 4:
  case 5: a = 5;
}
```

5.1 DECLARE ONE-DIMENSIONAL ARRAYS

In C, a one-dimensional array is a list of variables that are all of the same type and are referenced through a common name. An individual variable in the array is called an *array element*. Arrays form a convenient way to handle groups of related data.

To declare a one-dimensional array, use the general form

type var_name[size];

where *type* is a valid C data type, *var_name* is the name of the array, and size specifies the number of elements in the array. For example, to declare an integer array with 20 elements called **myarray**, use this statement.

```
int myarray[20];
```

An array element is accessed by indexing the array using the number of the element. In C, all arrays begin at 0. This means that if you want to access the first element in an array, use 0 for the index. To index an array, specify the index of the element you want inside square brackets. For example, the following statement accesses the second element of **myarray**:

```
myarray[1];
```

Remember, arrays start at 0, so an index of 1 references the second element.

To assign an array element a value, put the array on the left side of an assignment statement. For example, this gives the first element in **myarray** the value 100.

```
myarray[0] = 100;
```

C stores one-dimensional arrays in one contiguous memory location with the first element at the lowest address. For example, after this fragment executes,

```
int i[5];
int j;

for(j=0; j<5; j++) i[j] = j;
```

array **i** will look like this:

```
      0  1  2  3  4
  i [ 0 | 1 | 2 | 3 | 4 ]
```

You may use the value of an array element anywhere you would use a simple variable or constant. For example, the following program loads the **sqrs** array with the squares of the numbers 1 through 10 and then displays them.

```
#include "stdio.h"

main( )
{
  int sqrs[10];
  int i;

  for(i=1; i<11; i++) sqrs[i-1] = i*i;

  for(i=0; i<10; i++) printf("%d ", sqrs[i]);
}
```

When you want to use **scanf( )** to input a numeric value into an array element, simply put the **&** in front of the array name. For example, this **scanf( )** call reads an integer into **count[9]**.

```
scanf("%d", &count[9]);
```

C does not perform any bounds checking on array indexes. This means that it is possible to overrun the end of an array. For example, if an array called **a** is declared as having five elements, the compiler will still let you access the (non-existent) tenth element with a statement like **a[9]**. Of course, attempting to access non-existent elements will generally have disastrous results, often causing the program—even the computer—to crash. It is up to you, the programmer, to make sure that the ends of arrays are never overrun.

In C, you may not assign one entire array to another. For example, this fragment is incorrect.

```
char a1[10], a2[10];
.
.
.
a2 = a1; /* this is wrong */
```

If you wish to copy the values of all the elements of one array to another, you must do so by copying each element separately.

Examples

1. Arrays are very useful in programming when lists of information need to be managed. For example, this program reads the noonday temperature for each day of a month and then reports the month's average temperature, as well as its hottest and coolest days.

```c
#include "stdio.h"

main( )
{
  int temp[31], i, min, max, avg;
  int days;

  printf("How many days in the month? ");
  scanf("%d", &days);

  for(i=0; i<days; i++) {
    printf("Enter noonday temperature for day %d: ", i+1);
    scanf("%d", &temp[i]);
  }

  /* find average */
  avg = 0;
  for(i=0; i<days; i++) avg = avg + temp[i];
  printf("Average temperature: %d\n", avg/days);

  /* find min and max */
  min = 200;   /* initialize min and max */
  max = 0;
  for(i=0; i<days; i++) {
    if(min>temp[i]) min = temp[i];
```

```
   if(max<temp[i]) max = temp[i];
 }

 printf("Minimum temperature: %d\n", min);
 printf("Maximum temperature: %d\n", max);
}
```

2. As stated earlier, to copy the contents of one array to another, you must explicitly copy each element separately. For example, this program loads **a1** with the numbers 1 through 10 and then copies them into **a2**.

```
#include "stdio.h"

main( )
{
   int a1[10], a2[10];
   int i;

   for(i=1; i<11; i++) a1[i]=i;

   for(i=1; i<11; i++) a2[i] = a1[i];

   for(i=1; i<11; i++) printf("%d ", a2[i]);
}
```

3. The following program is an improved version of the code-machine program developed in Chapter 3. In this version, the user first enters the message, which is stored in a character array. When the user presses ENTER, the entire message is then encoded by adding 1 to each letter.

```
#include "stdio.h"
#include "conio.h"

main( )
{
   char mess [80];
   int i;
```

```
   printf("Enter message (less than 80 characters)/n");
   for(i=0; i<80; i++) {
     mess[i] = getche( );
     if(mess[i]=='\r') break;
   }

   for(i=0; temp[i]!='\r'; i++) printf("%c, temp[i]);
}
```

4. Arrays are especially useful when you want to sort information. For example, this program lets the user enter up to 100 numbers and then sorts them. The sorting algorithm is the bubble sort. The bubble sort algorithm is very poor, but it is simple to understand and easy to code. The general concept behind the bubble sort, indeed how it got its name, is the repeated comparisons and, if necessary, exchanges of adjacent elements. This is a little like bubbles in a tank of water with each bubble, in turn, seeking its own level.

```
#include "stdio.h"
#include "stdlib.h"

main( )
{
   int item[100];
   int a, b, t;
   int count;

   /* read in numbers */
   printf("How many numbers? ");
   scanf("%d", &count);
   for(a=0; a<count; a++) scanf("%d", &item[a]);

   /* now, sort them using a bubble sort */
   for(a=1; a<count; ++a).
     for(b=count-1; b>=a; --b) {
         /* compare adjacent elements */
       if(item[b-1] > item[b]) {
          /* exchange elements */
```

```
        t = item[b-1];
        item[b-1] = item[b];
        item[b] = t;
      }
    }


    /* display sorted list */
    for(t=0; t<count; t++) printf("%d ", item[t]);
  }
```

Exercises

1. What is wrong with this program fragment?

```
#include "stdio.h"

main( )
{
  int i, count[10];

  for(i=0; i<100; i++) {
    printf("Enter a number: ");
    scanf("%d", &count[i]);
  }
  .
  .
  .
```

2. Write a program that reads ten numbers entered by the user and reports if any of them match.

3. Change the sorting program shown in the examples so that it sorts data of type **float**.

5.2 USE STRINGS

The most common use of the one-dimensional array in C is the string. Unlike most other computer languages,

C has no built-in string data type. Instead, C supports strings using one-dimensional character arrays. A string is defined as a *null-terminated character array*. In C, a null is 0. The fact that the string must be terminated by a null means that you must define the array that is going to hold a string to be one byte larger than the largest string it will be required to hold, to make room for the null. A string constant is also null-terminated by the compiler automatically.

To read a string from the keyboard you must use another of C's standard library functions, **gets( )**, which requires the STDIO.H header file. To use **gets( )**, call it using the name of a character array without any index. The **gets( )** function reads characters until you press RETURN. The carriage return is not stored, but is replaced by a null, which terminates the string. For example, this program reads and writes a string entered at the keyboard.

```
#include "stdio.h"

main( )
{
  char str[80];
  int i;

  printf("Enter a string (less than 80 chars):\n");
  gets(str);
  for(i=0; str[i]; i++) printf("%c", str[i]);
}
```

Notice how the program uses the fact that a null is false to control the loop that outputs the string.

The **gets( )** function performs no bounds checking, so it is possible for the user to enter more characters than the string that **gets( )** is called with can hold.

Therefore, be sure to call it with an array large enough to hold the expected input.

In the previous program, the string that was entered by the user was output to the screen a character at a time. There is however, a much easier way to display a string, using **printf( )**. Here is the previous program rewritten.

```
#include "stdio.h"

main( )
{
  char str[80];

  printf("Enter a string (less than 80 chars):\n");
  gets(str);
  printf(str); /* output the string */
}
```

Since the first argument to **printf( )** is a string, you simply use **str** without any index as the first argument to **printf( )**. If you wanted to output a newline, you could output **str** like this:

```
printf("%s\n", str);
```

This method uses the %**s** format specifier followed by the newline character and uses the array as a second argument to be matched by the %**s** specifier.

The C standard library supplies many string-related functions. The four most important are **strcpy( )**, **strcat( )**, **strcmp( )**, and **strlen( )**. These functions require the header file STRING.H. Let's look at each now.

The **strcpy( )** function has this general form.

strcpy(*to, from*);

It copies the contents of *from* to *to*. The contents of *from* are unchanged. For example, this fragment copies the string "hello" into **str** and displays it on the screen.

```
char str[80];

strcpy(str, "hello");
printf("%s", str);
```

The **strcpy( )** function performs no bounds checking, so you must make sure that the array on the receiving end is large enough to hold what is being copied, including the null terminator.

The **strcat( )** function adds the contents of one string to another. This is called *concatenation*. Its general form is

strcat(*to, from*);

It adds the contents of *from* to the contents of *to*. It performs no bounds checking, so you must make sure that *to* is large enough to hold its current contents plus what it will be receiving. This fragment displays **hello there**.

```
char str[80];

strcpy(str, "hello");
strcat(str, " there");
printf(str);
```

The **strcmp( )** function compares two strings. It takes this general form.

strcmp(*s1*, *s2*);

It returns 0 if the strings are the same. It returns less than 0 if *s1* is less than *s2* and greater than 0 if *s1* is greater than *s2*. The strings are compared lexicographically; that is, in dictionary order. Therefore, a string is less than another when it would appear before the other in a dictionary. A string is greater than another when it would appear after the other. The comparison is not based upon the length of the string. Also, the comparison is case-sensitive, lowercase characters being greater than uppercase. This fragment prints **0**, because the strings are the same.

```
printf("%d", strcmp("one", "one"));
```

The **strlen( )** function returns the length, in characters, of a string. Its general form is

strlen(*str*);

The **strlen( )** function does not count the null terminator. This means that if **strlen( )** is called using the string "test", it will return 4.

Examples

1. This program requests input of two strings, then demonstrates the four string functions with them.

    ```
    #include "string.h"
    #include "stdio.h"

    main( )
    {
    ```

```
char str1[80], str2[80];
int i;

printf("Enter the first string: ");
gets(str1);
printf("Enter the second string: ");
gets(str2);

/* see how long the strings are */
printf("%s is %d chars long\n", str1, strlen(str1));
printf("%s is %d chars long\n", str2, strlen(str2));

/* compare the strings */
i = strcmp(str1, str2);
if(!i) printf("The strings are equal.\n");
else if(i<0) printf("%s is less than %s\n", str1, str2);
else printf("%s is greater than %s\n", str1, str2);

/* concatenate str2 to end of str1 if
   there is enough room */
if(strlen(str1) + strlen(str2) < 80) {
  strcat(str1, str2);
  printf("%s\n", str1);
}

/* copy str2 to str1 */
strcpy(str1, str2);
printf("%s %s\n", str1, str2);
}
```

2. One common use of strings is to support a *command-based interface*. Unlike a menu, which allows the user to make a selection, a command-based interface displays a prompting message, waits for the user to enter a command, and then does what the command requests. Many operating systems use command-line interfaces, for example. The following program is similar to a program developed in Section 3.1. It allows the user to add, subtract, multiply, or divide, but does not use a menu. Instead, it uses a command-line interface.

```c
#include "stdlib.h"
#include "stdio.h"
#include "string.h"

main( )
{
  char command[80], temp[80];
  int i, j;

  for( ; ;) {
    printf("Operation? ");
    gets(command);

    /* see if user wants to stop */
    if(!strcmp(command, "quit")) break;

    printf("Enter first number: ");
    gets(temp);
    i = atoi(temp);

    printf("Enter second number: ");
    gets(temp);
    j = atoi(temp);

    /* now, perform the operation */
    if(!strcmp(command, "add"))
      printf("%d\n", i+j);
    else if(!strcmp(command, "subtract"))
      printf("%d\n", i-j);
    else if(!strcmp(command, "divide")) {
      if(j) printf("%d\n", i/j);
    }
    else if(!strcmp(command, "multiply"))
      printf("%d\n", i*j);
    else printf("Unknown command.\n");
  }
}
```

Notice that this example also introduces another of C's standard library functions: **atoi( )**. The **atoi( )** function returns the integer equivalent of the number represented by its string argument. For example,

atoi("100") returns the value 100. The reason that **scanf( )** is not used to read the numbers is because it is incompatible with **gets( )**. (You will need to know more about C before you can understand the cause of this incompatibility.) The **atoi( )** function uses the header file STDLIB.H.

3. You can create a string of length 0, using a **strcpy( )** statement like this:

```
strcpy(str, "");
```

Such a string is called a *null string*. It contains only one element: the null terminator.

Exercises

1. Write a program that inputs a string, then displays it backward on the screen.

2. What is wrong with this program?

```
#include "string.h"
#include "stdio.h"

main( )
{
   char str[5];

   strcpy(str, "this is a test");
   printf(str);
}
```

3. Write a program that repeatedly inputs strings. Each time a string is input, concatenate it with a second string called **bigstr**. Add newlines to the end of each string. If the user types **quit**, stop inputting and display **bigstr** (which will contain a record of all

strings input). Also stop if **bigstr** will be overrun by the next concatenation.

5.3 CREATE MULTIDIMENSIONAL ARRAYS

In addition to one-dimensional arrays, you can create arrays of two or more dimensions. For example, to create a 10×12 two-dimensional integer array called **count**, you would use this statement.

```
int count[10][12];
```

As you can see in the example, to add a dimension, you simply specify its size inside square brackets.

A two-dimensional array is essentially an array of one-dimensional arrays and is most easily thought of in a row, column format. For example, given a 4×5 integer array called **two_d**, you can think of it looking like that shown in Figure 5-1. Assuming this conceptual view, a two-dimensional array is accessed a row at a time, from left to right. This means that the rightmost index will change most quickly when the array is accessed sequentially from the lowest to highest memory address.

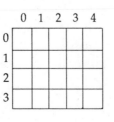

FIGURE 5-1.   A conceptual view of a two-dimansional array

Two-dimensional arrays are used like one-dimensional ones. For example, this program loads a 4×5 array with the products of the indices, then displays the array in row, column format.

```c
#include "stdio.h"

main( )
{
  int twod[4][5];
  int i, j;

  for(i=0; i<4; i++)
    for(j=0; j<5; j++)
      twod[i][j] = i*j;

  for(i=0; i; i++) {
    for(j=0; j<5; j++)
      printf("%d ", twod[i][j]);
    printf("\n");
  }
}
```

The program output looks like this:

```
0 0 0 0 0
0 1 2 3 4
0 2 4 6 8
0 3 6 9 12
```

To create arrays of three dimensions and greater, simply add the size of the additional dimension. For example, the following statement creates a 10×12×8 three-dimensional array.

```c
float values[10][12][8];
```

A three dimensional array is essentially an array of two-dimensional arrays.

You may create arrays of more than three dimensions, but this is seldom done because the amount of memory they consume increases exponentially with each additional dimension. For example, a 100-character one-dimensional array requires 100 bytes of memory. A 100×100 character array requires 10,000 bytes, and a 100×100×100 array requires 1,000,000. A 100×100×100×100 four-dimensional array would require 100,000,000 bytes of storage—large even by today's standards.

Example

1. A good use of a two-dimensional array is to manage lists of numbers. For example, you could use this two-dimensional array to hold the noontime temperature for each day of the year, grouped by month.

    ```
    float yeartemp[12][31];
    ```

    In the same vein, the following program can be used to keep track of the number of points scored per quarter by each member of a basketball team.

    ```
    #include "stdio.h"

    main( )
    {
      int bball[5][4];
      int i, j;

      for(i=0; i<4; i++)
        for(j=0; j<5; j++) {
    ```

```
      printf("Quarter %d, player %d, ", i+1, j+1);
      printf("enter number of points: ");
      scanf("%d", &bball[i][j]);
  }

  /* display results */
  for(i=0; i<4; i++)
    for(j=0; j<5; j++) {
      printf("Quarter %d, player %d, ", i+1, j+1);
      printf("%d\n", bball[i][j]);
    }
}
```

Exercises

1. Write a program that defines a 3×3×3 three-dimensional array, and load it with the numbers 1 to 27.

2. Have the program from the first exercise display the sum of its elements.

5.4 INITIALIZE ARRAYS

Like other types of variables, you can give the elements of arrays initial values. This is accomplished by specifying a list of values the array elements will have. The general form of array initialization for one-dimensional arrays is shown here:

type array-name[size] = { value-list };

The *value-list* is a comma-separated list of constants that are type compatible with the base type of the array. The first constant will be placed in the first position of the array, the second constant in the second position, and so on. Note that a semicolon follows the }. In the following example, a five-element integer array is initialized with the squares of the numbers 1 through 5.

```
int i[5] = {1, 4, 9, 16, 25};
```

This means that **i[0]** will have the value 1 and **i[4]** will have the value 25.

You can initialize character arrays two ways. First, if the array is not holding a null-terminated string, you simply specify each character using a comma-separated list. For example, this initializes **a** with the letters 'A,' 'B,' and 'C.'

```
char a[3] = {'A', 'B', 'C'};
```

If the character array is going to hold a string, you can initialize the array using a quoted string, as shown here.

```
char name[5] = "Herb";
```

Notice that no curly braces surround the string. They are not used in this form of initialization. Because strings in C must end with a null, you must make sure that the array you declare is long enough to include the null. This is why **name** is 5 characters long, even though "Herb" is only 4. When a string constant is used, the compiler automatically supplies the null terminator.

Multidimensional arrays are initialized in the same way as one-dimensional ones. For example, here the array **sqr** is initialized with the values 1 through 9, using row order.

```
int sqr[3][3] = {
   1, 2, 3,
   4, 5, 6,
   7, 8, 9
};
```

This initialization causes **sqr[0][0]** to have the value 1, **sqr[0][1]** to contain 2, **sqr[0][2]** to hold 3, and so forth.

If you are initializing a one-dimensional array, you need not specify the size of the array—simply put nothing inside the square brackets. If you don't specify the size, the compiler simply counts the number of initialization constants and uses that value as the size of the array. For example,

```
int pwr[] = {1, 2, 4, 8, 16, 32, 64, 128};
```

causes the compiler to create an initialized array eight elements long. Arrays that don't have their dimensions explicitly specified are called *unsized arrays*. An unsized array is useful because it is easier for you to change the size of the initialization list without having to count it and then change the array dimension. This helps avoid counting errors on long lists, which is especially important when initializing strings. Here, an unsized array is used to hold a prompting message.

```
char prompt[] = "Enter your name: ";
```

If, at a later date, you wanted to change the prompt to "Enter your last name: ", you would not have to count the characters and then change the array size.

Unsized array initializations are not restricted to only singly-dimensioned arrays. For multidimensional arrays you must specify all but the leftmost dimensions to allow C to index the array properly. In this way you may build tables of varying lengths with the compiler allocating enough storage for them automatically. For example, the declaration of **sqr** as an unsized array is shown here.

```
int sqr[][3] = {
    1, 2, 3,
    4, 5, 6,
    7, 8, 9
};
```

The advantage to this declaration over the sized version is that tables may be lengthened or shortened without changing the array dimensions.

Special note: Some compilers will not allow you to initialize an array within a function. For this reason, all initialized arrays are global variables in the examples. However, if your compiler allows locally initialized arrays, you should feel free to use them.

Examples

1. A common use of an initialized array is to create a lookup table. For example, in this program a 5×2 two-dimensional array is initialized so that the first element in each row is the number of a CPU, and the second element contains its average speed rating. The program allows a user to enter the number of a

processor, then it looks it up in the table and reports its average speed.

```c
#include "stdio.h"

long cpu[5][2] = {
  8088, 4,
  8086, 4,
  80286, 10,
  80386, 20,
  80486, 40
};

main( )
{
  long processor;
  int i;

  printf("Enter the number of the processor: ");
  scanf("%ld", &processor);

  /* look it up in the table */
  for(i=0; i<5; i++)
    if(processor == cpu[i][0]) {
      printf("Average speed is %d mhz.\n", cpu[i][1]);
      break;
    }

  /* report error if not found */
  if(i==5) printf("Processor not found.\n");
}
```

2. Even though an array has been given an initial value, its contents may be changed. For example, this program prints **hello** on the screen.

```c
#include "stdio.h"
#include "string.h"

main( )
{
  char str[80] = "I like C";
```

```
    strcpy(str, "hello");
    printf(str);
}
```

As this program illustrates, in no way does an initialization fix the contents of an array.

Exercises

1. Is this fragment correct?

    ```
    int balance[] = 10.0, 122.23, 100.0;
    ```

2. Is this fragment correct?

    ```
    #include "stdio.h"
    #include "string.h"

    main( )
    {
       char name[] = "Tom";

        strcpy(name, "Tom Brazwell");
    ```

3. Write a program that initializes a 10×3 array so that the first element of each row contains a number, the second element contains its square, and the third element contains its cube. Start with 1 and stop at 10. For example, the first few rows will look like this:

    1, 1, 1,
    2, 4, 8,
    3, 9, 27,
    4, 16, 64,
    .

    .

    .

Next, prompt the user for a cube, look up this value in the table, and report the cube's root and the root's square.

5.5 BUILD ARRAYS OF STRINGS

Arrays of strings, often called *string tables*, are very common in C programming. A two-dimensional string table is created like any other two-dimensional array. However, the way you think about it will be slightly different. For example, here is a small string table. What do you think it defines?

```
char names[10][40];
```

This statement specifies a table that can contain 10 strings, each up to 40 characters long (including the null terminator). To access a string within this table, specify only the first index. For example, to read a string from the keyboard into the third string in **names**, use this statement.

```
gets(names[2]);
```

By the same token, to output the first string, use this **printf( )** statement.

```
printf(names[0]);
```

The declaration that follows creates a three-dimensional table with three lists of strings. Each list is five strings long, and each string can hold 80 characters.

```
char animals[3][5][80];
```

To access a specific string in this situation, you must specify the first two dimensions. For example, to access the second string in the third list, specify **animals[2][1]**.

Examples

1. This program lets you enter ten strings, then lets you display them, one at a time, in any order you choose. To stop the program, enter a negative number.

    ```c
    #include "stdio.h"

    main( )
    {
      char text[10][80];
      int i;

      for(i=0; i<10; i++) {
        printf("%d: ", i+1);
        gets(text[i]);
      }

      do {
        printf("Enter number of string (1-10): ");
        scanf("%d", &i);
        i--;  /* adjust value to match array index */
        if(i>=0 && i) printf("%s\n", text[i]);
      } while(i>=0);
    }
    ```

2. You can initialize a string table as you would any other type of array. For example, the following program uses an initialized string table to translate

between German and English. Notice that curly braces are needed to surround the list. The only time they are not needed is when a single string is being initialized.

```c
/* English-to-German Translator. */

#include "stdio.h"
#include "string.h"

char words[][2][40] = {
  "dog", "Hund",
  "no", "nein",
  "year", "Jahr",
  "child", "Kind",
  "I", "Ich",
  "drive", "fahren",
  "house", "Haus",
  "to", "zu",
  "", ""
};

main( )
{
  char english[80];
  int i;

  printf("Enter English word: ");
  gets(english);

  /* look up the word */
  i = 0;
  /* search while null string not yet encountered */
  while(strcmp(words[i][0], "")) {
    if(!strcmp(english, words[i][0])) {
      printf("German translation: %s", words[i][1]);
      break;
    }
    i++;
  }
```

```
  if(!strcmp(words[i][0], ""))
    printf("Not in dictionary\n");
}
```

3. You can access the individual characters that comprise a string within a string table by using the rightmost index. For example, the following program prints the strings in the table one character at a time.

```
#include "stdio.h"

char text[][80] = {
  "When", "in", "the",
  "course", "of", "human",
  "events", ""
};

main( )
{
  int i, j;

  /* now, display them */
  for(i=0; text[i][0]; i++) {
    for(j=0; text[i][j]; j++)
      printf("%c", text[i][j]);
    printf(" ");
  }
}
```

Exercise

1. Write a program that creates a string table containing the English words for the numbers 0 through 9. Using this table, allow the user to enter a digit and then have your program display the word equivalent. (Hint: to obtain an index into the table, subtract 0 from the character entered, i.e., .).

EXERCISES

At this point you should be able to perform these exercises and answer these questions.

1. What is an array?

2. Given the array

    ```
    int count[10];
    ```

    Will this statement generate an error message?

    ```
    for(i=0; i<20; i++) count[i] = i;
    ```

3. In statistics, the mode of a group of numbers is the one that occurs the most often. For example, given the list 1, 2, 3, 6, 4, 7, 5, 4, 6, 9, 4, the mode is 4, because it occurs three times. Write a program that allows the user to enter a list of 20 numbers and then finds and displays the mode.

4. Show how to initialize an integer array called **items** with the values 1 through 10.

5. Write a program that repeatedly reads strings from the keyboard until the user enters **quit**.

6. Write a program that acts like an electronic dictionary. If the user enters a word in the dictionary, the program displays its meaning. Use a three-dimensional character array to hold the words and their meanings.

EXERCISES

This section checks how well you have integrated the material in this chapter with that from earlier chapters.

1. Write a program that inputs strings from the user. If the string is less than 80 characters long, pad it with periods. Print out the string to verify that you have correctly lengthened the string.

2. Write a program that inputs a string and then encodes it by alternately taking characters off of each end, starting with the left side, and stopping when the middle of the string has been reached. For example, the string "Hi there" would be "Heir eth".

3. Write a program that counts the number of spaces, commas, and periods in a string. Use a **switch** to categorize the characters.

4. What is wrong with this fragment?

```
char str[80];
str = getche( );
```

5. Write a program that plays a computerized version of Hangman. In the game of Hangman, you are shown the length of a magic word (using underscores) and you try to guess what the word is by entering letters. Each time you enter a letter, the magic word is checked to see if it contains that letter. If it does, that letter is shown. Keep a count on the number of letters entered to complete the word. For the sake of simplicity, a player wins when the magic word is entirely filled by characters using 15 or fewer guesses. For this exercise make the magic word "concatenation."

CHAPTER OBJECTIVES

6.1 Understand pointer basics

6.2 Learn restrictions to pointer expressions

6.3 Use pointers with arrays

6.4 Use pointers to string constants

6.5 Create arrays of pointers

6.6 Become acquainted with multiple indirection

6.7 Use pointers as parameters

·6·
Using Pointers

This chapter covers one of C's most important and sometimes its most troublesome feature: the *pointer*. A pointer is basically the address of an object. One reason that pointers are so important is that much of the power of the C language is derived from the unique way in which they are implemented in C. You will learn about the special pointer operators, pointer arithmetic, and how arrays and pointers are related. Also, you will be introduced to using pointers as parameters to functions.

EXERCISES

Before proceeding, you should be able to answer these questions and perform these exercises.

1. Write a program that inputs 10 integers into an array. Then have the program display the sum of the even numbers and the sum of the odd numbers.

2. Write a program that simulates a log-on to a remote system. The system can only be accessed if the user knows the password, which in this case is "Tristan." Give the user three tries to enter the correct password. If the user succeeds, simply print **log-on successful** and exit. If the user fails after three attempts to enter the correct password, display **access denied** and exit.

3. What is wrong with this fragment?

   ```
   char name[10] = "Thomas Jefferson";
   ```

4. What is a null string?

5. What does **strcpy( )** do? What does **strcmp( )** do?

6. Write a program that creates a string table consisting of names and telephone numbers. Initialize the array with some names of people you know and their phone numbers. Next, have the program request a name and print the associated telephone number. In other words, create a computerized telephone book.

6.1 UNDERSTAND POINTER BASICS

A pointer is a variable that holds the memory address of another object. For example, if a variable called **p** contains the address of another variable called **q**, then **p** is said to *point* to **q**. Therefore if **q** is at location 100 in memory, then **p** would have the value 100.

To declare a pointer variable, use this general form.

*type *var-name;*

Here, *type* is the *base type* of the pointer. The base type specifies the type of the object that the pointer can point to. Notice that the variable name is preceded by an asterisk. This tells the computer that a pointer variable is being created. For example, the following statement creates a pointer to an integer.

```
int *p;
```

C contains two special pointer operators: * and &. The & operator returns the address of the variable it precedes. The * operator returns the value stored at the address that it precedes. (The * pointer operator has no relationship to the multiplication operator, which uses the same symbol.) For example, examine this short program.

```
#include "stdio.h"

main( )
{
   int *p, q;

   q = 100; /* assign q 100 */

   p = &q;  /* assign p the address of q */

   printf("%d", *p); /* display q's value using pointer */
}
```

This program prints **100** on the screen. Let's see why. First, the line

```
int *p, q;
```

defines two variables: **p**, which is declared as an integer pointer, and **q**, which is an integer. Next, **q** is assigned the value 100. In the next line, **p** is assigned the *address of* **q**. You can verbalize the **&** operator as "address of." Therefore, this line can be read as "assign **p** the address of **q**." Finally, the value is displayed using the ***** operator applied to **p**. The ***** operator can be verbalized as "at address." Therefore, the **printf( )** statement can be read as "print the value at address **q**," which is 100.

When a variable's value is referenced through a pointer, the process is called *indirection*.

It is possible to use the ***** operator on the left side of an assignment statement in order to assign a variable a new value using a pointer to it. For example, this program assigns **q** a value indirectly using the pointer **p**.

```
#include "stdio.h"

main( )
{
   int *p, q;

   p = &q; /* get q's address */

   *p = 199; /* assign q a value using a pointer */

   printf("q's value is %d", q);
}
```

In the two simple example programs just shown, there is no reason to use a pointer. However, as you learn more about C, you will understand why pointers are important. Pointers are used to support linked lists and binary trees, for example.

The base type of a pointer is very important. Although C allows any type of pointer to point anywhere in memory, it is the base type that determines how the object pointed to will be treated. To understand the importance of this, consider the following fragment.

```
int  q;
float *fp;

fp = &q;

/* what does this line do? */
*fp = 100.23;
```

Although not syntactically incorrect, this fragment is wrong. The pointer **fp** is assigned the address of an integer. This address is then used on the left side of an assignment statement to assign a floating-point value. However, **ints** are shorter than **floats**, and this assignment statement causes memory adjacent to **q** to be overwritten. That is, assuming 2-byte **ints** and 4-byte **floats**, the assignment statement uses the 2 bytes allocated to **q** as well as two adjacent bytes, which will most likely be where **fp** is stored, thus causing an error.

In general, the C compiler uses the base type to determine how many bytes are in the object pointed to by the pointer. This is how C knows how many bytes to copy when an indirect assignment is made, or how many bytes to compare if an indirect comparison is made. Therefore, it is very important that you always use the proper base type for a pointer. Never use a pointer to one type to point to an object of a different type.

If you attempt to use a pointer before it has been assigned the address of a variable, your program will probably crash. Remember, declaring a pointer variable simply creates a variable capable of holding a memory address. It does not give it any meaningful initial value. This is why the following fragment is incorrect.

```
main( )
{
  int *p;

   *p = 10;   /* incorrect - p is not pointing to
                anything */
```

As the comment notes, the pointer **p** is not pointing to any known object. Hence, trying to indirectly assign a value using **p** is meaningless and dangerous.

As pointers are defined in C, a pointer that contains a null value (0) is assumed to be unused and pointing at nothing. In C, 0 is, by convention, assumed to be an invalid memory address. However, the compiler will still let you use a null pointer, usually with disastrous results.

Examples

1. To graphically illustrate how indirection works, assume these declarations.

   ```
   int *p, q;
   ```

   Further assume that **q** is located at memory address 102 and that **p** is right before it, at location 100. After this statement

   ```
   p = &q;
   ```

   the pointer **p** contains the value 102. Therefore, after this assignment, memory looks like this:

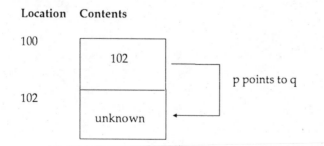

   After the statement

   ```
   *p = 1000;
   ```

   executes, memory looks like this.

Location   Contents

100

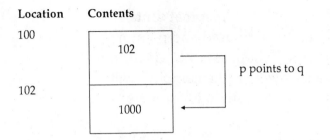

102

Remember, the value of **p** has nothing to do with the *value* of **q**. It simply holds **q**'s *address*, to which the indirection operators may be applied.

2. To illustrate why you must make sure that the base type of a pointer is the same as the object it points to, try this incorrect but benign program. (Some compilers may generate a warning message when you compile it, but none will issue an actual error message and stop compilation.)

```
/* This program is wrong, but harmless. */

#include "stdio.h"

main( )
{
   int *p;
   float q, temp;

   temp = 1234.34F;

   p = &temp; /* attempt to assign q a value */
   q = *p; /* using indirection through an integer
              pointer */

   printf("%f", q); /* this will not print 1234.34 */
}
```

Even though **p** points to **temp**, which does, indeed, hold the value 1234.34, the assignment

```
q = *p;
```

fails to copy the number because only 2 bytes (assuming 2-byte integers) will be transferred. Since **p** is an integer pointer, it cannot be used to transfer a 4-byte quantity (assuming 4-byte **float**s).

Exercises

1. What is a pointer?

2. What are the pointer operators and what are their effects.

3. Why is the base type of a pointer important?

4. Write a program with a **for** loop that counts from 0 to 9, displaying the numbers on the screen. Print the numbers using a pointer.

6.2 LEARN RESTRICTIONS TO POINTER EXPRESSIONS

In general, pointers may be used like other variables. However, you need to understand a few rules and restrictions.

In addition to the * and & operators, there are only four other operators that may be applied to pointer variables: the arithmetic operators +, ++, −, and −−. Further, you may add or subtract only integer quantities. You cannot, for example, add a floating-point number to a pointer.

Pointer arithmetic differs from "normal" arithmetic in one very important way: it is performed relative to the base type of the pointer. Each time a pointer is incremented, it will point to the next item, as defined by its base type, beyond the one currently pointed to. For example, assume that an integer pointer called **p** contains the address 200. After the statement

```
p++;
```

executes, **p** will have the value 202, assuming integers are two bytes long. By the same token, if **p** had been a **float** pointer (assuming 4-byte **float**s), then the resultant value contained in **p** would have been 204.

The only pointer arithmetic that appears as "normal" occurs when **char** pointers are used. Because characters are one byte long, an increment increases the pointer's value by one, and a decrement decreases its value by one.

You may add or subtract any integer quantity you want to or from a pointer. For example, the following is a valid fragment.

```
int *p
  .
  .
  .
p = p + 200;
```

This statement causes **p** to point to the 200th integer past the one to which **p** was currently pointing.

Aside from addition and subtraction of an integer, you may not perform any other type of arithmetic operations—you may not multiply, divide, or take the modulus of a pointer.

It is possible to apply the increment and decrement operators to either the pointer itself or the object to which it points. However, you must be careful when attempting to increment the object pointed to by a pointer. For example, assume that **p** points to an integer that contains the value 1. What do you think the following statement will do?

```
*p++;
```

Contrary to what you might think, this statement first increments **p** and then obtains the value at the new location. To increment what is pointed to by a pointer, you must use a form like this:

```
(*p)++;
```

The parentheses cause the value pointed to by **p** to be incremented.

You may compare two pointers using the relational operators. However, pointer comparisons only make sense if the pointers relate to each other—if they both point to the same object, for example. Shortly you will see an example of pointer comparisons.

At this point you might be wondering what use there is for pointer arithmetic. You will shortly see, however, that it is one of the most valuable components of the C language.

Examples

1. You can use **printf( )** to display the memory address contained in a pointer by using the **%p** format specifier. We can use this **printf( )** capability to illustrate several aspects of pointer arithmetic. The following

program, for example, shows how all pointer arithmetic is relative to the base type of the pointer.

```c
#include "stdio.h"

main( )
{
  char *cp, ch;
  int  *ip, i;
  float *fp, f;
  double *dp, d;

  cp = &ch;
  ip = &i;
  fp = &f;
  dp = &d;

  /* print the current values */
  printf("%p %p %p %p\n", cp, ip, fp, dp);

  /* now increment them by one */
  cp++;
  ip++;
  fp++;
  dp++;

  /* print their new values */
  printf("%p %p %p %p\n", cp, ip, fp, dp);
}
```

Although the values contained in the pointer variables in this program will vary widely between compilers and even between versions of the same compiler, you will see that the address pointed to by **ch** will be incremented by one byte. The others will be incremented by the number of bytes in their base types, typically 2 for **ints**, 4 for **floats**, and 8 for **doubles**.

2. The following program illustrates the need for parentheses when you want to increment the object pointed to by a pointer instead of the pointer itself.

```
#include "stdio.h"

main( )
{
   int *p, q;

   p = &q;

   q = 1;
   printf("%p ", p);

   *p++; /* this will not increment q */
   printf("%d %p", q, p);
}
```

After this program has executed, **q** still has the value 1, but **p** has been incremented.

   However, if the program is written like this

```
#include "stdio.h"

main( )
{
   int *p, q;

   p = &q;

   q = 1;
   printf("%p ", p);

   (*p)++;   /* now q is incremented and p is unchanged */
   printf("%d %p", q, p);
}
```

q is incremented to 2 and **p** is unchanged.

Exercises

1. What is wrong with this fragment?

   ```
   int *p, i;

   p = &i;

   p = p * 8;
   ```

2. Can you add a floating-point number to a pointer?

3. Assume that **p** is a **float** pointer that currently points to location 100 and that **float**s are 4 bytes long. What is the value of **p** after this fragment has executed?

   ```
   p = p + 2;
   ```

6.3 USE POINTERS WITH ARRAYS

In C, pointers and arrays are closely related. In fact, they are often interchangeable. It is this relationship between the two that makes their implementation both unique and powerful.

When you use an array name without an index, you are generating a pointer to the start of the array. This is why no indexes are used when you read a string using **gets( )**, for example. What is being passed to **gets( )** is not an array, but a pointer. In fact, you cannot pass an array to a function in C; you may only pass a pointer to the array. This important point was not mentioned in the preceding chapter on arrays because you had not yet learned about pointers. However, this fact is crucial to understanding the C language. The **gets( )** function uses the pointer to load the array it points to with the characters you enter at the keyboard. You will see how this is done later.

Since an array name without an index is a pointer to the start of the array, it stands to reason that you can assign that value to another pointer and access the array using pointer arithmetic. And, in fact, this is exactly what you can do. Consider this program.

```
#include "stdio.h"

int a[10] = {1, 2, 3, 4, 5, 6, 7, 8, 9, 10};

main( )
{
  int *p;

  p = a; /* assign p the address of start of a */

  /* this prints a's first, second and third elements */
  printf("%d %d %d\n", *p, *(p+1), *(p+2));

  /* this does the same thing using a */
  printf("%d %d %d", a[0], a[1], a[2]);
}
```

Here, both **printf( )** statements display the same thing. The parentheses in expressions such as ***(p+2)** are necessary because the ***** has a higher precedence than the **+** operator.

Now you should be able to fully understand why pointer arithmetic is done relative to the base type—it allows arrays and pointers to relate to each other.

To use a pointer to access multidimensional arrays, you must manually do what the compiler does automatically. For example, in this array

```
float balance[10][5];
```

each row is five elements long. Therefore, to access
balance[3][1] using a pointer, (assume **p** is a **float** pointer) you must use a fragment like this:

```
*(p + (3*5) + 1)
```

To reach the desired element, you must multiply the
row number by the number of elements in the row and
then add the number of the element within the row.
Generally, with multidimensional arrays it is easier to
use array indexing rather than pointer arithmetic.

Pointers and arrays are linked by more than the fact
that by using pointer arithmetic you can access array
elements. You might be surprised to learn that you can
index a pointer as if it were an array. The following
program, for example, is perfectly valid.

```c
#include "stdio.h"

char str[] = "Pointers are fun";

main( )
{
  char *p;
  int i;

  p = str;

  /* loop until null is found */
  for(i=0; p[i]; i++)
    printf("%c", p[i]);
}
```

Keep one point firmly in mind: you should only index
a pointer when that pointer points to an array. While
the following fragment is syntactically correct, it is

wrong; if you tried to execute it, you would probably crash your computer.

```
char *p, ch;
int i;

p = &ch;   /* wrong */
for(i=0; i<10; i++) p[i] = 'A'+i;
```

Since **ch** is not an array, it cannot be meaningfully indexed.

Although you can index a pointer as if it were an array, you will seldom want to do this. The reason is that, in general, using pointer arithmetic is faster than using array indexing. For somewhat complex reasons, a C compiler will generally create faster executable code for an expression such as

```
*(p+3)
```

than it will for the comparable array index

```
p[3]
```

Because an array name without an index is a pointer to the start of the array, you can, if you choose, use pointer arithmetic rather than array indexing to access elements of the array. For example, this program is perfectly valid and prints **c** on the screen.

```
#include "stdio.h"

main( )
{
  char str[80];
```

```
  *(str+3) = 'c';
  printf("%c", *(str+3));
}
```

You cannot, however, modify the value of the pointer generated by using an array name. For example, assuming the previous program, this is an invalid statement:

```
str++;
```

The pointer that is generated by **str** must be thought of as a constant that always points to the start of the array. Therefore, it is invalid to modify it and the compiler will report an error.

Examples

1. Two of C's library functions, **toupper( )** and **tolower( )**, are called using a character argument. In the case of **toupper( )**, if the character is a lowercase letter, the uppercase equivalent is returned; otherwise the character is returned unchanged. For **tolower( )**, if the character is an uppercase letter, the lowercase equivalent is returned; otherwise the character is returned unchanged. These functions use the header file CTYPE.H. The following program requests a string from the user and then prints the string, first in uppercase letters and then in lowercase. This version uses array indexing to access the characters in the string so they can be converted into the appropriate case.

```
#include "ctype.h"
#include "stdio.h"

main( )
{
```

```
char str[80];
int i;

printf("Enter a string: ");
gets(str);

for(i=0; str[i]; i++)
  str[i] = toupper(str[i]);

printf("%s\n", str);  /* uppercase string */

for(i=0; str[i]; i++)
  str[i] = tolower(str[i]);

printf("%s\n", str);  /* lowercase string */
}
```

The same program is shown below, only this time, a pointer is used to access the string. This second approach is the way you would see this program written by professional C programmers because incrementing a pointer is generally faster than indexing an array.

```
#include "ctype.h"
#include "stdio.h"

main( )
{
  char str[80], *p;

  printf("Enter a string: ");
  gets(str);
  p = str;

  while(*p) {
    *p = toupper(*p);
    p++;
  }

  printf("%s\n", str);  /* uppercase string */

  p = str; /* reset p */
```

```
  while(*p) {
    *p = tolower(*p);
    p++;
  }

  printf("%s\n", str);   /* lowercase string */
}
```

Before leaving this example, a small digression is in order. The routine

```
  while(*p) {
    *p = toupper(*p);
    p++;
  }
```

will generally be written like this by experienced programmers

```
while(*p)
  *p++ = toupper(*p);
```

Because the ++ follows the **p**, the value pointed to by **p** is first obtained and then **p** is incremented to point to the next element. Since this is the way C code is often written, this book will use the more compact form from time to time when it seems appropriate.

2. Remember that, although most of the examples have been incrementing pointers, you can decrement a pointer as well. For example, the following program uses a pointer to copy the contents of one string into another in reversed order.

```
#include "stdio.h"
#include "string.h"

char str1[] = "Pointers are fun to use";

main( )
```

```
{
  char str2[80], *p1, *p2;

  /* make p point to end of str1 */
  p1 = str1 + strlen(str1) - 1;

  p2 = str2;

  while(p1 >= str1)
    *p2++ = *p1--;

  /* null terminate str2 */
  *p2 = '\0';

  printf("%s %s", str1, str2);
}
```

This program works by setting **p1** to point to the end of **str1**, and **p2** to the start of **str2**. It then copies the contents of **str1** into str2 in reverse order. Notice the pointer comparison in the **while** loop. It is used to stop the copying process when the start of **str1** is reached.

Also, notice the use of the compacted forms ***p2++** and ***p1– –**. The loop is the equivalent of this one.

```
while(p1 >= str1) {
  *p2 = *p1;
  p1--;
  p2++;
}
```

Again, it is important for you to become familar with the compact form of this type of operation.

Exercises

1. Is this fragment correct?

```
int count[10];
 .
 .
 .
count = count + 2;
```

2. What value does this fragment display?

```
int temp[5] = {10, 19, 23, 8, 9};
int *p;

p = temp;

printf("%d", *(p+3));
```

3. Write a program that inputs a string. Then have the program look for the first space. If it finds one, print the remainder of the string.

6.4 USE POINTERS TO STRING CONSTANTS

As you know, C allows string constants enclosed between double quotes to be used in a program. When the compiler encounters such a string, it stores it in the program's string table and generates a pointer to the string. For this reason, the following program is correct and prints **one two three** on the screen.

```
#include "stdio.h"

main( )
{
  char *p;

  p = "one two three";

  printf(p);
}
```

Let's see how this program works. First, **p** is declared as a character pointer. This means that it may point to an array of characters. When the compiler compiles the line

```
p = "one two three";
```

it stores the string in the program's string table and assigns to **p** the address of the string in the table. Therefore, when **p** is used in the **printf( )** statement, **one two three** is displayed on the screen.

This program can be written more efficiently, as shown here.

```
#include "stdio.h"

char *p = "one two three";

main( )
{

  printf(p);
}
```

Here, **p** is initialized to point to the string.

Examples

1. This program continues to read strings until you enter **stop**.

    ```
    #include "stdio.h"
    #include "string.h"

    char *p = "stop";

    main( )
    ```

```
{
  char str[80];

  do {
   printf("Enter a string: ");
   gets(str);
  } while(strcmp(p, str));
}
```

2. Using pointers to string constants can be very helpful when those constants are quite long. For example, suppose that you had a program that at various
   different points would prompt the user to insert a
   diskette into drive A. To save youself some typing,
   you might elect to initialize a pointer to the string
   and then simply use the pointer when the message
   needed to be displayed; for example:

```
char *p = "Insert disk into drive A, then press ENTER";
  .
  .
  .
printf(p);
  .
  .
  .
printf(p);
```

   Another advantage to this approach is that to change
   the prompt, you only need to change it once, and all
   references to it will reflect the change.

Exercise

1. Write a program that creates three character pointers and initialize them so that one points to the string

"one", the second to the string "two", and the third to the string "three". Next, have the program print all 6 permutations of these three strings. (For example, one permutation is "one two three", another is "two one three".

6.5 CREATE ARRAYS OF POINTERS

Pointers may be arrayed like any other data type. For example, the following statement declares an integer pointer array that has 20 elements.

```
int *pa[20];
```

The address of an integer variable called **myvar** is assigned to the ninth element of the array as follows:

```
pa[8] = &myvar;
```

Because **pa** is an array of pointers, the only value that the array elements may hold are the addresses of integer variables. To assign the integer pointed to by the third element of **pa** the value 100, use the statement:

```
*pa[2] = 100;
```

Examples

1. Probably the single most common use of arrays of pointers is to create string tables in much the same way that unsized arrays were used in the previous chapter. For example, this function displays an error

message based upon the value of its parameter
err_num.

```c
char *p[] = {
  "Input exceeds field width",
  "Out of range",
  "Printer not turned on",
  "Paper out",
  "Disk full",
  "Disk write error"
};

error(int err_num)
{
  printf(p[err_num]);
}
```

2. The following program uses a two-dimensional array of pointers to create a string table that links apple varieties with their colors. To use the program, enter the name of the apple, and the program will tell you its color.

```c
#include "stdio.h"
#include "string.h"

char *p[][2] = {
  "Red Delicious", "red",
  "Golden Delicious", "yellow",
  "Winesap", "red",
  "Gala",  "reddish orange",
  "Lodi", "green",
  "Mutsu", "yellow",
  "Cortland", "red",
  "Jonathan", "red",
  "", ""  /* terminate the table with null strings */
};

main( )
{
  int i;
  char apple[80];
```

```
printf("enter name of apple: ");
gets(apple);

for(i=0; *p[i][0]; i++) {
  if(!strcmp(apple, p[i][0]))
    printf("%s is %s\n", apple, p[i][1]);
}
}
```

Look carefully at the condition controlling the **for** loop. The expression ***p[i][0]** gets the value of the first byte of the ith string. Since the list is terminated by null strings, this value will be 0 (false) when the end of the table is reached. In all other cases it will be non-0, and the loop will repeat.

Exercise

1. In this exercise, you will create an "executive decision aid." This is a program that answers yes, no, or maybe to a question entered at the keyboard. To create this program use an array of character pointers and initialize them to point to these three strings: "Yes", "No", and "Maybe. Rephrase the question". Next, input the user's question and find the length of the string. Next, use this formula to compute an index into the pointer array:

    index = length % 3

6.6 BECOME ACQUAINTED WITH MULTIPLE INDIRECTION

It is possible in C to have a pointer point to another pointer. This is called *multiple indirection* (see Figure 6-1). When a pointer points to another pointer, the first

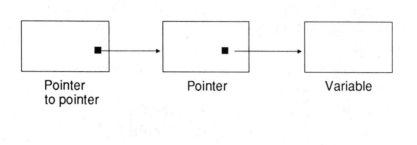

| Pointer to pointer | Pointer | Variable |

FIGURE 6-1. Multiple indirection

pointer contains the address of the second pointer, which points to the location containing the object.

To declare a pointer to a pointer an additional asterisk is placed in front of the pointer's name. For example, this declaration tells the compiler that **mp** is a pointer to a character pointer.

```
char **mp;
```

It is important to understand that **mp** is not a pointer to a character, but rather a pointer to a character pointer.

Accessing the target value indirectly pointed to by a pointer to a pointer requires that the asterisk operator be applied twice. For example,

```
char **mp, *p, ch;

p = &ch; /* get address of ch */
mp = &p; /* get address of p */

**mp = 'A'; /* assign ch the value A using
                multiple indirection */
```

As the comments suggest, **ch** is assigned a value indirectly by using two pointers.

Multiple indirection is not limited to merely "a pointer to a pointer." You can apply the * as often as needed. However, multiple indirection beyond a pointer to a pointer is very difficult to follow and is not recommended.

You may not see the need for multiple indirection at this time, but as you learn more about C, you will see some examples in which it is very valuable.

Examples

1. The following program assigns **val** a value using multiple indirection. It first displays the value directly, then through the use of multiple indirection.

    ```
    #include "stdio.h"

    main( )
    {
      float *fp, **mfp, val;

      fp = &val;
      mfp = &fp;

      **mfp = 123.903;
      printf("%f %f", val, **mfp);
    }
    ```

2. This program shows how you can input a string using **gets( )** by using a pointer to a pointer to the string.

    ```
    #include "stdio.h"

    main( )
    {
      char *p, **mp, str[80];
    ```

```
    p = str;
    mp = &p;

    printf("Enter your name: ");
    gets(*mp);
    printf("Hi %s", *mp);
}
```

Notice that when **mp** is used as an argument to both **gets( )** and **printf( )**, only one * is used. This is because both of these functions require a pointer to a string for their operation. Remember, ****mp** is a pointer to **p**. However, **p** is a pointer to the string **str**. Therefore, ***mp** is a pointer to **str**. If you are a little confused, don't worry. Over time, you will develop a clearer concept of pointers to pointers.

Exercise

1. To help you understand multiple indirection better, write a program that assigns an integer a value using a pointer to a pointer. Before the program ends, display the addresses of the integer variable, the pointer, and the pointer to the pointer. (Remember, use %**p** to display a pointer value.)

6.7 USE POINTERS AS PARAMETERS

Pointers may be passed to functions. For example, when you call a function like **strlen( )** with the name of a string, you are actually passing a pointer to a function. When you pass a pointer to a function, the function must be declared as receiving a pointer of the same type. In the case of **strlen( )**, this is a character pointer. A complete discussion of using pointers as parameters is presented in the next chapter. However, some basic concepts are discussed here.

When you pass a pointer to a function, the code inside that function has access to the variable pointed to by the parameter. This means that the function can change the variable used to call the function. This is why functions like **strcpy( )**, for example, can work. Because it is passed pointers, the function is able to modify the array that receives the string.

This is why you need to precede a variable's name with an **&** when using **scanf( )**. In order for **scanf( )** to modify the value of one of its arguments, it must be passed a pointer to that argument.

Examples

1. Another of C's standard library functions is called **puts( )**; it writes its string argument to the screen followed by a newline. The program that follows creates its own version of **puts( )** called **myputs( )**.

```
#include "stdio.h"

main( )
{
  myputs("this is a test");
}

myputs(char *p)
{
  while(*p) { /* as long as p does not point to the
                 null, which terminates the string */
    printf("%c", *p);
    p++; /* go to next character */
  }
  printf("\n");
}
```

This program illustrates a very important point that was mentioned earlier in this chapter. When the compiler encounters a string constant, it places it into the program's string table and generates a pointer to it. Therefore, the **myputs( )** function is actually called with a character pointer, and the parameter **p** must be declared as a character pointer in order to receive it.

2. The following program shows one way to implement the **strcpy( )** function, called **mystrcpy( )**.

```
#include "stdio.h"

main( )
{
  char str[80];

  mystrcpy(str, "this is a test");
  printf(str);
}

mystrcpy(char *to, char *from)
{
  while(*from) *to++ = *from++;
  *to = '\0'; /* null terminates the string */
}
```

Exercises

1. Write your own version of **strcat( )** called **mystrcat( )**, and write a short program that demonstrates it.

2. Write a program that passes a pointer to an integer variable to a function. Inside that function, assign the variable the value − 1. After the functon has returned, demonstrate that the variable does, indeed, contain − 1 by printing its value.

EXERCISES

At this point you should be able to perform these exercises and answer these questions.

1. Show how to declare a pointer to a **double**.

2. Write a program that assigns a value to a variable indirectly by using a pointer to that variable.

3. Is this fragment correct? If not, why not.

```
main( )
{
  char *p;

  printf("Enter a string: ");
  gets(p);
}
```

4. How do pointers and arrays relate to each other?

5. Given this fragment:

```
char *p, str[80] = "this is a test";

p = str;
```

    show two ways to access the 'i' in "this."

6. Assume that **p** is declared as a pointer to a **double** and contains the address 100. Further, assume that **doubles** are 8 bytes long. After **p** is incremented, what will its value be?

EXERCISES

This section checks how well you have integrated the material in this chapter with that from earlier chapters.

1. What is the advantage of using pointers over array indexing?

2. Below is a program that counts the number of spaces in a string entered by the user. Show how you can make this program more efficient.

```c
#include "stdio.h"

main( )
{
  char str[80];
  int i, spaces;

  printf("Enter a string: ");
  gets(str);

  spaces = 0;
  for(i=0; str[i]; i++)
    if(str[i]==' ') spaces++;

  printf("Number of spaces: %d", spaces);
}
```

3. Rewrite the following array reference using pointer arithmetic.

```c
int count[100][10];

count [44][8];
```

CHAPTER OBJECTIVES

7.1 Create functions that return values

7.2 Use function prototypes

7.3 Understand recursion

7.4 Take a closer look at parameters

7.5 Pass arguments to **main( )**

7.6 Compare classic to modern function
     parameter declarations

·7·
A Closer Look
at Functions

At the very foundation of C is the function. As you know, all action statements must appear within a function. This chapter takes a close look at several important aspects of functions.

EXERCISES

Before proceeding you should be able to answer these questions and perform these exercises.

1. What does this fragment do?

   ```
   int i, *p;

   p = &i;
   *p = 19;
   ```

2. What is generated when you use an array name without an index?

3. Is this fragment correct? If it is correct, explain why it works.

   ```
   char *p = "this is a string";
   ```

4. Write a short program that assigns a floating-point value to a variable indirectly using a pointer to the variable.

5. Write your own version of **strlen( )** (call it **mystrlen( )**) and demonstrate it in a program.

6. Is this fragment correct? If it is, what does the program display?

   ```
   char str[8];

   strcpy(str, "ABCDEFG");
   printf("%c", *(str+2));
   ```

7.1 CREATE FUNCTIONS THAT RETURN VALUES

Up to this point, we have only been working with functions that either did not return a value or returned an integer value. However, a function may return any type of data. In Chapter 1 you were introduced to a specific form of a function. Here is the general form of a C function.

type function-name(parameter-list)
{
  statements
}

Here, *type* specifies the return type of a function. A function can return any type of data except an array. If no data type specifier is present, then the C compiler automatically assumes that the function is returning an integer. In other words, **int** is the default type when no type specifier is present. This is why we have not had to use explicit type declarations on functions we wrote earlier in this book. However, when a function returns a type other than **int**, it must be explicitly declared. This function, for example, returns a **double**.

```
/* Compute the volume of a cube. */
double volume(double s1, double s2, double s3)
{
  return s1 * s2 * s3;
}
```

Before you can use a function that returns a noninteger value, you need to inform the compiler about its return type. If you don't, the compiler will generate code with the assumption that an integer is being returned. There are two ways to inform the compiler about the return type of a function: the traditional method and the function-prototype method. Let's begin with the traditional method. Function prototypes will be covered in the next section.

The traditional method of informing the compiler about the return type of a function is to specify, near the top of your program, the type and name of the function followed by opening and closing parentheses and a semicolon. For example, this statement

```
double volume( );
```

tells the compiler that **volume( )** will be returning a **double**. The following program uses **volume( )**. Notice where the function is declared.

```
#include "stdio.h"

double volume( ); /* tell the compiler about volume( ) */

main( )
{
  double vol;

  vol = volume(12.2, 5.67, 9.03);
  printf("Volume: %ld", vol);
}

/* Compute the volume of a cube. */
double volume(double s1, double s2, double s3)
{
  return s1 * s2 * s3;
}
```

If a function does not return a value and your compiler is compatible with the ANSI C standard, you can declare the function as **void**. This tells the compiler that the function does not return a value and prevents its use on the right side of an assignment statement. The following program uses a **void** function.

```
#include "stdio.h"

void message( );

main( )
{
  message( );
}

void message( )
{
  printf("This is a message");
}
```

The **main( )** function may return an integer value to the operating system. This return value is generally interpreted as a termination code. Usually, a return value of 0 indicates a successful termination. Any other value means that the program terminated because of an error. If you don't specify any return value, most compilers automatically return 0. Although not necessary, many programmers declare **main( )** as **void** when no explicit return value is used, as will this book from this point on. It is not necessary to declare **main ( )** in advance because it is not called by any other function in a program.

Examples

1. As you know, the standard library function **sqrt( )** returns a **double** value. You might be wondering

how the compiler knows this. The answer is that **sqrt( )** is declared as returning a **double** in its header file MATH.H. To see the importance of using the header file, try this program.

```c
#include "stdio.h"

void main( )
{
  double answer;

  answer = sqrt(9.0);
  printf("%ld", answer);
}
```

When you run this program, it displays something other than **3** because the compiler generates code that copies only two bytes (assuming two-byte integers) into **answer**. If you include MATH.H, the program will work correctly.

2. Quite commonly, when a function returns a character, the return type of the function is allowed to default to **int**. The reason for this is found in the fact that C very cleanly handles the conversion of characters to integers and integers back to characters. There is no loss of information. For example, the following program is perfectly valid.

```c
#include "stdio.h"

void main( )
{
  char ch;

  ch = get_a_char( );
  printf("%c", ch);
}
```

```
get_a_char( )
{
  return 'a';
}
```

When **get_a_char( )** returns, it elevates the character 'a' to an integer by adding a high-order byte containing zeros. When this value is assigned to **ch** in **main( )**, the high-order byte is removed. The reason few programmers bother to declare functions like **get_a_char( )** as returning a character instead of an **int** is that there is little (or, nothing) to gain.

Exercises

1. Write a program that creates a function, called **avg( )**, that reads ten floating-point numbers entered by the user and returns their average.

2. Is this program fragment correct? If not, why not?

```
#include "stdio.h"

float myfunc( );

void main( )
{
  double d;

  d = myfunc( );
  printf("%ld", d);
}

double myfunc( )
{
  .
  .
  .
```

7.2 USE FUNCTION PROTOTYPES

The second way to inform the compiler about the return value of a function is to use a *function prototype*. A prototype extends the method described in the previous section by also declaring the number and types of the function's arguments. Prototypes allow C to find and report any illegal type conversions between the type of arguments used to call a function and the type definition of its parameters. Prototypes also enable the compiler to report when the number of arguments to a function is not the same as the number of parameters declared in the function.

Function prototypes were not supported by the original version of C. They were added by the ANSI C standardization committee and are considered to be one of the most important additions made to the C language.

The general form of a function prototype definition is shown here.

type function-name(type parameter-name1,
        type parameter-name2,..., type parameter-nameN);

Here is the volume-computing program developed in the preceding section using a function prototype.

```
#include "stdio.h"

/* this is volume's prototype */
double volume(double s1, double s2, double s3);

void main( )
{
  double vol;
```

```
  vol = volume(12.2, 5.67, 9.03);
  printf("Volume: %ld", vol);
}

/* Compute the volume of a cube. */
double volume(double s1, double s2, double s3)
{
  return s1 * s2 * s3;
}
```

Prototyping may not seem important in programs as small as most of the examples in this book. However, as your programs become larger, prototyping will help you avoid errors.

When function prototypes were added to C by the ANSI C standardization committee, two minor compatibility problems between the old version of C and the ANSI version of C had to be resolved relative to prototypes. The first issue was how to handle the traditional declaration method, which does not use an argument list. The ANSI standard specifies that when a function declaration occurs without an argument list, nothing is being said about the arguments to the function. This leads to this question: how do you prototype a function that takes no arguments? For example, this function simply outputs a line of periods.

```
void line( )
{
  int i;

  for(i=0; i<80; i++) printf(".");
}
```

If you try to use this as a prototype, it won't work because the compiler will think that you are simply using the old-style declaration method.

```
void line( );
```

The ANSI committee resolved this problem by expanding the use of the **void** keyword. When a function has no parameters, its prototype uses **void** inside the parentheses. For example, here is **line( )**'s proper prototype.

```
void line(void);
```

This tells the compiler that the function has no parameters, and any call to that function that has parameters is an error. However, you must make sure to also use **void** when the function is defined. For example, **line( )** must look like this:

```
void line(void)
{
  int i;

  for(i=0; i<80; i++) printf(".");
}
```

Although not necessary, for consistency reasons many programmers declare **main( )** as follows:

```
void main(void)
```

This approach will also be used from this point forward in this book. However, as you shortly see, there are some parameters that **main( )** may have.

A second issue affected by prototyping is the way it affects C's automatic type promotions. Because of some features of the environment in which C was developed, when a nonprototyped function is called, all characters are converted to integers and all **floats** into **doubles**.

However, these type promotions seem to violate the purpose of the prototype. The resolution to this problem is that when a prototype exists, the types specified in the prototype are maintained, and no type promotions will occur.

Function prototypes help you write programs more easily because they help ensure that the functions in your programs are being called with correct types and numbers of arguments.

Now that you have learned about prototypes, this book will use them in all subsequent examples. Also, when new library functions are introduced, they will be shown using their prototype form.

Examples

1. To see how a function prototype can catch an error, try compiling this version of the volume program.

```c
#include "stdio.h"

/* this is volume( )'s full prototype */
double volume(double s1, double s2, double s3);

void main(void)
{
  double vol;

  vol = volume(12.2, 5.67, 9.03, 10.2);
  printf("Volume: %ld", vol);
}

/* Compute the volume of a cube. */
double volume(double s1, double s2, double s3)
{
  return s1 * s2 * s3;
}
```

As you will see, this program will not compile because the compiler knows that **volume( )** is declared as having only three parameters, but the program is attempting to call it with four parameters.

2. When you create functions that take no parameters, you should use **void** between the parentheses, both in the function prototype and when the function is actually declared, as shown in this program.

```c
#include "stdio.h"

int getnum(void);

void main(void)
{
    int i;

    i = getnum( );
    printf("%d", i);
}

getnum(void)
{
    int x;

    printf("Enter a number: ");
    scanf("%d", &x);
    return x;
}
```

Exercises

1. Rewrite the program from Exercise 1, Section 7.1, so that it uses a function prototype.

2. Is the following program correct? If not, why not? If it is, can it be made better?

```
#include "stdio.h"

double myfunc( );

void main(void)
{
  printf("%f", myfunc(10.2));
}

double myfunc(double num)
{
  return num / 2.0;
}
```

7.3 UNDERSTAND RECURSION

Recursion is the process by which something is defined in terms of itself. When applied to computer languages, recursion means that a function can call itself. Not all computer languages support recursive functions, but C does. A very simple example of recursion is shown in this program.

```
#include "stdio.h"

void recurse(int i);

void main(void)
{
  recurse(0);
}

void recurse(int i)
{
  if(i<10) {
    recurse(i+1);
    printf("%d ", i);
  }
}
```

This program prints

9 8 7 6 5 4 3 2 1 0

on the screen. Let's see why.

The **recurse( )** function is first called with 0. This is **recurse( )'s** first activation. Since 0 is less than 10, **recurse( )** then calls itself with the value of **i** (in this case 0) plus 1. This is the second activation of **recurse( )**, and **i** equals 1. This causes **recurse( )** to be called again using the value 2. This process repeats until **recurse( )** is called with the value 10. This causes **recurse( )** to return. Since it returns to the point of its call, it will execute the **printf( )** statement in its previous activation, print **9**, and return. This, then, returns the point of its call in the previous activation, which causes **8** to be displayed. The process continues until all the calls return, and the program terminates.

It is important to understand that there are not multiple copies of a recursive function. Instead, only one copy exists. When a function is called, storage for its parameters and local data are allocated on the stack. Thus, when a function is called recursively, the function begins executing with a new set of parameters and local variables, but the code that constitutes the function remains the same.

If you think about the preceding program, you may note that recursion is essentially a new type of program control mechanism. This is why every recursive function you write will have an **if** statement that controls whether the function will call itself again or return. Without such a statement, a recursive function will simply run wild, using up all the memory allocated to the stack and then crashing the program.

Recursion is generally employed sparingly. However, it can be quite useful in simplifying certain algorithms. For example, the Quicksort sorting algorithm is difficult to implement without the use of recursion. If you are new to programming in general, you might find yourself uncomfortable with recursion. Don't worry; as you become more experienced, the use of recursive functions will become more natural.

Examples

1. The recursive program described above can be altered to print the numbers 0 through 9 on the screen. To accomplish this, only the position of the **printf( )** statement needs to be changed, as shown here.

```
#include "stdio.h"

void recurse(int i);

void main(void)
{
  recurse(0);
}

void recurse(int i)
{
  if(i<10) {
    printf("%d ", i);
    recurse(i+1);
  }
}
```

Because the call to **printf( )** now precedes the recursive call to **recurse( )**, the numbers are printed in ascending order.

2. The following program demonstrates how recursion can be used to copy one string to another.

```
#include "stdio.h"

void rcopy(char *s1, char *s2);

void main(void)
{
  char str[80];

  rcopy(str, "this is a test");
  printf(str);
}

/* Copy s2 to s1 using recursion. */
void rcopy(char *s1, char *s2)
{
  if(*s2) { /* if not at end of s2 */
    *s1++ = *s2++;
    rcopy(s1, s2);
  }
  else *s1 = '\0'; /* null terminate the string */
}
```

The program works by assigning the character currently pointed to by **s2** to the one pointed to by **s1**, and then incrementing both pointers. These pointers are then used in a recursive call to **rcopy( )**, until **s2** points to the null that terminates the string.

Although this program makes an interesting example of recursion, no professional C programmer would actually code a function like this for one simple reason: efficiency. It takes more time to execute a function call than it does to execute a loop. Therefore, tasks like this will almost always be coded using an iterative approach.

3. It is possible to have a program in which two or more functions are *mutually recursive*. Mutual recursion

occurs when one function calls another, which in turn calls the first. For example, study this short program.

```
#include "stdio.h"

void f2(int b);
void f1(int a);

void main(void)
{
   f1(30);
}

void f1(int a)
{
   if(a) f2(a-1);
   printf("%d ", a);
}

void f2(int b)
{
   printf(".");
   if(b) f1(b-1);
}
```

This program displays

...............0 2 4 6 8 10 12 14 16 18 20 22 24 26 28 30

on the screen. Its output is caused by the way the two functions f1( ) and f2( ) call each other. Each time f1( ) is called, it checks to see if a is 0. If not, it calls f2( ) with a-1. The f2( ) function first prints a period and then checks to see if b is 0. If not, it calls f1( ) with b-1, and the process repeats. Eventually, b is 0 and the function calls start unraveling, causing f1( ) to display the numbers 0 to 30 counting by twos.

Exercises

1. One of the best known examples of recursion is the recursive version of a function that computes the factorial of a number. The factorial of a number is computed by multiplying the original number by all integers less than it and greater than 1. Therefore, 4 factorial is 4 x3 x2, or 24. Write a function, called **fact( )**, that uses recursion to compute the factorial of its integer argument. Have it return the result. Also, demonstrate its use in a program.

2. What is wrong with this recursive function?

```
void f( )
{
   int i;

   printf("in f( )\n");

   /* call f( ) 10 times */
   for(i=0; i<10; i++) f( );
}
```

3. Write a program that displays a string on the screen, one character at a time, using a recursive function.

7.4 TAKE A CLOSER LOOK AT PARAMETERS

Functions can be passed arguments in one of two ways. The first is called *call by value*. This method copies the *value* of an argument into the formal parameter of the function. Therefore, changes made to the parameters of the subroutine have no effect on the variables used to call it. The second way a function can have arguments passed to it is *call by reference*. In this method, the *address* of an argument is copied into the parameter. Inside the subroutine, the address is used to access the actual argument used in the call. This means that changes made to the parameter will affect the variable used to call the routine.

By default, C uses call by value to pass arguments. This means, in general, that you cannot alter the variables used to call the function. What occurs inside the function will have no effect on the variable used in the call. However, as you saw in Chapter 6, it is possible to cause a call by reference by passing a pointer to an argument. Since this causes the address of the argument to be passed to the function, it then is possible to change the value of the argument outside the function.

The classic example of a call-by-reference function is **swap( )**, shown here. It exchanges the value of its two integer arguments.

```c
#include "stdio.h"

void swap(int *i, int *j);

void main(void)
{
  int num1, num2;

  num1 = 100;
  num2 = 800;

  printf("num1: %d num2: %d\n", num1, num2);
  swap(&num1, &num2);
  printf("num1: %d num2: %d\n", num1, num2);
}

/* Exchange the values pointed to by two integer pointers.
*/
void swap(int *i, int *j)
{
  int temp;
```

```
  temp = *i;
  *i = *j;
  *j = temp;
}
```

Since pointers to the two integers are passed to the function, the actual values pointed to by the arguments are exchanged.

As you know, when an array is used as an argument to a function, only the address of the array is passed, not a copy of the entire array, which implies call-by-value. This means that the parameter declaration must be of a compatible pointer type. There are three ways to declare a parameter that is to receive a pointer to an array. First, the parameter may be declared as an array of the same type and size as that used to call the function. Second, it may be specified as an unsized array. Finally, and most commonly, it may be specified as a pointer to the base type of the array. The following program demonstrates all three methods.

```c
#include "stdio.h"

void f1(int num[5]), f2(int num[]), f3(int *num);

void main(void)
{
  int count[5] = {1, 2, 3, 4, 5};

  f1(count);
  f2(count);
  f3(count);
}

void f1(int num[5])
{
  int i;
```

```
  for(i=0; i<5; i++) printf("%d ", num[i]);
}

void f2(int num[])
{
   int i;

   for(i=0; i<5; i++) printf("%d ", num[i]);
}

void f3(int *num)
{
   int i;

   for(i=0; i<5; i++) printf("%d ", num[i]);
}
```

Even though each of the three methods of declaring a parameter that will receive a pointer to an array look different, they all result in a pointer parameter being created.

Example

1. Some computer languages, such as BASIC, provide an input function that allows you to specify a prompting message. C has no counterpart for this type of function. However, you can easily create one. The program shown here uses the function **prompt( )** to display a prompting message and then to read a string entered by the user.

   ```
   #include "stdio.h"

   void prompt(char *msg, int *num);

   void main(void)
   {
      int i;
   ```

```
    prompt("Enter a num: ", &i);
    printf("Your number is: %d", i);
}

void prompt(char *msg, int *num)
{
  printf(msg);
  scanf("%d", num);
}
```

Because the parameter **num** is already a pointer, you do not need to precede it with an **&**. (In fact, it would be an error to do so.)

Exercises

1. Is this program correct? If not, why not?

    ```
    #include "stdio.h"

    myfunc(int num, int min, int max);

    void main(void)
    {
      int i;

      printf("Enter a number between 1 and 10: ");
      myfunc(&i, 1, 10);
    }

    void myfunc(int num, int min, int max)
    {
      do {
        scanf("%d", num);
      } while (*num<min || *num>max);
    }
    ```

2. Write a program that creates an input function similar to **prompt( )** described earlier in this section. Have it input a string rather than an integer.

7.5 PASS ARGUMENTS TO main( )

Many programs allow command-line arguments to be specified when they are run. A *command-line argument* is the information that follows the program's name on the command line of the operating system. Command-line arguments are used to pass information to the program. For example, when you use a text editor, you probably specify the name of the file you want to edit after the name of the word processing program. For example, if you use a word processor called WP, then this line causes the file TEST to be edited.

WP TEST

Here, TEST is a command-line argument.

Your C programs may also utilize command-line arguments. These are passed to a C program through two arguments to the **main( )** function. The parameters are called **argc** and **argv**. As you probably guessed, these parameters are optional and are not used when no command line arguments are being used. Let's look at **argc** and **argv** more closely.

The **argc** parameter holds the number of arguments on the command line and is an integer. It will always be at least 1 because the name of the program qualifies as the first argument.

The **argv** parameter is an array of string pointers. The most common method for declaring **argv** is shown here.

```
char *argv[ ];
```

The empty brackets indicate that it is an array of unde-termined length. All command-line arguments are passed to **main( )** as strings. To access an individual string, index **argv**. For example, **argv[0]** points to the program's name and **argv[1]** points to the first argument. This program displays all the command-line arguments that it is called with.

```
#include "stdio.h"

void main(int argc, char *argv[ ])
{
  int i;

  for(i=1; i<argc; i++) printf("%s ", argv[i]);
}
```

The ANSI C standard does not specify what constitutes a command-line argument, because operating systems vary considerably on this point. However, the most common convention is as follows: Each command-line argument must be separated by a space or a tab character. Commas, semicolons, and the like are not considered separators. For example,

```
This is a test
```

is made up of four strings, but

```
this,that,and,another
```

is one string.

If you need to pass a command-line argument that does, in fact, contain spaces, you must place it between quotes, as shown in this example.

```
"this is a test"
```

The names of **argv** and **argc** are arbitrary—you can use any names you like. However, **argc** and **argv** have traditionally been used since C's origin. It is a good idea to use these names so that anyone reading your program can quickly identify them as the command-line parameters.

One last point: the ANSI C standard only defines the **argc** and **argv** parameters. However, your compiler may allow additional parameters to **main( )**. For example, most DOS-based compilers allow access to DOS's environmental information. Check your compiler's user manual.

Examples

1. As mentioned earlier, when you need to pass numeric data to a program, that data will be received in its string form. Your program will need to convert it into the proper internal format using one or another of C's standard library functions. The most common conversion functions are shown here, using their prototypes.

```
int atoi(char *str);
double atof(char *str);
long atol(char *str);
```

These functions use the STDLIB.H header file. The **atoi( )** function returns the **int** equivalent of its string argument. The **atof( )** returns the **double** equivalent of its string argument, and the **atol( )** returns the **long** equivalent of its string argument. If you call one of these functions with a string that is not a valid number, 0 will be returned. The following program demonstrates these functions. To use it, enter an integer, a long integer, and a floating-point number on the command line. It will then redisplay them on the screen.

```c
#include "stdio.h"
#include "stdlib.h"

void main(int argc, char *argv[])
{
  int i;
  double d;
  long l;

  i = atoi(argv[1]);
  l = atol(argv[2]);
  d = atof(argv[3]);

  printf("%d %ld %lf", i, l, d);
}
```

2. This program converts ounces to pounds. To use it, specify the number of ounces on the command line.

```c
#include "stdio.h"
#include "stdlib.h"

void main(int argc, char *argv[ ])
{
  double pounds;
  pounds = atof(argv[1]) / 16.0;
  printf("%lf pounds", pounds);
}
```

3. Although the examples up to this point haven't done so, you should verify, in real programs, that the right number of command-line arguments have been supplied by the user prior to using one. The way to do this is to test the value of **argc**. For example, the ounces-to-pounds program can be improved as shown here.

```
#include "stdio.h"
#include "stdlib.h"

void main(int argc, char *argv[ ])
{
  double pounds;

  if(argc!=2) {
    printf("usage: CONVERT <ounces>\n");
    printf("try again");
  }
  else {
    pounds = atof(argv[1]) / 16.0;
    printf("%lf pounds", pounds);
  }
}
```

This way the program will only perform a conversion if a command-line argument is present. (Of course, you may prompt the user for any missing information, if you choose.)

Generally the preceding program will be written by a professional C programmer like this:

```
#include "stdio.h"
#include "stdlib.h"

void main(int argc, char *argv[ ])
{
  double pounds;

  if(argc!=2) {
    printf("usage: CONVERT <ounces>\n");
    printf("try again");
    exit(1); /* stop the program */
  }

  pounds = atof(argv[1]) / 16.0;
  printf("%lf pounds", pounds);
}
```

When some condition necessary for a program's execution has not been met, most C programmers call the standard library function **exit( )** to terminate the program. The **exit( )** has this prototype

void exit(int *return-code*);

and uses the STDLIB.H header file. When **exit( )** terminates the program, it returns the value of *return-code* to the operating system. By convention, most operating systems use a return code of 0 to mean that a program has terminated normally. Non-0 values indicate abnormal termination.

Exercises

1. Write a program that accepts two arguments. Have the program compare them and report which is lexicographically greater than the other.

2. Write a program that takes two numeric arguments and displays their sum.

3. Expand the program in Exercise 2 so that it takes three arguments. The first argument must be one of these words: add, subtract, multiply, or divide. Based on the value of the first argument, perform the requested operation on the remaining two numeric arguments.

7.6 COMPARE CLASSIC TO MODERN FUNCTION PARAMETER DECLARATIONS

The original version of C used a different parameter declaration method than has been shown in this book.

This original declaration method is now called the *classic form*. The form used in this book, the *modern form*, was introduced in the ANSI C standard.

The general form of the classic parameter declaration is shown here.

type function-name(parameter1, parameter2,...parameterN)
type parameter1;
type parameter2;
.

.

.

type parameterN;
{
    function-code
}

Notice that the declaration is divided into two parts. Within the parentheses, only the names of the parameters are specified. Outside the parentheses, the types and names are specified. For example, given the following modern declaration

```
float f(char ch, long size, double max)
{
    .
    .
    .
}
```

the equivalent classic declaration is

```
float f(ch, size, max)
char ch;
long size;
```

```
double max;
{
    .
    .
    .

}
```

One other aspect of the classic form is that you can specify more than one parameter after its type. For example, this is perfectly valid.

```
myfunc(i, j, k)
int i, j, k;
{
    .
    .
    .

```

The ANSI C standard specifies that either the classic or the modern declaration form may be used. The reason for this is to maintain compatibility with older C programs. (There are literally millions of lines of C code that use the classic form.) So, if you see programs in books or magazines that use the classic form, don't worry; your compiler will be able to compile them. However for all new programs, you should definitely use the modern form.

Example

1. This program uses the classic declaration form.

```
#include "stdio.h"

void main(void)
{
   printf("area is %d", area(10, 13));
}
```

```
area(l, w)
int l, w;
{
   return l * w;
}
```

Exercise

1. Convert this program so that **f_to_m( )** uses the classic declaration form.

    ```
    #include "stdio.h"

    double f_to_m(double f);

    void main(void)
    {
      double feet;

      printf("Enter feet: ");
      scanf("%lf", &feet);
      printf("Meters: %lf", f_to_m(feet));
    }

    double f_to_m(double f)
    {
      return f / 3.28;
    }
    ```

EXERCISES

At this point you should be able to answer these questions and perform these exercises.

MASTERY SKILLS CHECK

√

1. How do you declare a function that does not return a value?

2. What is a function prototype, and what are the benefits of it?

3. How do command-line arguments get passed to a C program?

4. Write a program that uses a recursive function to display the letters of the alphabet.

5. Write a program that takes one command-line string argument. It then outputs the string in coded form. To code the string, add 1 to each character.

6. What is the prototype for this function?

```
double myfunc(int x, int y, char ch)
{
    .
    .
    .
}
```

7. Show how the function in Exercise 6 would be coded using the classic function declaration.

8. What does the **exit( )** function do?

9. What does the **atoi( )** function do?

EXERCISES

This section checks how well you have integrated the material in this chapter with that from earlier chapters.

INTEGRATING NEW SKILLS CHECK

√

1. Write a program that only allows access to it if the user enters the correct password as a command-line parameter. If the user enters the right word, print **Access permitted**; otherwise print **Access denied**.

2. Create a function called **string_up( )** that transforms the string it is called with into uppercase characters.

Demonstrate its use in a program. (Hint, use the **toupper( )** function to convert lowercase characters into uppercase.)

3. Write a function called **avg( )** that averages a list of floating-point values. The function will have two arguments. The first is a pointer to the array containing the numbers; the second is an integer value, which is the size of the array. Demonstrate its use in a program.

4. Explain how pointers allow C to generate a call-by-reference function call.

CHAPTER OBJECTIVES

8.1 Learn another preprocessor directive

8.2 Examine character and string input and output

8.3 Examine some nonstandard console functions

8.4 Take a closer look at **gets( )** and **puts( )**

8.5 Master **printf( )**

8.6 Master **scanf( )**

·8·
Console I/O

In this chapter you will learn about C's console I/O functions. These are the functions that read or write information to and from the console. You have already been using some of these functions. However, in this chapter, these functions are discussed in detail. This chapter begins with a short but necessary digression that introduces another of C's preprocessor directives: **#define**.

EXERCISES

Before proceeding, you should be able to answer these questions and perform these exercises.

1. If a function is returning a type other than an integer, what must you do so that the compiler can compile code that will correctly call this function?

2. What are the principle advantages of using function prototypes.

3. Write a program that uses a function called **hypot( )** that returns the length of the hypotenuse of a right triangle when passed the length of the two opposing sides. Have the function return a **double** value. The type of the parameters must be **double** as well. Demonstrate the function in a program. (The Pythagorean Theorem states that the sum of the squares of the two opposing sides equals the square of the hypotenuse.)

4. What return type should you use for a function that returns no value?

5. Write a recursive function called **rstrlen( )** that uses recursion to compute the length of a string. Demonstrate it in a program.

6. Write a program that reports how many command line arguments it has been called with. Also, have it display the contents of the last one.

7. How is this declaration coded using the classic function-declaration form?

```
void func(int a, char ch, double d)
{
  .
  .
  .
```

8.1 LEARN ANOTHER PREPROCESSOR DIRECTIVE

Up to this point, you have learned about and have been using one preprocessor directive, **#include**. Before you can learn more about C's console I/O functions, you need to learn about another of its preprocessor directives, **#define**.

As you recall, the C preprocessor performs various manipulations on the source code of your program before it is actually compiled. A preprocessor directive is simply an instruction to the preprocessor. The **#define** directive is used to tell the preprocessor to substitute one string for another throughout your entire program. This process is generally referred to as *macro substitution*. The general form of the **#define** statement is shown here

#define *macro-name string*

Notice that this line does not end in a semicolon. Each time the *macro-name* is encountered in the program, the associated string is substituted for it. For example, consider this program.

```
#include "stdio.h"

#define MAX 100

void main(void)
{
  int i;

  for(i=0; i<MAX; i++) printf("%d ", i);
}
```

When the identifier **MAX** is encountered by the pre-processor, the string **100** is automatically substituted. Thus, the **for** loop will actually look like this to the compiler.

```
for(i=0; i<100; i++) printf("%d ", i);
```

Keep one thing clearly in mind: At the time of the substitution, **100** is simply a string of characters composed of a 1 and two 0s. The preprocessor does not convert a number into any sort of internal format. This is left to the compiler.

The macro name can be any valid C identifier. Although macro names can appear in either upper- or lowercase letters, most programmers have adopted the convention of using uppercase for macro names. This makes it easy for anyone reading your program to know when a macro name is being used.

There may one or more spaces after the macro name before the substitution string begins. This string may contain any type of character and is terminated by the end of the line.

Preprocessor directives in general and **#define** in particular are not affected by C's code blocks. That is, whether you define a macro name outside of all functions or within a function, once it is defined, all code after that point may have access to it. For example, this program prints **80386** on the screen.

```
#include "stdio.h"

void f(void);

void main(void)
{
  #define PROCESSOR 80386

  f( );
}

void f(void)
{
  printf("%ld", PROCESSOR);
}
```

There is one important point you must remember: each preprocessor directive must appear on its own line.

Macro substitutions are useful for two main reasons. First, many C library functions use certain predefined values to indicate special conditions or results. Your programs will need access to these values when they use one of these functions. However, many times the actual value will vary between programming environments. For this reason, many of these values are specified using macro names. These macro names are defined inside the header file that relates to each specific function. You will see an example of this in the next section.

The second reason macro substitution is important is that it can help make it easier to maintain programs. For example, if you know that a value, such as an array size, is going to be used several places in your program, it is better to create a macro for this value. Then if you ever need to change this value, you simply change the macro definition. All references to it will be automatically changed when the program is recompiled.

Examples

1. Since a macro substitution is simply a string replacement, you can use a macro name in place of a string. For example, the following program prints **Macro Substitutions are Fun**.

```
#include "stdio.h"

#define FUN "Macro Substitutions are Fun"

void main(void)
{
  printf(FUN);
}
```

To the compiler, the **printf( )** statement looks like this:

```
printf("Macro Substitutions are Fun");
```

2. Once a macro name has been defined, it can be used to help define another macro name. For example, examine this program.

```
#include "stdio.h"

#define SMALL 1
#define MEDIUM SMALL+1
#define LARGE MEDIUM+1

void main(void)
{
  printf("%d %d %d", SMALL, MEDIUM, LARGE);
}
```

As you might expect, it prints **1 2 3** on the screen.

3. If a macro name appears inside of a quoted string, no substitution will take place. For example, given this definition

```
#define ERROR "catastrophic error occurred"
```

the following statement will not be affected.

```
printf("ERROR: Try again");
```

Exercises

1. Create a program that defines two macro names, **MAX** and **COUNTBY**. Have the program count from 0 to **MAX-1** by whatever value **COUNTBY** is defined as. (Give **COUNTBY** the value 3 for demonstration purposes.)

2. Is this fragment correct?

```
#define MAX MIN+100
#define MIN 10
```

3. Is this fragment correct?

```
#define STR this is a test
    .
    .
    .
printf(STR);
```

4. Is this program correct?

```
#define STDIO "stdio.h"
#include STDIO

void main(void)
{
  printf("this is a test");
}
```

8.2 EXAMINE CHARACTER AND STRING INPUT AND OUTPUT

Although you have already learned how to input and output characters and strings, this section looks at these processes more formally.

The ANSI C standard defines these two functions that perform character input and output, respectively:

```
int getchar(void);
int putchar(int ch);
```

They both use the header file STDIO.H. As mentioned earlier in this book, many compilers implement **getchar( )** in a line-buffered manner, which makes it unusable in an interactive environment. Most compilers contain a nonstandard function called **getche( )**, which operates like **getchar( )**, except that it is interactive. Discussion of **getche( )** and other nonstandard functions will occur in a later section.

The **getchar( )** function returns the next character typed on the keyboard. This character is read as an **unsigned char** converted to an **int**. However, most commonly, your program will assign this value to a **char** variable, even though **getchar( )** is declared as returning an **int**. If you do this, the high-order byte of the integer is simply discarded. The reason that **getchar( )** returns an integer is that if an error occurs reading input, **getchar( )** returns the macro **EOF** , which is a negative integer, generally −1. The **EOF** macro, defined in STDIO.H, stands for end-of-file. Although it may seem hard to see how a keyboard could generate an end-of-file condition, this is the traditional value used for **getchar( )** when an error occurs. Therefore, to allow the **EOF** value to be returned, **getchar( )** must return an integer. In the vast majority of circumstances, if an error occurs when reading from the keyboard, it generally means that the computer has died. Therefore, most programmers don't bother checking for EOF when using **getchar( )** and simply assign the value to a character value.

The **putchar( )** function outputs a single character to the screen. Although its parameter is declared to be of type **int**, this value is converted into an **unsigned char** by the function. If the output operation is successful, **putchar( )** returns the character written. If an output error occurs, **EOF** is returned. For reasons similar to those given for **getchar( )**, if output to the screen fails, the computer has probably crashed anyway, so most programmers don't bother checking the return value of **putchar( )** for errors.

The reason that you might want to use **putchar( )** rather than **printf( )** with the %c specifier to output a character is that **putchar( )** is faster and more efficient. Although **printf( )** is very powerful and flexible, a call to **printf( )** generates more overhead than a call to **putchar( )**.

Examples

1. As stated earlier, **getchar( )** is generally implemented using line buffering. When input is line buffered, no characters are actually passed back to the calling program until the user presses ENTER. The following program demonstrates this.

```
#include "stdio.h"

void main(void)
{
  char ch;
```

```
do {
  ch = getchar( );
  putchar('.');
} while(ch != '\n');
}
```

Instead of printing a period between each character, what you will see on the screen is all the letters you typed before pressing ENTER, followed by a string of periods.

One other point: When entering characters using **getchar( )**, pressing ENTER will cause the newline character to be returned. However, when using one of the alternative nonstandard functions, pressing ENTER will cause the carriage return character **\r** to be returned. Keep this difference in mind.

2. The following program illustrates the fact that you can use C's backslash character constants with **putchar( )**.

```
#include "stdio.h"

void main(void)
{
  putchar('A');
  putchar('\n');
  putchar('B');
}
```

This program displays

```
A
B
```

on the screen.

Exercises

1. Rewrite the program shown in the first example so that it checks for errors on both input and output operations.

2. What is wrong with this fragment?

```
char str[80] = "this is a test";
 .
 .
 .
putchar(str);
```

8.3 EXAMINE SOME NONSTANDARD CONSOLE FUNCTIONS

Because of the noninteractive nature of **getchar( )** as commonly implemented, many compilers supply additional input routines that provide interactive character input. You are already familiar with **getche( )**. Here are the prototypes of **getche( )** and **getch( )**.

int getche(void);
int getch(void);

Both functions use the header file CONIO.H. The **getche( )** function waits until the next keystroke is entered at the keyboard and then reads the character and echoes it to the screen. The character is read as an **unsigned char** and elevated to **int**. However, your routines can simply assign this value to a **char** value. The **getch( )** function is the same as **getche( )**, except that the keystroke is not echoed to the screen.

Another very useful non-ANSI-standard function commonly supplied with a C compiler is **kbhit( )**. It has this prototype.

int kbhit(void);

The **kbhit( )** function requires the header file CONIO.H. This function is used to determine whether a key has been pressed or not. If the user has pressed a key, this function returns true (non-0), but does not read the character. If a keystroke is waiting, you may read it with **getche( )** or **getch( )**. If no keystroke is pending, **kbhit( )** returns false (0).

Examples

1. The **getch( )** function lets you take greater control of the screen because you can determine what is displayed each time a key is struck. For example, this program reads characters until a 'q' is typed. All characters displayed are uppercase.

    ```c
    #include "stdio.h"
    #include "conio.h"
    #include "ctype.h"

    void main(void)
    {
      char ch;

      do {
    ```

```
      ch = getch( );
      putchar(toupper(ch));
    } while (ch != 'q');
  }
```

2. The **kbhit( )** function is very useful when you want to let a user interrupt a routine without actually forcing the user to continually respond to a prompt like "Continue?". For example, this program prints a 5-percent sales-tax table in increments of 20 cents. The program continues to print the table until either the user strikes a key or the maximum value is printed.

```
#include "stdio.h"
#include "conio.h"

void main(void)
{
  double amount;

  amount = 0.20;

  printf("Printing 5-percent tax table\n");
  printf("Press a key to stop.\n\n");
  do {
    printf("amount: %lf, tax: %lf\n", amount, amount*0.05);
    if(kbhit( )) break;
    amount = amount + 0.20;
  } while(amount < 100.0);
}
```

Exercises

1. Write a program that displays the ASCII code of each character typed. Do not display the actual character, however.

2. Write a program that prints periods on the screen until you press a key.

8.4 TAKE A CLOSER LOOK AT gets( ) AND puts( )

Although both **gets( )** and **puts( )** were introduced earlier, let's take a close look at them now. Their function prototypes are

char *gets(char *str);
int puts(char *str);

These functions use the header file STDIO.H. The **gets( )** function reads characters entered at the keyboard until a carriage return is entered. It stores the characters in the array pointed to by str. The carriage return is not added to the string. Instead, it is converted into the null terminator. If successful, **gets( )** returns a pointer to the start of str. If an error occurs, a null pointer is returned.

The **puts( )** function outputs the string pointed to by str to the screen. It automatically appends a carriage return, line-feed sequence. If successful, **puts( )** returns a non-negative value. If an error occurs, **EOF** is returned.

The main reason you may want to use **puts( )** instead of **printf( )** to output a string is that **puts( )** is much smaller and faster. While this is not important to the example programs shown in this book, it may be in some applications.

Examples

1. This program shows how you can use the return
    value of **gets( )** to access the string holding the input
    information. Notice that this program also confirms
    that no error has occurred before attempting to use
    the string.

    ```c
    #include "stdio.h"

    void main(void)
    {
      char *p, str[80];

      printf("Enter a string: ");
      p = gets(str);
      if(p)   /* if not null */
        printf("%s %s", p, str);
    }
    ```

2. If you simply want to make sure that **gets( )** did not
    encounter an error before proceeding, you can place
    gets( ) directly inside an **if** statement, as illustrated
    by the following program.

    ```c
    #include "stdio.h"

    void main(void)
    {
      char str[80];

      printf("Enter a string: ");
      if(gets(str))   /** if not null */
        printf("Here is your string: %s", str);
    }
    ```

    Because a null pointer is false, there is no need for
    the intermediary variable **p**, and the **gets( )** state-
    ment can be put directly inside the **if**.

3. It is important to understand that, even though **gets( )** returns a pointer to the start of the string, it still must be called with a pointer to an actual array. For example, the following is wrong.

```
char *p;

p = gets(p); /* wrong!!! */
```

Here, there is no array defined into which **gets( )** can put the string. This will probably result in a program crash.

4. This program outputs the words **one**, **two**, and **three** on three separate lines, using **puts( )**.

```
#include "stdio.h"

void main(void)
{
  puts("one");
  puts("two");
  puts("three");
}
```

Exercises

1. Compile the program shown in Example 2, above. Note the size of the compiled code. Next, convert it so that it uses **printf( )** statements, instead of **puts( )**. You will find that the **printf( )** version is several bytes larger.

2. Is this program correct? If not, why not?

```
#include "stdio.h"

void main(void)
{
  char *p, *q;
```

```
    printf("Enter a string: ");
    p = gets(q);
    printf(p);
}
```

8.5 MASTER printf( )

Although you already know many things about **printf( )**, you will be surprised by how many more features it has. In this section you will learn about some more of them. To begin, let's review what you know so far.

The **printf( )** function has this prototype.

int printf(char *control-string, ...);

The periods indicate a variable-length parameter list. The **printf( )** function returns the number of characters output. If an error occurs, it returns a negative number. Frankly, few programmers bother with the return value of **printf( )** because, as mentioned earlier, if the console is not working, the computer is probably nonfunctional anyway.

The control string may contain two types of items: characters to be output and format specifiers. All format specifiers begin with %. A *format specifier* determines how its matching argument will be displayed. Format specifiers and their arguments are matched from left to right, and there must be as many arguments as there are specifiers.

The format specifiers accepted by **printf( )** are shown in Table 8-1. You have already learned about the %**c**, %**d**, %**s**, %**u**, %**p**, and %**f** specifiers. The others will be examined now.

The %**i** command is the same as %**d** and is redundant.

TABLE 8-1.   printf( ) Format Commands

Code	Format
%c	Character.
%d	Signed decimal integers.
%i	Signed decimal integers.
%e	Scientific notation (lowercase 'e').
%E	Scientific notation (uppercase 'E').
%f	Decimal floating point.
%g	Uses %e or %f, whichever is shorter.
%G	Uses %E or %f, whichever is shorter.
%o	Unsigned octal.
%s	String of characters.
%u	Unsigned decimal integers.
%x	Unsigned hexadecimal (lowercase letters).
%X	Unsigned hexadecimal (uppercase letters).
%p	Displays a pointer.
%n	The associated argument shall be an integer pointer into which is placed the number of characters written so far.
%%	Prints a % sign.

You can display numbers of type **float** using scientific notation by using either %e or %E. The only difference between the two is that %e uses a lowercase 'e' and %E uses an uppercase 'E.' These specifiers may have the l and L modifiers applied to them to allow them to display values of type **double** and **long double** respectively.

The %g and %G specifiers cause output to be in either normal or scientific notation, depending upon which is shorter. The difference between the %g and the %G is whether a lower- or uppercase 'e' is used in cases where scientific notation is shorter. These specifiers may have the l and L modifiers applied to them to allow them to display values of type **double** and **long double** respectively.

You can display an integer in octal format using %**o** or in hexadecimal using %**x** or %**X**. Using %**x** causes the letters 'a' through 'f' to be displayed in lowercase. Using %**X** causes them to be displayed in uppercase. These specifiers may have the **h** and **l** modifiers applied to allow them to display **short** and **long** data types, respectively.

The argument that matches the %**n** specifier must be a pointer to an integer. When the %**n** is encountered, **printf( )** assigns the integer pointed to by the associated argument the number of characters output so far.

Since all format commands begin with a percent sign, you must use %% to output a percent sign.

All but the %%, %**p**, and %**c** specifiers may have a minimum-field-width specifier and/or a precision specifier associated with them. Both of these are **int** quantities. If the item to output is shorter than the specified minimum field width, the output is padded with spaces, so that it equals the minimum width. However, if the output is longer than the minimum, output is *not* truncated. The minimum field width specifier is placed after the % sign and before the format specifier.

The precision specifier follows the minimum-field-width specifier. The two are separated by a period. The precision specifier affects different types of format specifiers differently. If it is applied to the %**d**, %**i**, %**o**, %**u** or %**x** specifiers, it determines how many digits are to be shown. Leading zeros are added if needed. When applied to %**f**, %**e**, or %**g**, it determines how many digits will be displayed after the decimal point. When applied to the %**s**, it specifies a maximum field width. If a string is longer than the maximum field width specifier, it will be truncated.

By default, all numeric output is right justified. To left justify output, put a minus sign directly after the % sign.

The general form of a format specifier is shown here. Optional items are shown between brackets

%[-][*minimum-field- width*][.][*precision*]*format-specifier*

For example, this format specifier tells **printf( )** to output a **double** value using a field width of 15, with 2 digits after the decimal point.

```
%15.2lf
```

Examples

1. If you don't want to specify a minimum field width, you can still specify the precision. Simply put a period in front of the precision value, as illustrated by the following program.

```
#include "stdio.h"

void main(void)
{
  printf("%.5d\n", 10);
  printf("$%.2f\n", 99.95);
  printf("%.10s", "Not all of this will be printed\n");
}
```

The output from this program looks like this:

```
00010
$99.95
Not all of
```

Notice the effect of the precision specifier as applied to each data type.

2. The minimum-field-width specifier is especially useful for creating tables that contain columns of

numbers that must line up. For example, this program prints 1000 random numbers in three columns. It uses another of C's standard library functions, **rand( )**, to generate the random numbers. The **rand( )** function returns a random integer value each time it is called. It uses the header STDLIB.H.

```
#include "stdio.h"
#include "stdlib.h"

void main(void)
{
  int i;

  for(i=0; i<1000; i++)
    printf("%10d %10d %10d\n", rand( ), rand( ), rand( ));
}
```

Part of the output from this program is shown here. Notice how the columns are aligned. (Remember, if you try the program, you will probably see different numbers.)

```
10982        130        346
 7117      11656       1090
22948       6415      17595
14558       9004      31126
18492      22879       3571
26721       5412       1360
27119      25047      22463
13985       7190      31441
30252      27509      31214
19816      14779      26571
17995      19651      21681
13310       3734      23593
15561      21995       3979
11288      18489      16092
 5892       8664      28466
 5364      22766      13863
20427      21151      17639
 8812      25795        100
12347      12666      15108
```

3. This program prints the value 90 four different ways: decimal, octal, lowercase hexadecimal, and uppercase hexadecimal. It also, prints a floating-point number using scientific notation with a lowercase 'e' and an uppercase 'E.'

```
#include "stdio.h"

void main(void)
{
  printf("%d %o %x %X\n", 90, 90, 90, 90);
  printf("%e %E\n", 99.231, 99.231);
}
```

The output from this program is shown here.

```
90 132 5a 5A
9.92310e+01 9.92310E+01
```

4. The following program demonstrates the %n specifier.

```
#include "stdio.h"

void main(void)
{
  int i;

  printf("%d %f\n%n", 100, 123.23, &i);
  printf("%d characters output so far", i);
}
```

Its output looks like this:

```
100 123.230000
15 characters output so far
```

The fifteenth character is the newline.

Exercises

1. Write a program that prints a table of numbers, each line consisting of a number, its square, and its cube. Have the table begin at 2 and end at 100. Make the columns line up, and left justify each column.

2. How would you output this line using **printf( )**?

   ```
   Clearance price: 40% off as marked
   ```

3. Show how to display **1024.03** so that only two decimal places are printed.

8.6 MASTER scanf( )

Like **printf( )**, **scanf( )** has many more features than we have used so far. In this section several of these additional features are explored. Let's begin by reviewing what you have already learned.

The prototype for **scanf( )** is shown here.

int scanf(char *control-string, ...);

The *control-string* consists mostly of format specifiers. However, it can contain other characters. (You will learn about the effect of other characters in the control string soon.) The format specifiers determine how **scanf( )** reads information into the variables pointed to by the arguments that follow the control string. The specifiers are matched in order, from left to right, with

TABLE 8-2.   scanf( ) Format Codes

Code	Meaning
%c	Read a single character
%d	Read a decimal integer
%i	Read a decimal integer
%e	Read a floating-point number
%f	Read a floating-point number
%g	Read a floating-point number
%o	Read an unsigned octal number
%s	Read a string
%x	Read an unsigned hexadecimal number
%p	Read a pointer
%n	Receives an integer value equal to the number of characters read so far
%u	Read an unsigned integer
%[ ]	Scan for a set of characters

the arguments. There must be as many arguments as their are specifiers. The format specifiers are shown in Table 8-2. As you can see, the **scanf( )** specifiers are very much like the **printf( )** specifiers.

The **scanf( )** function returns the number of fields assigned values. If an error occurs before any assignments are made, **EOF** is returned.

The specifiers %x and %o are used to read an unsigned integer using hexadecimal and octal number bases, respectively.

The specifiers %d, %i, %u, %x, and %o may be modified by the **h** when inputting into a **short** variable and by **l** when inputting into a **long** variable.

The specifiers %e, %f, and %g are equivalent. They all read floating-point numbers represented in either scientific notation or standard decimal notation. Unmodified, they input information into a **float** variable.

You can modify them using an **l** when inputting into a **double**. To read a **long double**, modify them with an **L**.

You can use **scanf( )** to read a string using the **%s** specifier, but you probably won't want to. Here's why: When **scanf( )** inputs a string, it stops reading that string when the first whitespace character is encountered. A whitespace character is either a space, a tab, or a newline. This means that you cannot easily use **scanf( )** to read input like this into a string:

this is one string

Because there is a space after "this," **scanf( )** will stop inputting the string at that point. This is why **gets( )** is generally used to input strings.

The **%p** specifier inputs a memory address using the format determined by the host environment. The **%n** specifier assigns the number of characters input up to the point the **%n** is encountered to the integer variable pointed to by its matching argument. The **%n** may be modified by either **l** or **h** so that it may assign its value to either a **long** or **short** variable.

A very interesting feature of **scanf( )** is called a *scanset*. A scanset specifier is created by putting a list of characters inside square brackets. For example, here is a scanset specifier containing the letters 'ABC.'

```
%[ABC]
```

When **scanf( )** encounters a scanset, it begins reading input into the character array pointed to by the scanset's matching argument. It will only continue reading characters as long as the input character is part of the scanset. As soon as a character that is not part of the scanset is found, **scanf( )** stops reading input for this specifier and moves on to any others in the control string.

You can specify a range in a scanset using the - (hyphen). For example, this scanset specifies the characters 'A' through 'Z.'

```
%[A-Z]
```

When the scanset is very large, sometimes it is easier to specify what is *not* part of a scanset. To do this, precede the set with a ^. For example,

```
%[^0123456789]
```

When **scanf( )** encounters this scanset, it will read any characters *except* the digits 0 through 9.

You can suppress the assignment of a field by putting an asterisk immediately after the % sign. This can be very useful when inputting information that contains needless characters. For example, given this **scanf( )** statement

```
int first, second;
scanf("%d%*c%d", &first, &second);
```

this input

```
555-2345
```

will cause **scanf( )** to assign **555** to **first**, discard the -, and assign **2345** to **second**. Since the hyphen is not needed, there is no reason to assign it to anything. Hence, no associated argument is supplied.

You can specify a maximum field width for all specifiers except **%c**, for which a field is always one character, and **%n**, to which the concept does not apply. The maximum field width is specified as an unsigned integer, and it immediately precedes the format specifier character. For example, this limits the maximum length of a string assigned to **str** to 20 characters.

```
scanf("%20s", str);
```

If a space appears in the control string, then **scanf( )** will begin reading and discarding whitespace characters until the first non-whitespace character is encountered. If any other character appears in the control string, **scanf( )** reads and discards all matching characters until it reads the first character that does not match that character.

One final point: As **scanf( )** is generally implemented, it line buffers input in the same way that **getchar( )** often does. While this makes little difference when inputting numbers, its lack of interactivity tends to make **scanf( )** unusable for other types of input. Most users will simply not tolerate (nor should they have to tolerate) line-buffered input.

Examples

1. To see the effect of the **%s** specifier, try this program. When prompted, type **this is a test** and press ENTER. You will see only **this** redisplayed on the screen. This is because, when reading strings, **scanf( )** stops when it encounters the first whitespace character.

```
#include "stdio.h"

void main(void)
{
  char str[80];

  /* Enter "this is a test" */
  printf("Enter a string: ");
  scanf("%s", str);
  printf(str);
}
```

2. Here's an example of a scanset that accepts both the upper- and lowercase characters. Try entering some letters, then any other character, and then some more letters. After you press ENTER, only the letters that you entered before pressing the nonletter key will be contained in **str**.

```
#include "stdio.h"

void main(void)
{
  char str[80];

  printf("Enter letters, anything else to stop\n");
  scanf("%[a-zA-Z]", str);

  printf(str);
}
```

3. If you want to read a string containing spaces using **scanf( )**, you can do so using the scanset shown in this slight variation of the previous program.

```
#include "stdio.h"

void main(void)
{
  char str[80];
```

```
   printf("Enter letters and spaces\n");
   scanf("%[a-zA-Z ]", str);

   printf(str);
}
```

You could also specify punctuation symbols and digits, so that you can read virtually any type of string. However, this is a fairly cumbersome way of doing things.

4. This program lets the user enter a number followed by an operator followed by a second number. It then performs the specified operation on the two numbers and displays the results.

```
#include "stdio.h"

void main(void)
{
   int i, j;
   char op;

   printf("Enter operation: ");
   scanf("%d%c%d", &i, &op, &j);

   switch(op) {
     case '+': printf("%d", i+j);
       break;
     case '-': printf("%d", i-j);
       break;
     case '/': if(j) printf("%d", i/j);
       break;
     case '*': printf("%d", i*j);
   }
}
```

Notice that the format for entering the information is somewhat restricted, because no spaces are allowed between the first number and the operator. As you know, **scanf( )** automatically discards leading whitespace characters except when you use the **%c** specifier. However, since you know that the operator will not be a whitespace character, you can modify the **scanf( )** command to look like this:

```
scanf("%d %c%d", &i, &op, &j);
```

Whenever there is a space in the control string, **scanf( )** will match and discard whitespace characters until the first non-whitespace character is found. This includes matching 0 whitespace characters. With this change in place, you can enter the information into the program using one or more spaces between the first number and the operator.

5. This program illustrates the maximum-field-width specifier.

```
#include "stdio.h"

void main(void)
{
  int i, j;

  printf("Enter an integer: ");
  scanf("%3d%d", &i, &j);
  printf("%d %d", i, j);
}
```

If you run this program and enter the number **12345**, **i** will be assigned 123, and **j** will have the value 45. The reason for this is that **scanf( )** was told that **i**'s field is only three characters long. The remainder of the input was then sent to **j**.

6. This program illustrates the effect of having non-whitespace characters in the control string. It allows

you to enter a decimal value, but it assigns the digits to the left of the decimal point to one integer and those to the right of the decimal to another. The decimal point between the two **%d** specifiers causes the decimal point in the number to be matched and discarded.

```
#include "stdio.h"

void main(void)
{
  int i, j;

  printf("Enter a decimal number: ");
  scanf("%d.%d", &i, &j);
  printf("left part: %d, right part: %d", i,j);
}
```

Exercises

1. Write a program that prompts you for your name and then inputs your first, middle, and last names. Have the program read no more than 20 characters for each part of your name. Finally, have the program redisplay your name.

2. Write a program that reads a floating-point number as a string using a scanset.

3. Is this fragment correct? If not why not?

```
char ch;

scanf("%2c", &ch);
```

4. Write a program that inputs a string, a **double**, and an integer. After these items have been read, have

the program display how many characters had been input. (Hint: use the %n specifier.)

5. Write a program that converts a hexadecimal number entered by the user into its corresponding decimal and octal equivalents.

EXERCISES

Before proceeding you should be able to answer these questions and perform these exercises.

MASTERY
SKILLS CHECK
√

1. What is the difference between **getchar( )**, **getche( )**, and **getch( )**?

2. What is the difference between the %**e** and the %**E** **printf( )** format specifiers?

3. What is a scanset?

4. Write a program, using **scanf( )**, that inputs your first name, birth date (using the format mm/dd/yy), and telephone number. Redisplay the information on the screen to verify that it was input correctly.

5. What is one advantage to using **puts( )** over **printf( )** when you only need to output a string? What is one disadvantage to **puts( )**?

6. Write a program that defines a macro called **COUNT** as the value 100. Have the program then use this macro to control a **for** that displays the numbers 0 through 99.

7. What is **EOF**, and where is it defined?

EXERCISES

This section checks how well you have integrated the material in this chapter with that from earlier chapters.

1. Write a program that allows you to enter the batting averages for the players on a little league team. (Assume there are exactly 9 players.) Have the user enter the first name and batting average of each player. Use a two-dimensional character array to hold the names and a one-dimensional **double** array to hold the batting averages. Once all the names are entered, have the program report the name and average of the highest and lowest averages. Also, have the program display the team average.

2. Write a program that is a simple electronic library card catalog. Have the program display this menu:

   Card Catalog:
   1. Enter
   2. Search by Author
   3. Search by Title
   4. Quit

   Choose your selection:

   If you choose **Enter**, have the program repeatedly input the name, author, and publisher of a book.

   Have this process continue until the user enters a blank line for the name of the book. For searches, prompt the user for the specified author or title and then, if a match is found, display the rest of the information. After you finish this program, keep your file, because in the next chapter you will learn how to save the catalog to a disk file.

CHAPTER OBJECTIVES

9.1 Understand streams

9.2 Master file-system basics

9.3 Understand **foef( )** and **ferror( )**

9.4 Learn some higher-level text functions

9.5 Learn to read and write binary data

9.6 Understand random access

9.7 Learn about various file-system functions

9.8 Learn about the standard
    streams

·9·
File I/O

Although C does not have any built-in method of performing file I/O, the C standard library contains a very rich set of I/O functions. As you will see in this chapter, C's approach to I/O is efficient, powerful, and flexible.

Note: Most C compilers supply two complete sets of disk I/O functions. One is called the *ANSI file system* (sometimes called the *buffered file system*). This file system is defined by the ANSI C standard. The second file system is based upon the original UNIX operating environment and is called the *UNIX- like file system* (sometimes called the *unbuffered file system*). This file system is not defined by the ANSI standard. The ANSI standard only defines one file system because the two file systems are redundant. Further, not all environments may be able to adapt to the UNIX-like system. For these reasons, this book only discusses the ANSI file system. For a discussion of the UNIX-like file system, see the book *C: The Complete Reference* by Herb Schildt (Berkeley, Calif.: Osborne/McGraw-Hill, 1989)

EXERCISES

Before proceeding you should be able to perform these exercises and answer these questions.

SKILLS CHECK

√

1. What is the difference between **getchar( )** and **getche( )**?

2. Give one reason why you probably won't use **scanf( )**'s %s option to read strings from the keyboard.

3. Write a program that prints a four-column table of the prime numbers between 2 and 1000. Make sure that the columns are aligned.

4. Write a program that inputs a **double**, a character, and a string not longer than 20 characters. Redisplay the values to confirm that they were input correctly.

5. Write a program that reads and discards leading digits and then reads a string. (Hint: Use a scanset to read past any leading digits.)

9.1 UNDERSTAND STREAMS

Before we can begin our discussion of disk file I/O, you must understand a very important concept in C: the *stream*. In C, the stream is a common, logical interface to the various devices that comprise the computer. In its most common form, a stream is a logical interface to a *file*. As C defines the term "file," it can refer to a disk file, the screen, the keyboard, a port, a file on tape, and so on. Although files differ in form and capabilities, all streams are the same. The advantage to this approach is that to you, the programmer, one hardware device will look much like any other. The stream provides a consistent interface.

A stream is linked to a file using an *open operation*. A stream is disassociated from a file using a *close operation*.

There are two types of streams: text and binary. A *text stream* is used with ASCII characters. When a text stream is being used, some character translations may take place. For example, when the newline character is output, it is converted into a carriage-return/linefeed sequence. For this reason, there may not be a one-to-one correspondence between what is sent to the stream and what is written to the file. A *binary stream* may be used with any type of data. No character translations will occur, and there is a one-to-one correspondence between what is sent to the stream and what is actually contained in the file.

One final concept you need to understand is that of the *current location*. The current location, also referred to as the *current position,* is the location in a file where the next file access will occur. For example, if a file is 100 bytes long and half the file has been read, the next read operation will occur at byte 50, which is the current location.

To summarize: In C, disk I/O (like certain other types of I/O) is performed through a logical interface called a stream. All streams have similar properties, and all are operated on by the same I/O functions, no matter what type of file the stream is associated with. A file is the actual physical entity that receives the data. Even though files differ, streams do not. (Of course, some devices may not support the random-access operations, for example, so their associated stream will not support such operations either.)

Now that you are familiar with the theory behind C's file system, it is time to begin learning about it.

9.2 MASTER FILE-SYSTEM BASICS

In this section you will learn how to open and close a file. You will also learn how to read and write characters to and from the file.

To open a file and associate it with a stream, use **fopen( )**. Its prototype is shown here.

FILE *fopen(char *fname, char *mode);

The **fopen( )** function, like all the file-system functions, uses the header STDIO.H. The name of the file to open is pointed to by *fname*. It must be a valid file name, as

TABLE 9-1.   The Legal Values for Mode

Mode	Meaning
r	Open a text file for reading
w	Create a text file for writing
a	Append to a text file
rb	Open a binary file for reading
wb	Create a binary file for writing
ab	Append to a binary file
r+	Open a text file for read/write
w+	Create a text file for read/write
a+	Append or create a text file for read/write
r+b	Open a binary file for read/write
w+b	Create a binary file for read/write
a+b	Append a binary file for read/write

defined by the operating system. The string pointed to by *mode* determines how the file may be accessed. The legal values for *mode* are shown in Table 9-1.

If the open operation is successful, **fopen( )** returns a valid file pointer. The type **FILE** is defined in STDIO.H. It is a structure that holds various information about the file, such as its size, the current location of the file, and its access modes. It essentially identifies the file. (A structure is a group of variables accessed under one name. You will learn about structures in the next chapter. However, you do not need to know anything about them to learn and fully use C's file system.) The **fopen( )** function returns a pointer to the structure associated with the file by the open process. You will use this pointer with all other functions that operate on the file. However, you must never alter it or the object it points to.

If the **fopen( )** function fails, it returns a null pointer. The header STDIO.H defines the macro **NULL**, which is defined to be a null pointer. It is very important to ensure that a valid file pointer has been returned. You must check the value returned by **fopen( )** to be sure that it is not **NULL**. For example, the proper way to open a file called **myfile** for text input is shown in this fragment.

```
FILE *fp;

if((fp = fopen("myfile", "r"))==NULL) {
  printf("Error opening file\n");
  exit(1); /* or substitute your own error handler */
}
```

Although most of the file modes are self-explanatory, a few comments are in order. If, when opening a file for read-only operations, the file does not exist, **fopen( )** will fail. If it does not exist when opening a file for append mode, one will be created. Further, all new data written to the file will be written to the end of the file. The original contents will remain unchanged. If, when a file is opened for writing, the file does not exist, it will be created. If it does exist, the contents of the original file will be destroyed and a new file created. The difference between modes **r+** and **w+** is that **r+** will not create a file if it does not exist; however, **w+** will. Further, if the file already exists, opening it with **w+** destroys its contents; opening it with **r+** does not.

To close a file, use **fclose( )**, whose prototype is

int fclose(FILE *fp);

The **fclose( )** function closes the file associated with *fp*, which must be a valid file pointer previously obtained using **fopen( )**, and disassociates the stream from the file. In order to improve efficiency, most file system implementations write data to disk one sector at a time. Therefore, data is buffered until a sector's worth of information has been output before the buffer is physically written to disk. When you call **fclose( )**, it automatically writes any information remaining in a partially full buffer to disk. This is often referred to as *flushing the buffer*.

You must never call **fclose( )** with an invalid argument. Doing so will damage the file system and possibly cause irretrievable data loss.

The **fclose( )** function returns 0 if successful. If an error occurs, **EOF** is returned.

Once a file has been opened, depending upon its mode, you may read and/or write bytes to or from it using these two functions.

```
int fgetc(FILE *fp);
int fputc(int ch, FILE *fp);
```

The **fgetc( )** function reads the next byte from the file described by *fp* as an **unsigned char** and returns it as an integer. The reason that it returns an integer is that if an error occurs, **fgetc( )** returns **EOF**, which is an integer value. The **fgetc( )** function also returns **EOF** when the end of the file is reached. Your routine can assign the **fgetc( )**'s return value to a **char**. You don't have to assign it to an integer. The **fputc( )** function writes the byte contained in *ch* to the file associated with *fp* as an **unsigned char**. Although *ch* is defined as an **int**, you may call it using simply a **char**, which is the common procedure. The **fputc( )** function returns the character written if successful or **EOF** if an error occurs.

Historical note: The traditional names for **fgetc( )** and **fputc( )** are **getc( )** and **putc( )**. The ANSI standard still defines these names, and they are essentially inter-changeable with **fgetc( )** and **fputc( )**. One reason the new names were added was for consistency. All other ANSI file system function names begin with 'f,' so the 'f' was added to **getc( )** and **putc( )**. The ANSI standard still supports the traditional names, however, because there are so many existing programs that use them. If you see programs that use **getc( )** and **putc( )**, don't worry. They are essentially different names for **fgetc( )** and **fputc( )**.

Examples

1. This program demonstrates the four file-system functions you have learned about so far. First, it opens a file called MYFILE for output. Next, it writes the string "This is a file system test" to the file. Then, it closes the file and reopens it for read operations. Finally, it displays the contents of the file on the screen and closes the file.

```c
#include "stdio.h"
#include "stdlib.h"

char str[80] = "This is a file system test";

void main(void)
{
  FILE *fp;
  char *p;
  int i;

  /* open myfile for output */
  if((fp = fopen("myfile", "w"))==NULL) {
    printf("Cannot open file\n");
    exit(1);
  }
```

```
  /* write str to disk */
  p = str;
  while(*p) {
    if(fputc(*p, fp)==EOF) {
      printf("Error writing file\n");
      exit(1);
    }
    p++;
  }
  fclose(fp);

  /* open myfile for input */
  if((fp = fopen("myfile", "r"))==NULL) {
    printf("Cannot open file\n");
    exit(1);
  }

  /* read back the file */
  for(; ;) {
    i = fgetc(fp);
    if(i == EOF) break;
    putchar(i);
  }
  fclose(fp);
}
```

In this version, the return value of **fgetc( )** is assigned to an **int**. The value of this integer is then checked to see if the end of the file has been reached. For most compilers, however, you can simply assign the value returned by **fgetc( )** to a **char** and still check for **EOF**, as is shown in the following version.

```
#include "stdio.h"
#include "stdlib.h"

char str[80] = "This is a file system test";

void main(void)
{
  FILE *fp;
  char ch, *p;
```

```
/* open myfile for output */
if((fp = fopen("myfile", "w"))==NULL) {
  printf("Cannot open file\n");
  exit(1);
}

/* write str to disk */
p = str;
while(*p) {
  if(fputc(*p, fp)==EOF) {
    printf("Error writing file\n");
    exit(1);
  }
  p++;
}
fclose(fp);

/* open myfile for input */
if((fp = fopen("myfile", "r"))==NULL) {
  printf("Cannot open file\n");
  exit(1);
}

/* read back the file */
for(; ;) {
  ch = fgetc(fp);
  if(ch == EOF) break;
  putchar(ch);
}
fclose(fp);
}
```

The reason this approach works with most compilers is that when a **char** is being compared to an **int**, the **char** value is automatically elevated to an equivalent **int** value. When doing this, most compilers assume that the character is **signed** and automatically provide an equivalent integer value.

There is, however, even a better way to code this program. For example, there is no need for a separate comparison step because the assignment and the comparison can be performed at the same time, within the **if**, as shown here.

```c
#include "stdio.h"
#include "stdlib.h"

char str[80] = "This is a file system test";

void main(void)
{
  FILE *fp;
  char ch, *p;

  /* open myfile for output */
  if((fp = fopen("myfile", "w"))==NULL) {
    printf("Cannot open file\n");
    exit(1);
  }

  /* write str to disk */
  p = str;
  while(*p) {
    if(fputc(*p, fp)==EOF) {
      printf("Error writing file\n");
      exit(1);
    }
    p++;
  }
  fclose(fp);

  /* open myfile for input */
  if((fp = fopen("myfile", "r"))==NULL) {
    printf("Cannot open file\n");
    exit(1);
  }

  /* read back the file */
  for(; ;) {
    if((ch = fgetc(fp)) == EOF) break;
    putchar(ch);
  }
  fclose(fp);
}
```

Don't let the statement

```
if((ch = fgetc(fp)) == EOF) break;
```

fool you. Here's what is happening. First, inside the
if, the return value of **fgetc( )** is assigned to **ch**. As
you may recall, the assignment operation in C is an
expression. The entire value of **(ch = fgetc(fp))** is
equal to the return value of **fgetc( )**. Therefore, it is
this integer value that is tested against **EOF**.

Expanding upon this approach, you will normally see this program written by a professional C
programmer as follows:

```c
#include "stdio.h"
#include "stdlib.h"

char str[80] = "This is a file system test";

void main(void)
{
  FILE *fp;
  char ch, *p;

  /* open myfile for output */
  if((fp = fopen("myfile", "w"))==NULL) {
    printf("Cannot open file\n");
    exit(1);
  }

  /* write str to disk */
  p = str;
  while(*p)
    if(fputc(*p++, fp)==EOF) {
      printf("Error writing file\n");
      exit(1);
    }

  fclose(fp);

  /* open myfile for input */
  if((fp = fopen("myfile", "r"))==NULL) {
```

```
        printf("Cannot open file\n");
        exit(1);
    }

    /* read back the file */
    while((ch = fgetc(fp)) != EOF) putchar(ch);
    fclose(fp);
}
```

Notice that now, each character is read, assigned to **ch**, and tested against **EOF**, all within the expression of the **while** loop that controls the input process. If you compare this with the original version, you can see how much more efficient this one is. In fact, the ability to integrate such operations is one reason C is so powerful. It is important that you get used to the kind of approach just shown. Later on in this book we will explore such assignment statements more fully.

2. The following program takes two command-line arguments. The first is the name of a file, the second is a character. The program searches the specified file, looking for the character. If the file contains at least one of these characters, it reports this fact. Notice how it uses **argv** to access the file name and the character for which to search.

```
/* Search specified file for specified character. */
#include "stdio.h"
#include "stdlib.h"

void main(int argc, char *argv[])
{
    FILE *fp;
    char ch;

    /* see if correct number of command line
       arguments
    */
```

```
if (argc!=3) {
  printf("Usage: find <filename> <ch>\n");
  exit(1);
}

/* open file for input */
if ((fp = fopen(argv[1], "r"))==NULL) {
  printf("Cannot open file\n");
  exit(1);
}

/* look for character */
while ((ch = fgetc(fp)) != EOF)
  if (ch==*argv[2]) {
    printf("%c found", ch);
    break;
  }
fclose(fp);
}
```

Exercises

1. Write a program that displays the contents of the text file specified on the command line.

2. Write a program that reads a text file and counts how many times each letter from 'A' to 'Z' occurs. Have it display the results. (Do not differentiate between upper- and lowercase letters.)

3. Write a program that copies the contents of one text file to another. Have the program accept three command-line arguments. The first is the name of the source file, the second is the name of the destination file, the third is optional. If present and if it equals "watch," have the program display each character as it copies the files; otherwise, do not have the program display any screen output. If the destination file does not exist, create it.

9.3 UNDERSTAND feof( ) AND ferror( )

As you know, when **fgetc( )** returns **EOF**, either an error has occurred or the end of the file has been reached, but how do you know which event has occurred? Further, if you are operating on a binary file, all values are valid. This means it is possible that a byte will have the same value (when elevated to an **int**) as **EOF**, so how do you know if valid data has been returned or if the end of the file has been reached? The solution to these problems are the functions **feof( )** and **ferror( )**, whose prototypes are shown here.

int feof(FILE *fp);
int ferror(FILE *fp);

The **feof( )** function returns non-0 if the file associated with *fp* has reached the end of the file. Otherwise it returns 0. This function works for both binary files and text files. The **ferror( )** function returns non-0 if the file associated with *fp* has experienced an error; otherwise, it returns 0.

Using the **feof( )** function, this code fragment shows how to read to the end of a file.

```
FILE *fp;
   .
   .
   .
while(!feof(fp)) fgetc(fp);
```

This code works for any type of file and is better in general than checking for **EOF**. However, it still does not provide any error checking, as illustrated here.

```
FILE *fp;
.
.
.
while(!feof(fp)) {
  fgetc(fp);
  if(ferror(fp)) {
    printf("file error\n");
    break;
  }
}
```

Keep in mind that **ferror( )** only reports the status of the file system relative to the last file access. Therefore, to provide the fullest error checking, you must call it after each file operation.

The most damaging file errors occur at the operating-system level. Frequently, it is the operating system that intercepts these errors and displays its own error messages. For example, if a bad sector is found on the disk, most operating systems will, themselves, stop the execution of the program and report the error. Often the only types of errors that actually get passed back to your program are relatively minor. Perhaps these errors have occurred because some bug in your program has caused a file to be accessed in a way inconsistent with the mode used to open it or an out-of-range condition has occurred. For this reason, you will frequently see examples of C code in which there are relatively few (if any) calls to **ferror( )**. Not all of the file system examples in this book will provide full error checking, mostly in the interest of keeping the programs short and easy to understand. However, if you are writing programs for actual use, you should pay special attention to error checking.

Examples

1. This program copies any type of file, binary or text.
   It takes two command-line arguments. The first is
   the name of the source file, the second is the name
   of the destination file. If the destination file does not
   exist, it is created. It includes full error checking.
   (You might want to compare this version with the
   copy program you wrote for text files in the preceding section.)

```c
/* Copy a file. */
#include "stdio.h"
#include "stdlib.h"

void main(int argc, char *argv[])
{
  FILE *from, *to;
  char ch;

  /* see if correct number of command line
     arguments
  */
  if(argc!=3) {
    printf("Usage: copy <source> <destination>\n");
    exit(1);
  }

  /* open source file */
  if((from = fopen(argv[1], "rb"))==NULL) {
    printf("Cannot open source file\n");
    exit(1);
  }

  /* open destination file */
  if((to = fopen(argv[2], "wb"))==NULL) {
    printf("Cannot open file\n");
    exit(1);
  }
```

```
/* copy the file */
while(!feof(from)) {
  ch = fgetc(from);
  if(ferror(from)) {
    printf("error reading source file\n");
    exit(1);
  }
  if(!feof(from)) fputc(ch, to);
  if(ferror(to)) {
    printf("error writing destination file\n");
    exit(1);
  }
}
fclose(from);
fclose(to);
}
```

2. This program compares the two files whose names
    are specified on the command line. It either prints
    Files are the same, or it displays the byte of the first
    mismatch.

```
/* Compare files. */
#include "stdio.h"
#include "stdlib.h"

void main(int argc, char *argv[])
{
  FILE *fp1, *fp2;
  char ch1, ch2, same;
  unsigned long l;

  /* see if correct number of command line
     arguments
  */
  if(argc!=3) {
    printf("Usage: compare <file 1>  <file 2>\n");
    exit(1);
  }

  /* open first file */
  if((fp1 = fopen(argv[1], "rb"))==NULL) {
    printf("Cannot open source file\n");
```

```
    exit(1);
  }

  /* open second file */
  if((fp2 = fopen(argv[2], "rb"))==NULL) {
    printf("Cannot open file\n");
    exit(1);
  }

  l = 0;
  same = 1;
  /* compare the files */
  while(!feof(fp1)) {
    ch1 = fgetc(fp1);
    if(ferror(fp1)) {
      printf("error reading first file\n");
      exit(1);
    }
    ch2 = fgetc(fp2);
    if(ferror(fp2)) {
      printf("error reading second file\n");
      exit(1);
    }
    if(ch1!=ch2) {
      printf("Files differ at byte number %ul", l);
      same = 0;
      break;
    }
    l++;
  }
  if(same) printf("Files are the same.");

  fclose(fp1);
  fclose(fp2);
}
```

Exercises

1. Write a program that counts the number of bytes in
    a file (text or binary) and displays the result. Have

the user specify the file to count on the command line.

2. Write a program that exchanges the contents of the two files whose names are specified on the command line. That is, given two files called FILE1 and FILE2, after the program has run, FILE1 will contain the contents that originally were in FILE2, and FILE2 will contain FILE1's original contents. (Hint: Use a temporary file to aid in the exchange process.)

9.4 LEARN SOME HIGHER-LEVEL TEXT FUNCTIONS

When working with text files, C provides four functions which make file operations easier. The first two are called **fputs( )** and **fgets( )**, which write a string and read a string from a file, respectively. Their prototypes are

int fputs(char *str*, FILE *fp*);
char *fgets(char *str*, int *num,* FILE *fp*);

The **fputs( )** function writes the string pointed to by *str* to the file associated with *fp.* It returns **EOF** if an error occurs and a non-negative value if successful. The null that terminates *str* is not written. Also, unlike its related function **puts( )** it does not automatically append a carriage-return/linefeed sequence.

The **fgets( )** function reads characters from the file associated with *fp* into the string pointed to by *str* until *num*−1 characters have been read, a newline character is encountered, or the end of the file is reached. In any case, the string is null-terminated. Unlike its related function **gets( )**, the newline character is retained. The function returns *str* if successful and a null pointer if an error occurs.

The C file system contains two very powerful functions similar to two you already know. They are **fprintf( )** and **fscanf( )**. These functions operate exactly like **printf( )** and **scanf( )** except that they work with files. Their prototypes are

inf fprintf(FILE *fp, char *control-string, ...);
int fscanf(FILE *fp, char *control-string, ...);

Instead of directing their I/O operations to the console, these functions operate on the file specified by *fp*. Otherwise their operations are the same as their console-based relatives.

The advantage to **fprintf( )** and **fscanf( )** is that they make it very easy to write a wide variety of data to a file using a text format.

Examples

1. This program demonstrates **fputs( )** and **fgets( )**. It reads lines entered by the user and writes them to the file specified on the command line. When the user enters a blank line, the input phase terminates, and the file is closed. Next, the file is reopened for input, and the program uses **fgets( )** to display the contents of the file.

```c
#include "stdio.h"
#include "stdlib.h"
#include "string.h"

void main(int argc, char *argv[])
{
  FILE *fp;
```

```
char str[80];

/* check for command line arg */
if(argc!=2) {
  printf("specify file name\n");
  exit(1);
}

/* open file for output */
if((fp = fopen(argv[1], "w"))==NULL) {
  printf("Cannot open file\n");
  exit(1);
}

printf("Enter a blank line to stop\n");
do {
  printf(": ");
  gets(str);
  strcat(str, "\n"); /* add newline */
  if(*str!='\n') fputs(str, fp);
} while(*str!='\n');
fclose(fp);

/* open file for input */
if((fp = fopen(argv[1], "r"))==NULL) {
  printf("Cannot open file\n");
  exit(1);
}

/* read back the file */
do {
  fgets(str, 79, fp);
  printf(str);
} while(!feof(fp));
fclose(fp);
}
```

2. This program demonstrates **fprintf( )** and **fscanf( )**.
   It first writes a **double**, an **int**, and a string to the file
   specified on the command line. Next, it reads them
   back and displays their values as verification. If you
   examine the file created by this program, you will

see that it contains human-readable text. This is
because **fprintf( )** writes to a disk file what **printf( )**
would write to the screen. No internal data formats
are used.

```c
#include "stdio.h"
#include "stdlib.h"
#include "string.h"

void main(int argc, char *argv[])
{
  FILE *fp;
  double ld;
  int d;
  char str[80];

  /* check for command line arg */
  if(argc!=2) {
    printf("specify file name\n");
    exit(1);
  }

  /* open file for output */
  if((fp = fopen(argv[1], "w"))==NULL) {
    printf("Cannot open file\n");
    exit(1);
  }

  fprintf(fp, "%lf %d %s", 12345.342, 1908, "hello");
  fclose(fp);

  /* open file for input */
  if((fp = fopen(argv[1], "r"))==NULL) {
    printf("Cannot open file\n");
    exit(1);
  }

  fscanf(fp, "%lf%d%s", &ld, &d, str);
  printf("%lf %d %s", ld, d, str);
  fclose(fp);
}
```

Exercises

1. In Chapter 6 you wrote a very simple telephone-directory program. Write a program that expands on this concept by allowing the directory to be saved to a disk file. Have the program present a menu that looks like this:

   1. Enter names and numbers
   2. Find numbers
   3. Save directory to disk
   4. Load directory from disk
   5. Quit

   The program should be capable of storing 100 names and numbers. (Use only first names if you like.) Use **fprintf( )** to save the directory to disk and **fscanf( )** to read it back into memory.

2. Write a program that uses **fgets( )** to display the contents of a text file, one screenful at a time. After each screen is displayed, have the program prompt the user for more.

3. Write a program that copies a text file. Specify both the source and destination file names on the command line. Use **fgets( )** and **fputs( )** to copy the file. Include full error checking.

9.5 LEARN TO READ AND WRITE BINARY DATA

As useful and convenient as **fprintf( )** and **fscanf( )** are, they are not necessarily the most efficient way to read and write data to a file. The reason for this is that both functions perform conversions on the data. For example, when you output a number using **fprintf( )** the number is converted from its internal format into ASCII text. Conversely, when you read a number using **fscanf( )**, it must be converted back into its internal representation. For many applications, this conversion time will not be meaningful; for others, it will be a severe limitation. Further, for some types of data, a file created by **fprintf( )** will also be larger than one that contains a mirror image of the data using its internal format. For these reasons, the C file system includes two important functions: **fread( )** and **fwrite( )**. These functions can read and write any type of data, using any kind of representation. Their prototypes are

size_t fread(void *buffer, size_t size, size_t num, FILE *fp);
size_t fwrite(void *buffer, size_t size, size_t num, FILE *fp);

As you can see, these prototypes introduce some unfamiliar elements. However, before discussing them, a brief description of each function is necessary.

The **fread( )** function reads from the file associated with fp, num number of objects, each object size bytes long, into the buffer pointed to by buffer. It returns the number of objects actually read. If this value is 0, no objects have been read, and either the end of the file has been encountered or an error has occurred. You can use **feof( )** or **ferror( )** to find out which.

The **fwrite( )** function is the opposite of **fread( )**. It writes to the file associated with fp, num number of objects, each object size bytes long, from the buffer pointed to by buffer. It returns the number of objects written. This value will be less than num only if an output error has occurred.

Before looking at any examples, let's take a look at the concepts introduced by the functions' prototypes.

The first concept is that of the **void** pointer. A **void** pointer, simply put, is a pointer that can point to any type of data without the use of a type cast. This is generally referred to as a *generic pointer*. In C, **void** pointers are used for two primary purposes. First, as illustrated by **fread( )** and **fwrite( )**, they are a way for a function to receive a pointer to any type of data without causing a type mismatch error. As stated earlier, **fread( )** and **fwrite( )** can be used to read or write any type of data. Therefore, the functions must be capable of receiving any sort of data pointed to by *buffer*. This is why **void** pointers were invented. A second purpose they serve is to allow a function to return a generic pointer. You will see an example of this later in this book.

The second new concept is the type **size_t**. This type is defined in the STDIO.H header file. A variable of this type is defined by the ANSI C standard as being able to hold a value equal to the size of the largest object supported by the compiler. For our purposes, you can think of **size_t** as being the same as **unsigned** or **unsigned long**. The reason that **size_t** is used instead of its equivalent built-in type is to allow C compilers running in different environments to accommodate the needs and confines of those environments.

As a simple example, this program writes an integer value to a file called MYFILE using its internal, binary representation. (The program assumes that integers are two bytes long.)

```c
#include "stdio.h"
#include "stdlib.h"

void main(void)
{
  FILE *fp;
  int i;

  /* open file for output */
  if((fp = fopen("myfile", "w"))==NULL) {
    printf("Cannot open file\n");
    exit(1);
  }

  i = 100;

  if(fwrite(&i, 2, 1, fp)!=1) {
    printf("Write error occurred");
    exit(1);
  }
  fclose(fp);

  /* open file for input */
  if((fp = fopen("myfile", "r"))==NULL) {
    printf("Cannot open file\n");
    exit(1);
  }

  if(fread(&i, 2, 1, fp)!=1) {
    printf("Read error occurred");
    exit(1);
  }
  printf("i is %d", i);
  fclose(fp);
}
```

Notice how error checking is easily performed in this program by simply comparing the number of items written or read with that requested. In some situations, however, you will still need to use **feof( )** or **ferror( )** to determine if the end of the file has been reached or if an error has occurred.

One thing wrong with the preceding example is that an assumption about the size of an integer has been made and is hardcoded into the program. Therefore, this program will not work properly with compilers that use four-byte integers, for example. More generally, the size of many different types of data changes between systems or is difficult to determine manually. For this reason, C includes the keyword **sizeof**, which is a compile-time operator that returns the size, in bytes, of the type or variable that follows it. It takes the general forms

sizeof (*type*)

or

sizeof *var_name*;

For example, if **float**s are four bytes long and **f** is a **float** variable, the following statements evaluate to 4.

```
sizeof f;
sizeof (float);
```

When using **sizeof** with a type, the type must be enclosed between parentheses. No parentheses are needed when using a variable name, although the use of parentheses is not an error.

By using **sizeof**, not only do you save yourself the drudgery of computing the size of some object by hand, but you also ensure the portability of your code to new environments. An improved version of the preceding program is shown here, using **sizeof**.

```c
#include "stdio.h"
#include "stdlib.h"

void main(void)
{
  FILE *fp;
  int i;

  /* open file for output */
  if((fp = fopen("myfile", "w"))==NULL) {
    printf("Cannot open file\n");
    exit(1);
  }

  i = 100;

  if(fwrite(&i, sizeof(int), 1, fp)!=1) {
    printf("Write error occurred");
    exit(1);
  }
  fclose(fp);

  /* open file for input */
  if((fp = fopen("myfile", "r"))==NULL) {
    printf("Cannot open file\n");
    exit(1);
  }

  if(fread(&i, sizeof i, 1, fp)!=1) {
    printf("Read error occurred");
    exit(1);
  }
  printf("i is %d", i);
  fclose(fp);
}
```

Examples

1. This program fills a ten-element array with floating-point numbers, writes them to a file, and then reads them back. This program writes each element of the array separately. Because binary data is being written using its internal format, the file must be opened for binary I/O operations.

```c
#include "stdio.h"
#include "stdlib.h"

double d[10] = {
  10.23, 19.87, 1002.23, 12.9, 0.897,
  11.45, 75.34, 0.0, 1.01, 875.875
};

void main(void)
{
  int i;
  FILE *fp;

  if((fp = fopen("myfile", "wb"))==NULL) {
    printf("cannot open file");
    exit(1);
  }

  for(i=0; i<10; i++)
    if(fwrite(&d[i], sizeof(double), 1, fp)!=1) {
      printf("write error");
      exit(1);
    }
  fclose(fp);

  if((fp = fopen("myfile", "rb"))==NULL) {
    printf("cannot open file");
    exit(1);
  }

  /* clear the array */
  for(i=0; i<10; i++) d[i] = -1.0;
```

```
    for(i=0; i<10; i++)
      if(fread(&d[i], sizeof(double), 1, fp)!=1) {
        printf("read error");
        exit(1);
      }
    fclose(fp);

    /* display the array */
    for(i=0; i<10; i++) printf("%lf ", d[i]);
}
```

2. The following program does the same thing as the first, but here only one call to **fwrite( )** and **fread( )** is used because the entire array is written in one step, which is much more efficient. This example helps illustrate how powerful these functions are.

```
#include "stdio.h"
#include "stdlib.h"

double d[10] = {
  10.23, 19.87, 1002.23, 12.9, 0.897,
  11.45, 75.34, 0.0, 1.01, 875.875
};

void main(void)
{
  int i;
  FILE *fp;

  if((fp = fopen("myfile", "wb"))==NULL) {
    printf("cannot open file");
    exit(1);
  }

  /* write the entire array in one step */
  if(fwrite(d, sizeof d, 1, fp)!=1) {
      printf("write error");
      exit(1);
    }
  fclose(fp);

  if((fp = fopen("myfile", "rb"))==NULL) {
```

```
      printf("cannot open file");
      exit(1);
  }

  /* clear the array */
  for(i=0; i<10; i++) d[i] = -1.0;

  /* read the entire array in one step */
  if(fread(d, sizeof d, 1, fp)!=1) {
      printf("read error");
      exit(1);
  }
  fclose(fp);

  /* display the array */
  for(i=0; i<10; i++) printf("%lf ", d[i]);
}
```

Exercises

1. Write a program that allows a user to input as many **double** values as desired (up to 32,767) and writes them to a disk file as they are entered. Call this file VALUES. Keep a count of the number of values entered, and write this number to a file called COUNT.

2. Using the file you created in Exercise 1, write a program that first reads the number of items in VALUES from COUNT. Next, read the number of values in VALUES and display their average.

9.6 UNDERSTAND RANDOM ACCESS

So far, the examples have either written or read a file sequentially from its beginning to its end. However, using another of C's file system functions, you can access any point in a file at any time. The function that lets you do this is called **fseek( )**, and its prototype is

int fseek(FILE *fp*, long *offset*, int *origin*);

Here, *fp* is associated with the file being accessed. The value of *offset* determines the number of bytes from *origin* to make the new current position. *Origin* must be one of these macros, shown here with their meanings.

Value of Origin	Meaning
SEEK_SET	Seek from start of file
SEEK_CUR	Seek from current location
SEEK_END	Seek from end of file

These macros are defined in STDIO.H. For example, if you wanted to make the current location 100 bytes from the start of the file, then *origin* will be **SEEK_SET** and *offset* will be 100.

The **fseek( )** function returns 0 when successful and non-0 if a failure occurs. In most implementations, you may seek past the end of the file, but you may never seek to a point before the start of the file.

You can determine the current location of a file using **ftell( )**, another of C's file system functions. Its prototype is

long ftell(FILE *fp*);

It returns the location of the file position indicator within the file associated with *fp*. If a failure occurs, it returns −1L.

In general, you will want to use random access only on binary files. The reason for this is simple. Because text files may have character translations performed on them, there may not be a direct correspondence between what is in the file and the byte to which it would appear that you need to seek. The only time you should use **fseek( )** with a text file is when seeking to a position previously determined by **ftell( )**, using **SEEK_SET** as the origin.

Remember one important point: Even a file that contains only text can be opened as a binary file, if you like. There is no inherent restriction about random access on files containing text. The restriction applies only to files opened *as* text files.

Examples

1. The following program uses **fseek( )** to report the value of any byte within the file specified on the command line.

```
#include "stdio.h"
#include "stdlib.h"

void main(int argc, char *argv[])
{
  long loc;
  FILE *fp;

  /* see if filename is specified */
  if(argc!=2) {
    printf("File name missing");
    exit(1);
  }

  if((fp = fopen(argv[1], "rb"))==NULL) {
    printf("cannot open file");
    exit(1);
  }
```

```
  printf("Enter byte to seek to: ");
  scanf("%ld", &loc);
  if(fseek(fp, loc, SEEK_SET)) {
    printf("seek error");
    exit(1);
  }

  printf("Value at loc %ld is %d", loc, getc(fp));
  fclose(fp);
}
```

2. The following program uses **ftell( )** and **fseek( )** to copy the contents of one file into another in reverse order. Pay special attention to how the end of the input file is found. Also, notice that many files are terminated by an end-of-file marker, which must not be copied. This is true especially for text files. For this reason, the program backs up, so that the current location of the file associated with **in** is on the last actual character in the file.

```
/* Copy a file in reverse order */
#include "stdio.h"
#include "stdlib.h"

void main(int argc, char *argv[])
{
  long loc;
  FILE *in, *out;
  char ch;

  /* see if filename is specified */
  if(argc!=3) {
    printf("File name missing");
    exit(1);
  }

  if((in = fopen(argv[1], "rb"))==NULL) {
    printf("cannot open file");
    exit(1);
```

```
   }
   if((out = fopen(argv[2], "wb"))==NULL) {
     printf("cannot open file");
     exit(1);
   }

   /* find end of source file */
   fseek(in, 0L, SEEK_END);
   loc = ftell(in);

   /* copy file in reverse order */
   loc = loc-2;   /* back up past end-of-file mark */
   while(loc>=0L) {
     fseek(in, loc, SEEK_SET);
     ch = fgetc(in);
     fputc(ch, out);
     loc--;
   }
   fclose(in);
   fclose(out);
}
```

3. This program writes ten **double** values to disk. It then asks you which one you want to see. This example shows how you can access data of any type. You simply need to multiply the size of the base data type by its index in the file. You will see more examples of this procedure in the next chapter.

```
#include "stdio.h"
#include "stdlib.h"

double d[10] = {
   10.23, 19.87, 1002.23, 12.9, 0.897,
   11.45, 75.34, 0.0, 1.01, 875.875
};

void main(void)
{
  long loc;
  double value;
```

```
FILE *fp;

if((fp = fopen("myfile", "wb"))==NULL) {
  printf("cannot open file");
  exit(1);
}

/* write the entire array in one step */
if(fwrite(d, sizeof d, 1, fp)!=1) {
    printf("write error");
    exit(1);
  }
fclose(fp);

if((fp = fopen("myfile", "rb"))==NULL) {
  printf("cannot open file");
  exit(1);
}

printf("Which element? ");
scanf("%ld", &loc);
if(fseek(fp, loc*sizeof(double), SEEK_SET)) {
  printf("seek error");
  exit(1);
}

fread(&value, sizeof(double), 1, fp);
printf("Element %ld is %lf", loc, value);

fclose(fp);
}
```

Exercises

1. Write a program that uses **fseek( )** to display every
   other byte in a text file. (Remember, you must open
   the text file as a binary file in order for **fseek( )** to
   work properly.) Have the user specify the file on the
   command line.

2. Write a program that searches a file, specified on the command line, for a specific integer value (also specified on the command line). If this value is found, have the program display its location, relative, in bytes, to the start of the file.

9.7 LEARN ABOUT VARIOUS FILE-SYSTEM FUNCTIONS

You can erase a file using **remove( )**. Its prototype is

int remove(char *file-name);

This function will erase the file whose name matches that pointed to by *file-name*. It returns 0 if successful and non-0 if an error occurs.

You can position a file's current location to the start of the file using **rewind**. Its prototype is

void rewind(FILE *fp);

It rewinds the file associated with *fp*. The **rewind( )** function has no return value, because any file that has been successfully opened can be rewound.

Although seldom necessary because of the way C's file system works, you can cause a file's disk buffer to be flushed using **fflush( )**. Its prototype is

int fflush(FILE *fp);

It flushes the buffer of the file associated with *fp*. The function returns 0 if successful, **EOF** if a failure occurs.

If you call **fflush( )** using a null, all existing disk buffers are flushed.

Examples

1. This program demonstrates **remove( )**. It prompts the user for the file to erase and also provides a safety check in case the user entered the wrong name.

```
#include "stdio.h"
#include "stdlib.h"
#include "conio.h"
#include "ctype.h"

void main(void)
{
  char fname[80];

  printf("Enter name of file to erase: ");
  gets(fname);
  printf("Are you sure? (Y/N) ");
  if(toupper(getche())=='Y') remove(fname);
}
```

2. The following program demonstrates **rewind( )** by displaying the contents of the file specified on the command line twice.

```
#include "stdio.h"
#include "stdlib.h"

void main(int argc, char *argv[])
{
  FILE *fp;

  /* see if filename is specified */
  if(argc!=2) {
    printf("File name missing");
```

```
        exit(1);
    }

    if((fp = fopen(argv[1], "r"))==NULL) {
        printf("cannot open file");
        exit(1);
    }

    /* show it once */
    while(!feof(fp))
        putchar(getc(fp));

    rewind(fp);

    /* show it twice */
    while(!feof(fp))
        putchar(getc(fp));

    fclose(fp);
}
```

3. This fragment causes the buffer associated with **fp** to be flushed to disk.

```
FILE *fp;
    .
    .
    .
fflush(fp);
```

Exercises

1. Improve the erase program so that it notifies the user if he/she tries to remove a nonexistent file .

2. On your own, think of ways that **rewind( )** and **fflush( )** could be useful in real applications.

9.8 LEARN ABOUT THE STANDARD STREAMS

When a C program begins execution, three streams are automatically opened and available for use. These streams are called *standard input* (**stdin**); *standard output* (**stdout**), and *standard error* (**stderr**). By default, they refer to the console, but in environments that support redirectable I/O, they may be redirected by the operating system to some other device.

Normally, **stdin** inputs from the keyboard; **stdout** and **stderr** write to the screen. These standard streams are **FILE** pointers and may be used with any function that uses a variable of type **FILE** *. For example, you can use **fprintf( )** to print formatted output to the screen. The following two statements are functionally the same.

```
fprintf(stdout, "%d %c %s", 100, 'c', "this is a string");
printf("%d %c %s", 100, 'c', "this is a string");
```

One important point: **stdin**, **stdout**, and **stderr** are not variables. They may not be assigned a value using **fopen( )**, nor should you attempt to close them using **fclose( )**. These streams are maintained internally by the compiler. You are free to use them, but not to change them.

In actuality, C makes little distinction between console I/O and file I/O. As just described, it is possible to perform console I/O using several of the file-system functions. However, it is also possible to perform disk file I/O using console I/O functions, such as **printf( )**! Here's why.

All of the functions described in Chapter 8 and referred to as "console I/O functions" are actually special-case file-system functions that operate on **stdin** and **stdout**. The "console" I/O functions are simply conveniences for you, the programmer. As far as C is concerned, the console is simply another hardware device. You don't actually need the "console" functions to access the console. Any file-system function can access it. (Of course, nonstandard I/O functions like **getche( )** are differentiated from the standard file-system functions and do, in fact, operate only on the console.) In environments that allow redirection of I/O, **stdin** and **stdout** could refer to devices other than the keyboard and screen. When this is done, you can use a "console" I/O function to write to a disk file, for example.

Examples

1. Consider this program.

```
#include "stdio.h"

void main(void)
{
  char str[80];

  printf("this is an example of redirection");
}
```

Assume that this program is called TEST. If you execute TEST normally, it displays the string on the screen. However, if an environment supports redirection of I/O, **stdout** can be redirected to a file. For example, in a DOS, OS/2, or UNIX environment, executing TEST like this

```
TEST > OUTPUT
```

causes the output of TEST to be written to a file called OUTPUT. You might want to try this now for yourself.

2. Input can also be redirected. For example, consider the following program:

```
#include "stdio.h"

void main(void)
{
  int i;

  scanf("%d", &i);
  printf("%d", i);
}
```

Assuming it is called TEST, executing it as

```
TEST < INPUT
```

causes **stdin** to be directed to the file called INPUT. Assuming that INPUT contained the ASCII representation for an integer, the value of this integer will be read from the file and printed on the screen.

Exercise

1. Write a program that copies the contents of one text file to another. However, use only "console" I/O functions and use redirection to accomplish the file copy.

EXERCISES

Before continuing, you should be able to answer these questions and complete these exercises.

1. Write a program that displays the contents of a text file (specified on the command line), one line at a time. After each line is displayed, ask the user if he/she wants to see another line.

2. Write a program that copies a text file. Have the user specify both file names on the command line. Have the copy program convert all lowercase letters into uppercase ones.

3. What do **fprintf( )** and **fscanf( )** do?

4. Write a program that uses **fwrite( )** to write 100 randomly generated integers to a file called RAND.

5. Write a program that uses **fread( )** to display the integers stored in the file called RAND, created in Exercise 4.

6. Using the file called RAND, write a program that uses **fseek( )** to allow the user to access and display the value of any integer in the file.

7. How do the "console" I/O functions relate to the file system?

EXERCISES

This section checks how well you have integrated the material in this chapter with that from earlier chapters.

1. Enhance the card-catalog program you wrote in Chapter 8 so that it stores its information in a disk file called CATALOG. When the program begins, have it read the catalog into memory. Also, add an option to save the information to disk.

2. Write a program that copies a file. Have the user specify both the source and destination files on the command line. Have the program remove tab characters, substituting the appropriate number of spaces.

3. On your own, create a small database to keep track of anything you desire—your record collection, for example.

CHAPTER OBJECTIVES

10.1 Master structure basics

10.2 Declare pointers to structures

10.3 Work with nested structures

10.4 Understand bit-fields

10.5 Create unions

·10·
Structures and Unions

In this chapter you will learn about two of C's most important user-defined types: the structure and the union.

EXERCISES

Before proceeding you should be able to answer these questions and perform these exercises.

SKILLS CHECK

√

1. Write a program that copies a file. Have the user specify both the source and destination file names on the command line. Include full error checking.

2. Write a program using **fprintf( )** to create a file that contains this information.

   this is a string 1230.23 1FFF A

   Use a string, a **double**, a hexadecimal integer, and character format specifiers and values.

3. Write a program that contains a 20-element integer array. Initialize the array so that it contains the numbers 1 through 20. Using only one **fwrite( )** statement, save this array to a file called TEMP.

4. Write a program that reads the TEMP file created in Exercise 3 into an integer array using only one **fread( )** statement. Display the contents of the array.

5. What are **stdin**, **stdout**, and **stderr**?

6. How do functions like **printf( )** and **scanf( )** relate to the C file system?

10.1 MASTER STRUCTURE BASICS

A *structure* is a conglomerate data type that is comprised of two or more related elements. Unlike arrays, each element of a structure can have its own types, which may differ from the types of any other elements. Structures are defined in C using the general form

```
struct tag-name {
    type element1;
    type element2;
    type element3;
        .
        .
        .
    type elementN;
} variable-list;
```

The keyword **struct** tells the compiler that a structure type is being defined. Here, each *type* is a valid C type. The types need not be the same. The *tag-name* is essentially the type name of the structure, and the *variable-list* is where actual variables of the structure are declared. Either the *tag-name* or the *variable-list* is optional, but one must be present. (You will see why shortly.)

The elements of a structure are also commonly referred to as *fields* or *members*. This book will use these terms interchangeably.

Generally, the information contained in a structure is logically related. For example, you might use a structure to hold a person's address. Another structure might be used to support an inventory program in which each item's name, its retail and wholesale cost, and the number of each item on hand is stored. The structure shown here expands the card-catalog example developed in the preceding two chapters.

```
struct catalog {
  char name[40]; /* author's name */
  char title[40]; /* book title */
  char pub[40]; /* publisher */
  unsigned date; /* publication date */
  unsigned char ed; /* edition number */
} card;
```

Here, **catalog** is the type name of the structure. It is not the name of a variable. The only variable defined by this structure is **card**. Figure 10-1 shows how this structure will appear in memory.

To access a field with a structure variable, you must specify both the structure name and the field name, separated by a period. For example, using the **card** structure variable, the following statement assigns the **date** field the value 1992.

```
card.date = 1992;
```

C programmers often refer to the period as the *dot operator*.

To print the date of publication, you can use a statement such as

```
printf("Publication date: %u", card.date);
```

name	40 bytes
title	40 bytes
pub	40 bytes
date	2 bytes
ed	2 bytes

FIGURE 10-1. How the **card** structure variable appears in memory

To input the date, use a **scanf( )** statement such as:

```
scanf("%u", &card.date);
```

Notice that the **&** goes before the structure name, not before the field name. In a similar fashion, these statements input the author's name and output the title.

```
gets(card.name);
.
.
.
printf("%s", card.title);
```

To access an individual character in the **title** field, simply index **title**. For example, the following statement prints the third letter.

```
printf("%c", card.title[2]);
```

Once you have defined a structure type, you can create more variables of that type using this general form.

struct *tag_name var_list*;

Assuming, for example, that **catalog** has been defined as shown earlier in this section, this statement declares three variables of type **struct catalog**.

```
struct catalog var1, var2, var3;
```

This is why it is not necessary to declare any variables when the structure type is defined. You can declare them separately, as needed.

If you know you only need a fixed number of structure variables, you do not need to specify the tag name. For example, this code creates two structure variables, but the structure is unnamed.

```
struct {
  int a;
  char ch;
} var1, var2;
```

In actual practice, however, you will seldom want to leave your structures nameless.

Structures can be arrayed in the same fashion as other data types. For example, the following structure definition creates a 100-element array of structures of type **catalog**.

```
struct catalog cat[100];
```

To access an individual structure of the array, you must index the array name. For example, the following accesses the first structure.

```
cat[0]
```

To access an element within a specific structure, follow the index with a period and the name of the element you want. For example, the following statement loads the **ed** field of structure 34 with the value 2.

```
cat[33].ed = 2;
```

Structures may be passed as parameters to functions just like any other type of value. A function may also return a structure.

You may assign the contents of one structure variable to another structure variable of the same type. For example, this fragment is perfectly valid.

```
struct s_type {
   int a;
   float f;
} var1, var2;

var1.a = 10;
var1.f = 100.23;

var2 = var1;
```

After this fragment executes, **var2** will contain exactly the same thing as **var1**.

One final point: When you pass a structure to a function, the entire structure is passed using C's normal call-by-value parameter-passing convention. However, some very old C compilers may only pass a pointer to the structure in much the same way that pointers to arrays are passed. If you are using an older compiler, you will want to check on this point.

Examples

1. This program demonstrates some ways to access structure elements.

   ```
   #include "stdio.h"

   struct  s_type {
     int i;
     char ch;
   ```

```
  double d;
  char str[80];
} s;

void main(void)
{
  printf("Enter an integer: ");
  scanf("%d", &s.i);
  printf("Enter a character: ");
  scanf(" %c", &s.ch);
  printf("Enter a floating point number: ");
  scanf("%lf", &s.d);
  printf("Enter a string: ");
  scanf("%s", s.str);

  printf("%d %c %lf %s", s.i, s.ch, s.d, s.str);
}
```

2. When you need to know the size of a structure, you should use the **sizeof** compile-time operator. Do not try to manually add up the number of bytes in each element. There are three good reasons for this. First, as you learned in the preceding chapter, using **sizeof** ensures that your code is portable to different environments. Second, in some situations, the compiler may need to align certain types of data on even word boundaries. In this case, the size of the structure will be larger than the sum of its individual elements. Finally, for 8086-based computers, there are several different ways the compiler can organize memory. Some of these ways cause pointers to take up twice the space they do when memory is arranged differently.

   When using **sizeof** with a structure type, you must precede the tag name with the keyword **struct**, as shown in this program.

```
#include "stdio.h"

struct  s_type {
  int i;
  char ch;
  int *p;
  double d;
} s;

void main(void)
{
  printf("s_type is %d bytes long", sizeof (struct
    s_type));
}
```

3. To see how useful arrays of structures are, examine an improved version of the card-catalog program developed in the preceding two chapters. Notice how using a structure makes it easier to organize the information about each book. Also notice how the entire structure array is written and read from disk in a single operation.

```
/* An electronic card catalog. */
#include "stdio.h"
#include "conio.h"
#include "string.h"
#include "stdlib.h"

#define MAX 100

int menu(void);
void display(int i);
void author_search(void), title_search(void);
void enter(void), save(void), load(void);

struct catalog {
  char name[80];  /* author name */
```

```c
  char title[80];  /* title */
  char pub[80];    /* publisher */
  unsigned date; /* date of publication */
  unsigned char ed; /* edition */
} cat[MAX];

int top = 0;  /* last location used */

void main(void)
{
  int choice;

  load(); /* read in catalog */

  do {
    choice = menu();
    switch(choice) {
      case 1: enter(); /* enter books */
        break;
      case 2: author_search(); /* search by author */
        break;
      case 3: title_search(); /* search by title */
        break;
      case 4: save();
    }
  } while(choice!=5);
}

/* Return a menu selection. */
menu(void)
{
  int i;

  printf("Card Catalog:\n");
  printf("  1. Enter\n");
  printf("  2. Search by Author\n");
  printf("  3. Search by Title\n");
  printf("  4. Save catalog\n");
  printf("  5. Quit\n");

  do {
    printf("Choose your selection: ");
    i = getche()-'0';
```

```
      printf("\n");
    } while(i<1 || i>5);

    return i;
}

/* Enter books into database. */
void enter(void)
{
  int i;
  char temp[80];

  for(i=top; i<MAX; i++) {
    printf("Enter author name (ENTER to quit): ");
    gets(cat[i].name);
    if(!*cat[i].name) break;
    printf("Enter title: ");
    gets(cat[i].title);
    printf("Enter publisher: ");
    gets(cat[i].pub);
    printf("Enter date of publication: ");
    gets(temp);
    cat[i].date = (unsigned) atoi(temp);
    printf("Enter edition: ");
    gets(temp);
    cat[i].ed = (unsigned char) atoi(temp);
  }
  top = i;
}

/* Search by author. */
void author_search(void)
{
  char name[80];
  int i, found;

  printf("Name: ");
  gets(name);

  found = 0;
  for(i=0; i<top; i++)
    if(!strcmp(name, cat[i].name)) {
      display(i);
```

```
        found = 1;
        printf("\n");
      }

    if(!found) printf("not found\n");
}

/* Search by title. */
void title_search(void)
{
  char title[80];
  int i, found;

  printf("Title: ");
  gets(title);

  found = 0;
  for(i=0; i<top; i++)
    if(!strcmp(title, cat[i].title)) {
      display(i);
      found = 1;
      printf("\n");
    }
  if(!found) printf("not found\n");
}

/* Display catalog entry. */
void display(int i)
{
  printf("%s\n", cat[i].title);
  printf("by %s\n", cat[i].name);
  printf("Published by %s\n", cat[i].pub);
  printf("Printed: %u, %u edition\n", cat[i].date, cat[i].ed);
}

/* Load the catalog file. */
void load(void)
{
  FILE *fp;

  if((fp = fopen("catalog", "r"))==NULL) {
    printf("Catalog file not on disk\n");
    return;
```

```
    }

    fread(&top, sizeof top, 1, fp); /* read count */
    fread(cat, sizeof cat, 1, fp);

    fclose(fp);
}

/* Save the catalog file. */
void save(void)
{
  FILE *fp;

  if((fp = fopen("catalog", "w"))==NULL) {
    printf("Cannot open catalog file\n");
    exit(1);
  }

  fwrite(&top, sizeof top, 1, fp);
  fwrite(cat, sizeof cat, 1, fp);

  fclose(fp);
}
```

4. In the preceding example, the entire catalog array is
    stored on disk, even if the array is not full. If you
    like, you can change the **load( )** and **save( )** routines
    as follows, so that only structures actually holding
    data are stored on disk.

```
/* Load the catalog file. */
void load(void)
{
  FILE *fp;
  int i;

  if((fp = fopen("catalog", "r"))==NULL) {
    printf("Catalog file not on disk\n");
    return;
  }

  fread(&top, sizeof top, 1, fp); /* read count */
  for(i=0; i<=top; i++)
```

```
      fread(&cat[i], sizeof (struct catalog), 1, fp);

    fclose(fp);
}

/* Save the catalog file. */
void save(void)
{
  FILE *fp;
  int i;

  if((fp = fopen("catalog", "w"))==NULL) {
    printf("Cannot open catalog file\n");
    exit(1);
  }

  fwrite(&top, sizeof top, 1, fp); /* write count */
  for(i=0; i<=top; i++)
    fwrite(&cat[i], sizeof (struct catalog), 1, fp);

  fclose(fp);
}
```

5. The names of structure elements will not conflict with other variables using the same names. Because the element name is linked with the structure name, it is separate from other variables of the same name. For example, this program prints **10 100 101** on the screen.

```
#include "stdio.h"

void main(void)
{
  struct s_type {
    int i;
    int j;
  } s;

  int i;
```

```
  i = 10;
  s.i = 100;
  s.j = 101;

  printf("%d %d %d", i, s.i, s.j);
}
```

The variable **i** and the structure element **i** have no relationship to each other.

6. As stated earlier, a function may return a structure to the calling procedure. The following program, for example, loads the elements of **var1** with the values 100 and 123.23 and then displays them on the screen.

```
#include "stdio.h"

struct s_type {
   int i;
   double d;
} var1;

struct s_type f(void);

void main(void)
{
  var1 = f();
  printf("%d %lf", var1.i, var1.d);
}

struct s_type f(void)
{
  struct s_type temp;

  temp.i = 100;
  temp.d = 123.23;

  return temp;
}
```

7. This program passes a structure to a function.

```
#include "stdio.h"

struct s_type {
  int i;
  double d;
} var1;

void f(struct s_type temp);

void main(void)
{
  var1.i = 99;
  var1.d = 98.6;
  f(var1);
}

void f(struct s_type temp)
{
  printf("%d %lf", temp.i, temp.d);
}
```

Exercises

1. In Chapter 9, you wrote a program that created a telephone directory that was stored on disk. Improve the program so that it uses an array of structures, each containing a person's name, area code, and telephone number. Store the area code as an integer. Store the name and telephone number as strings. Make the array **MAX** elements long, where **MAX** is any convenient value that you choose.

2. What is wrong with this fragment?

```
struct s_type {
  int i;
  long l;
  char str[80];
} s;
```

.
.
.

```
i = 10;
```

3. On your own, examine the header file STDIO.H and
    look at how the **FILE** structure is defined.

10.2 DECLARE POINTERS TO STRUCTURES

It is very common to access a structure through a pointer. You declare a pointer to a structure in the same way
that you declare a pointer to any other type of variable.
For example, the following fragment defines a structure
called **s_type** and declares two variables. The first, **s**, is
an actual structure variable. The second, **p**, is a pointer
to structures of type **s_type**.

```
struct s_type {
   int i;
   char str[80];
} s, *p;
```

Given this definition, the following statement assigns
to **p** the address of **s**.

```
p = &s;
```

Now that **p** points to **s** you can access **s** through **p**.
However, to access an individual element of s using **p**
you cannot use the dot operator. Instead, you must use
the *arrow operator*, as shown in the following example.

```
p->i = 1;
```

This statement assigns the value 1 to element **i** of **s** through **p**. The arrow operator is formed using a minus sign followed by a greater-than sign. There must be no spaces between the two.

C passes structures to functions in their entirety. However, if the structure is very large, the passing of a structure can cause a considerable reduction in a program's execution speed. For this reason, when working with large structures, you might want to pass a pointer to a structure in situations that allow it instead of passing the structure itself.

Remember this very important point: When accessing a structure element using a structure variable, use the dot operator. When accessing a structure element using a pointer to the structure, however, you must use the arrow operator.

Examples

1. The following program illustrates how to use a pointer to a structure.

```
#include "stdio.h"
#include "string.h"

struct s_type {
   int i;
   char str[80];
} s, *p;

void main(void)
{
   p = &s;

   s.i = 10;  /* this is functionally the same */
   p->i = 10; /* as this */
```

```
   strcpy(p->str, "I like structures");

   printf("%d %d %s", s.i, p->i, p->str);
}
```

2. One very useful application of structure pointers is found in C's time and date functions. Several of these functions use a pointer to hold the current time and date of the system. The time and date functions require the header file TIME.H, in which a structure called **tm** is defined. This structure can hold the date and time broken down into its elements. This is called the *broken-down time*. The **tm** structure is defined as

```
struct tm {
   int tm_sec;   /* seconds, 0-59 */
   int tm_min;   /* minutes, 0-59 */
   int tm_hour;  /* hours, 0-23 */
   int tm_mday;  /* day of the month, 1-31 */
   int tm_mon;   /* months since Jan, 0-11 */
   int tm_year;  /* years from 1900 */
   int tm_wday;  /* days since Sunday, 0-6 */
   int tm_yday;  /* days since Jan 1, 0-365 */
   int tm_isdst  /* Daylight Savings Time indicator */
}
```

The value of **tm_isdst** will be positive if Daylight Savings Time is in effect, 0 if it is not in effect, and negative if there is no information available. Also defined in TIME.H is the type **time_t**. It is essentially a **long** integer capable of representing the time and date of the system in an encoded implementation-specific internal format. This is referred to as the *calendar time*.

To obtain the calendar time of the system, you must use the **time( )** function, whose prototype is

time_t time(time_t *time)

The **time( )** function returns the encoded calendar time of the system or −1 if no system type is available. It also places this encoded form of the time into the variable pointed to by *time*. However, if *time* is null, the argument is ignored.

Since the calendar time is represented using an implementation-specific internal format, you must use another of C's time and date functions to convert it into a form that is easier to use. One of these functions is called **localtime( )**. Its prototype is

struct tm *localtime(time_t *time)

The **localtime( )** function returns a pointer to the broken-down form of *time*. The structure that holds the broken-down time is internally allocated by the compiler and will be overwritten by each subsequent call.

This program demonstrates **time( )** and **localtime( )** by displaying the current time of the system.

```c
#include "stdio.h"
#include "time.h"

void main(void)
{
  struct tm *systime;
  time_t t;

  t = time(NULL);
  systime = localtime(&t);

  printf("Time is %.2d:%.2d:%.2d\n", systime->tm_hour,
        systime->tm_min, systime->tm_sec);
  printf("Date: %.2d/%.2d/%.2d", systime->tm_mon+1,
        systime->tm_mday, systime->tm_year);
}
```

Exercises

1. Is this program fragment correct?

```
struct s_type {
  int a;
  int b;
} s, *p;

void main(void)
{
  p = &s;

  p.a = 100;
  .
  .
  .
```

2. Another of C's time and date functions is called **gmtime( )**. Its prototype is

struct tm *gmtime(time_t *time);

The **gmtime( )** function works exactly like **localtime( )**, except that it returns the Greenwich Mean time of the system. Change the program in Example 2 so that it displays both local time and Greenwich Mean time.

10.3 WORK WITH NESTED STRUCTURES

So far, we have only been working with structures whose elements consist solely of C's basic types. However, structure elements can also be other structures. These are referred to as *nested structures*. For example, here is an example that uses nested structures to hold information on the performance of two assembly lines, each with ten workers.

```
#define NUM_ON_LINE 10

struct worker {
  char name[80];
  int avg_units_per_hour;
  int avg_errs_per_hour;
};

struct asm_line {
  int product_code;
  double material_cost;
  struct worker wkers[NUM_ON_LINE];
} line1, line2;
```

To assign the value 12 to the **avg_units_per_hour** of the second **wkers** structure of **line1**, use this statement:

```
line1.wkers[1].avg_units_per_hour = 12;
```

As you see, the structures are referenced from the outer to the inner. This is also the general case. Whenever you have nested structures, you begin referencing with the outermost and end with the innermost.

Example

1. A nested structure can be used to improve the book catalog program. Here, the mechanical information about each book is stored in its own structure, which, in turn, is part of the **catalog** structure. The entire catalog program, using this approach is

shown here. Notice how the program now stores the
length of the book, in pages.

```c
/* An electronic card catalog - 3rd Improvement. */
#include "stdio.h"
#include "conio.h"
#include "string.h"
#include "stdlib.h"

#define MAX 100

int menu(void);
void display(int i);
void author_search(void), title_search(void);
void enter(void), save(void), load(void);

struct book_type {
  unsigned date; /* date of publication */
  unsigned char ed; /* edition */
  unsigned pages; /* length of book */
} ;

struct catalog {
  char name[80];   /* author name */
  char title[80];  /* title */
  char pub[80];    /* publisher */
  struct book_type book; /* mechanical info */
} cat[MAX];
int top = 0;  /* last location used */

void main(void)
{
  int choice;

  load(); /* read in catalog */

  do {
    choice = menu();
    switch(choice) {
      case 1: enter(); /* enter books */
        break;
      case 2: author_search(); /* search by author */
```

```
        break;
      case 3: title_search(); /* search by title */
        break;
      case 4: save();
    }
  } while(choice!=5);
}

/* Return a menu selection. */
menu(void)
{
  int i;

  printf("Card Catalog:\n");
  printf("  1. Enter\n");
  printf("  2. Search by Author\n");
  printf("  3. Search by Title\n");
  printf("  4. Save catalog\n");
  printf("  5. Quit\n");

  do {
    printf("Choose your selection: ");
    i = getche()-'0';
    printf("\n");
  } while(i<1 || i>5);

  return i;
}

/* Enter books into database. */
void enter(void)
{
  int i;
  char temp[80];

  for(i=top; i<MAX; i++) {
    printf("Enter author name (ENTER to quit): ");
    gets(cat[i].name);
    if(!*cat[i].name) break;
    printf("Enter title: ");
    gets(cat[i].title);
    printf("Enter publisher: ");
    gets(cat[i].pub);
```

```
      printf("Enter date of publication: ");
      gets(temp);
      cat[i].book.date = (unsigned) atoi(temp);
      printf("Enter edition: ");
      gets(temp);
      cat[i].book.ed = (unsigned char) atoi(temp);
      printf("Enter number of pages: ");
      gets(temp);
      cat[i].book.pages = (unsigned) atoi(temp);
   }
   top = i;
}

/* Search by author. */
void author_search(void)
{
  char name[80];
  int i, found;

  printf("Name: ");
  gets(name);

  found = 0;
  for(i=0; i<top; i++)
    if(!strcmp(name, cat[i].name)) {
      display(i);
      found = 1;
      printf("\n");
    }

  if(!found) printf("not found\n");
}

/* Search by title. */
void title_search(void)
{
  char title[80];
  int i, found;

  printf("Title: ");
  gets(title);

  found = 0;
```

```
  for(i=0; i<top; i++)
    if(!strcmp(title, cat[i].title)) {
      display(i);
      found = 1;
      printf("\n");
    }
  if(!found) printf("not found\n");
}

/* Display catalog entry. */
void display(int i)
{
  printf("%s\n", cat[i].title);
  printf("by %s\n", cat[i].name);
  printf("Published by %s\n", cat[i].pub);
  printf("Printed: %u, edition: %u\n", cat[i].book.date,
          cat[i].book.ed);
  printf("Pages: %u\n", cat[i].book.pages);
}

/* Load the catalog file. */
void load(void)
{
  FILE *fp;

  if((fp = fopen("catalog", "r"))==NULL) {
    printf("Catalog file not on disk\n");
    return;
  }

  fread(&top, sizeof top, 1, fp); /* read count */
  fread(cat, sizeof cat, 1, fp);

  fclose(fp);
}

/* Save the catalog file. */
void save(void)
{
  FILE *fp;

  if((fp = fopen("catalog", "w"))==NULL) {
    printf("Cannot open catalog file\n");
```

```
        exit(1);
    }

    fwrite(&top, sizeof top, 1, fp);
    fwrite(cat, sizeof cat, 1, fp);

    fclose(fp);
}
```

Exercise

1. Improve the telephone-directory program you wrote earlier in this chapter so that it includes each person's mailing address. Store the address in its own structure, called **address**, which is nested inside the directory structure.

10.4 UNDERSTAND BIT-FIELDS

C allows a variation on the structure element called a *bit-field*. A bit-field is an element of a structure that is comprised of one or more bits. Using a bit-field, you can access by name one or more bits within a byte or word. To define a bit-field, use the general form

type name : size;

where *type* is either **int** or **unsigned**. If you specify a **signed** bit-field, then the high-order bit is treated as a sign bit. Notice that a colon separates the name of the bit-field from its size in bits.

Bit-fields are very useful when you want to pack information into the smallest possible space. For example, here is a structure that uses bit-fields to hold inventory information.

```
struct b_type {
  unsigned department: 3; /* up to 7 departments */
  unsigned instock: 1;  /* 1 if in stock, 0 if out */
  unsigned backordered: 1; /* 1 if backordered, 0 if not */
  unsigned lead_time: 3; /* order lead time in months */
} inv[MAX_ITEM];
```

In this case one byte can be used to store information on an inventory item that would normally have taken four bytes without the use of bit-fields. You refer to a bit-field variable just like any other element of a structure. The following statement, for example, assigns the value 3 to the **department** field of item 10.

```
inv[9].department = 3;
```

The following statement determines whether item 5 is out of stock.

```
if(!inv[4].instock) printf("out of stock");
else printf("in stock");
```

It is not necessary to completely define all bits within a byte or word. For example, this is perfectly valid:

```
struct b_type {
  int a: 2;
  int b: 3;
} ;
```

The C compiler is free to store bit-field variables as it sees fit. However, generally the compiler will automatically store bit-fields in the smallest unit of memory that will hold them. Whether the bit-fields are stored high-order to low-order or the other way around is implementation-dependent. However, many compilers use high-order to low-order.

You can mix bit-fields with regular variables in a structure's definition. For example, this version of the inventory structure also includes room for the name of each item.

```
struct b_type {
  char name[40]; /* name of item */
  unsigned department: 3; /* up to 7 departments */
  unsigned instock: 1;   /* 1 if in stock, 0 if out */
  unsigned backordered: 1; /* 1 if backordered, 0 if not */
  unsigned lead_time: 3; /* order lead time in months */
} inv[MAX_ITEM];
```

Because the smallest addressable unit of memory is a byte, you cannot obtain the address of a bit-field variable.

Bit-fields are often used to store Boolean (true/false) data because they allow the efficient use of memory— remember, you can pack eight Boolean values into a single byte.

Examples

1. It is not necessary to name every bit when using bit-fields. Here, for example, is a structure that uses bit-fields to access the first and last bit in a byte.

```
struct b_type {
  unsigned first: 1;
  int : 6;
  unsigned last: 1;
} ;
```

The use of unnamed bit-fields makes it easy to reach the bits you are interested in.

2. To see how useful bit-fields can be when working with Boolean data, here is a a crude simulation of a spaceship flight recorder. By packing all the relevant information into one byte, comparatively little disk space is used by the flight recorder.

```
/* Simulation of a 100 minute spaceship
   flight recorder.
*/
#include "stdlib.h"
#include "stdio.h"

/* all fields indicate OK if 1,
   malfunctioning or low if 0 */
struct telemetry {
  unsigned fuel: 1;
  unsigned radio: 1;
  unsigned tv: 1;
  unsigned water: 1;
  unsigned food: 1;
  unsigned waste: 1;
} flt_recd;

void display(struct telemetry i);

void main(void)
{
  FILE *fp;
  int i;

  if((fp = fopen("flight", "wb"))==NULL) {
    printf("Cannot open file");
```

```
        exit(1);
      }

      /* imagine that each minute a status report of
         the spaceship is recorded on disk
      */

      for(i=0; i<100; i++) {
        flt_recd.fuel = rand()%2;
        flt_recd.radio = rand()%2;
        flt_recd.tv = rand()%2;
        flt_recd.water = rand()%2;
        flt_recd.food = rand()%2;
        flt_recd.waste = rand()%2;

        display(flt_recd);
        fwrite(&flt_recd, sizeof flt_recd, 1, fp);
      }

      fclose(fp);
    }

    void display(struct telemetry i)
    {
      if(i.fuel) printf("Fuel OK\n");
      else printf("Fuel low\n");
      if(i.radio) printf("Radio OK\n");
      else printf("Radio failure\n");
      if(i.tv) printf("TV system OK\n");
      else printf("TV malfuction\n");
      if(i.water) printf("Water supply OK\n");
      else printf("Water supply low\n");
      if(i.food) printf("Food supply OK\n");
      else printf("Food supply low\n");
      if(i.waste) printf("Waste containment OK\n");
      else printf("Waste containment failure\n");
      printf("\n");
    }
```

After you run this program, the file on disk will be only 100 bytes long. Now try the program after modifying the **telemetry** structure as shown here.

```
struct telemetry {
  char fuel;
  char radio;
  char tv;
  char water;
  char food;
  char waste;
} flt_recd;
```

In this version, no bit-fields are used—the resulting file is 600 bytes long!

Exercises

1. Write a program that creates a structure that contains three bit-fields called **a**, **b**, and **c**. Make **a** and **b** three bits long and make **c** two bits long. Make all three **signed** variables. Next, assign each a value and display the values.

2. Many compilers supply library functions that return the status of various hardware devices, such as a serial port or the keyboard, by encoding information in a bit-by-bit fashion. On your own, consult the user's manual for your compiler to see if it supports such functions. If it does, write some programs that read and decode the status of one or more devices.

10.5 CREATE UNIONS

In C, a *union* is a single memory location that is shared by two or more variables. The variables that share the memory may be of different types. However, only one variable may be in use at any one time. A union is defined much like a structure. Its general form is

```
union tag-name {
    type element1;
    type element2;
    type element3;

        .

        .

        .

    type elementN;
} variable-names;
```

Like a structure, either the *tag-name* or the *variable_names* may be missing. Elements may be of any valid C data type. For example, here is a **union** that contains three elements: an integer, a character array, and a **double**.

```
union u_type {
    int i;
    char c[2];
    double d;
} sample;
```

This **union** will appear in memory as shown in Figure 10-2.

To access an element of a union, use the dot and arrow operators just as you do for structures. For example, this statement assigns 123.098 to **d** of **sample**.

```
sample.d = 123.098;
```

If you are accessing a **union** through a pointer, you must use the arrow operator. For example, assume that **p** points to **sample**. The following statement assigns **i** the value 101.

```
p->i = 101;
```

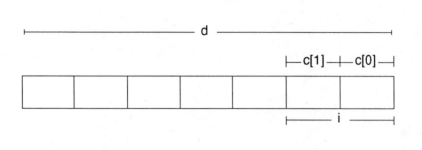

FIGURE 10-2. How **union** appears in memory (assuming 8-byte
         doubles)

It is important to understand that the size of a union is fixed at compile time and is large enough to accommodate the largest element in the union. Assuming 8-byte **doubles**, this means that **sample** will be 8 bytes long. Even if **sample** is currently used to hold an **int** value, it will still be using 8 bytes of memory. However, as is the case with structures, you should use the **sizeof** compile-time operator to determine the size of a **union**. You should not simply assume that it will be the size of the largest element, because in some environments, the compiler may pad the union so that it aligns on a word boundary.

Examples

1. Unions are very useful when you need to deal with data in two or more different ways. For example, the **encode( )** function shown below uses a union to encode an integer by swapping its two bytes. (The function assumes that integers are two bytes long.) The same function can also be used to decode an

encoded integer by swapping the already exchanged bytes back to their original positions.

```
#include "stdio.h"

int encode(int i);

void main(void)
{
  int i;

  i = encode(10); /* encode it */
  printf("10 encoded is %d\n", i);
  i = encode(i); /* decode it */
  printf("i decoded is %d", i);
}

/* Encode an integer, decode an encoded integer */
encode(int i)
{
  union crypt_type {
    int num;
    char c[2];
  } crypt;
  unsigned char ch;

  crypt.num = i;

  /* swap bytes */
  ch = crypt.c[0];
  crypt.c[0] = crypt.c[1];
  crypt.c[1] = ch;

  /* return encoded integer */
  return crypt.num;
}
```

The program displays the following.

```
10 encoded is 2560
i decoded is 10
```

2. The following program uses the union of a bit-field structure and a character to display the binary representation of the character typed at the keyboard.

```c
/* This program displays the binary code for a
   character entered at the keyboard.
*/
#include "stdio.h"
#include "conio.h"

struct sample {
  unsigned a: 1;
  unsigned b: 1;
  unsigned c: 1;
  unsigned d: 1;
  unsigned e: 1;
  unsigned f: 1;
  unsigned g: 1;
  unsigned h: 1;
};

union key_type {
  char ch;
  struct sample bits;
} key;

void main(void)
{
  printf("Strike a key: ");

  key.ch = getche();
  printf("\nBinary code is: ");

  if(key.bits.h) printf("1 ");
  else printf("0 ");
  if(key.bits.g) printf("1 ");
  else printf("0 ");
  if(key.bits.f) printf("1 ");
  else printf("0 ");
  if(key.bits.e) printf("1 ");
  else printf("0 ");
  if(key.bits.d) printf("1 ");
  else printf("0 ");
```

```
    if(key.bits.c) printf("1 ");
    else printf("0 ");
    if(key.bits.b) printf("1 ");
    else printf("0 ");
    if(key.bits.a) printf("1 ");
    else printf("0 ");
}
```

Exercises

1. Using a union composed of a **double** and an 8-byte
    character array, write a function that writes a **dou-
    ble** to a disk file, a character at a time. Write another
    function that reads this value from the file and re-
    constructs the value using the same union. (Note: If
    the length of a **double** for your compiler is not 8
    bytes, use an appropriately sized character array.)

2. Write a program that uses a union to convert an **int**
    into a **long**. Demonstrate that it works.

EXERCISES

At this point you should be able to answer these questions and perform these exercises.

MASTERY
SKILLS CHECK

√

1. In general terms what is a structure, and what is a
    union?

2. Show how to create a structure called **s_type** that
    contains these five elements:

```
char ch;
float d;
int i;
char str[80];
double balance;
```

Also, define one variable called **s_var** using this structure.

3. What is wrong with this fragment?

```
struct s_type {
   int a;
   char b;
   float bal;
} myvar, *p;

p = &myvar;

p.a = 10;
```

4. Write a program that uses an array of structures to store employee names, telephone numbers, hours worked, and hourly wages. Allow for 10 employees. Have the program input the information and save it to a disk file. Call the file EMP.

5. Write a program that reads the EMP file created in exercise 4 and displays the information on the screen.

6. What is a bit-field?

7. Write a program that displays individually the values of the high- and low-order bytes of an integer. (Hint: Use a union that contains as its two elements an integer and a two-byte character array.)

EXERCISES

This section checks how well you have integrated the material in this chapter with that from earlier chapters.

INTEGRATING
NEW SKILLS
CHECK

√

1. Write a program that contains two structure variables defined as

```
struct s_type {
  int i;
  char ch;
  double d;
} var1, var2;
```

   Have the program give each element of both structures initial values, but make sure that the value of the elements differs between the two structures. Using a function called **struct_swap( )**, have the program swap the contents of **var1** with **var2**.

2. As you know from Chapter 9, **fgetc( )** returns an integer value, even though it only reads a character from a file. Write a program that copies one file to another. Assign the return value of **fgetc( )** to a union that contains an integer and character. Use the integer element to check for **EOF**. Write the character element to the destination file. Have the user specify both the source and destination file names on the command line.

3. What is wrong with this fragment?

```
struct s_type {
  int a;
  int b: 2;
  int c: 6;
} var;
  .
  .
  .
scanf("%d", &var);
```

4. In C, as you know, you cannot pass an array to a function as a parameter. However, there is one way around this restriction. If you enclose the array within a structure, the array is passed using the standard call-by-value convention. Write a program that demonstrates this by passing a string inside a structure to a function, altering its contents inside the function and demonstrating that the original string is not altered after the function returns.

CHAPTER OBJECTIVES

11.1 Use the storage class specifiers

11.2 Use the access modifiers

11.3 Define enumerations

11.4 Understand **typedef**

11.5 Use C's bitwise operators

11.6 Master the shift operators

11.7 Understand the **?** operator

11.8 Do more with the assignment operator

11.9 Understand the comma
     operator

11.10 Know the precedence
      summary

·11·
Advanced Data Types and Operators

The C language includes a rich set of data type modifiers that allow you to better fit the type of a variable to the information it will be storing. Also, C includes a number of special operators that permit the creation of very efficient routines. Both of these items are the subject of this chapter.

EXERCISES

Before proceeding, you should be able to answer these questions and perform these exercises.

SKILLS CHECK

√

1. Write a program that uses an array of structures to hold the squares and cubes of the numbers 1 through 10. Display the contents of the array.

2. Write a program that uses a **union** to display as a character the bytes that make up an integer entered by the user.

3. What does this fragment display? (Assume two-byte **int**s and eight-byte **double**s.)

```
union {
   int i;
   double d;
} uvar;

printf("%d", sizeof uvar);
```

4. What is wrong with this fragment?

```
struct {
   int i;
   char str[80];
   double balance;
} svar;

svar->i = 100;
```

5. What is a bit-field?

11.1 USE THE STORAGE CLASS SPECIFIERS

C defines four type modifiers that affect how a variable is stored. They are

auto
extern
register
static

These specifiers precede the type name. Let's look at each now.

The specifier **auto** is completely unnecessary. It is provided in C to allow compatibility with its predecessor, B. Its use is to declare *automatic variables*. Automatic variables are simply local variables, which are **auto** by default. You will almost never see **auto** used in any C program.

Although the programs we have been working with in this book are fairly short, programs in the real world tend to be quite long. As the size of a program grows, it takes longer to compile. For this reason, C allows you to break a program into two or more files. You can separately compile these files and then link them together. (The actual method of separate compilation and linking will be explained in the user's manual for your compiler.) In C, global data may only be declared once. Because global data may need to be accessed by two or more files that form the program, a method of informing the compiler about the global data used by the program must be available. For example, consider the following program, which is split between two files.

```
FILE #1:

#include "stdio.h"

int count;

void f1(void);

void main(void)
{
  int i;

  f1( ); /* set count's value */

  for(i=0; i<count; i++)
    printf("%d ");
}
```

```
FILE #2:

#include "stdlib.h"

void f1(void)
{
  count = rand( );
}
```

If you try to compile the second file, an error will be reported because **count** is not defined. However, you *cannot* change FILE #2 as follows:

```
#include "stdlib.h"

int count;

void f1(void)
{
  count = rand( );
}
```

If you declare **count** a second time, the linker will report a duplicate-symbol error, which means that **count** is defined twice, and the linker doesn't know which to use.

The solution to this problem is C's **extern** specifier. By placing **extern** in front of **count**'s declaration in FILE #2, you are telling the compiler that **count** is an integer declared elsewhere. In other words, using **extern** informs the compiler about the existence and the type of the variable it precedes, but it does not cause storage for that variable to be allocated. The correct version of FILE #2 is

```
#include "stdlib.h"

extern int count;

void f1(void)
{
  count = rand( );
}
```

Although rarely done, it is not incorrect to use **extern** inside a function that uses a global variable defined in that file. For example, the following is valid.

```
#include "stdio.h"

int count;
```

```
void main(void)
{
  extern count;

  count = 10;
  printf("%d", count);
}
```

The reason you will rarely see this use of **extern** is that it is redundant. Whenever the compiler encounters a variable name not defined by the function as a local variable, it assumes that it is global.

One very important storage class specifier is **register**. When you specify a **register** variable you are telling the compiler that you want access to that variable to be as fast as possible. In the original version of C, **register**, which could only be applied to local variables (including formal parameters) of types **int** and **char**, caused the variables to be held in a register of the CPU. (This is how the name **register** came about.) By using a register of the CPU, extremely fast access times are achieved. The ANSI standard has broadened the definition to include all types of variables and has removed the requirement that **register** variables must be held in a CPU register. Instead, the ANSI standard stipulates that a **register** variable will be stored in such a way as to minimize access time. In practice, however, this means that **int** and **char register** variables continue to be held in a CPU register—this is still the fastest way to access them.

No matter what storage method is used, only so many variables can be granted the fastest possible access time. For example, the CPU has a limited number of registers. When fast-access locations are exhausted, the compiler is free to make **register** variables into regular variables. For this reason, you must choose carefully which variables you modify with **register**.

One good choice is to make a frequently used variable, such as the variable that controls a loop, into a **register** variable. The more times a variable is accessed, the greater the increase in performance when its access time is decreased. Generally, you can assume that at least two variables per function can be truly optimized for access speed.

Important: Because a **register** variable may be stored in a register of the CPU, it may not have a memory address. This means that you *cannot* use the & to find the address of a register variable.

When you use the **static** modifier, you can cause the contents of a local variable to be preserved between calls. Also, unlike normal local variables, which are initialized each time a function is entered, a **static** local variable is initialized only once. For example, take a look at this program,

```c
#include "stdio.h"

void f(void);

void main(void)
{
  int i;

  for(i=0; i<10; i++) f( );
}

void f(void)
{
  static int count = 0;

  count++;
  printf("count is %d\n", count);
}
```

which displays the following output.

```
count is 1
count is 2
count is 3
count is 4
count is 5
count is 6
count is 7
count is 8
count is 9
count is 10
```

As you can see, **count** retains its value between function calls. The advantage to using a **static** local variable over a global one is that the **static** local variable is still known to and accessible by only the function in which it is declared.

The **static** modifier may also be used on global variables. When it is, it causes the global variable to be known to and accessible by only the functions in the same file in which it is declared. Not only is a function not declared in the same file as a **static** global variable unable to access that global variable, it does not even know its name. This means that there are no name conflicts if a **static** global variable in one file has the same name as another global variable in a different file of the same program. For example, consider these two fragments, which are parts of the same program.

```
FILE #1                        FILE #2

int count;                     static int count;
.                              .
.                              .
.                              .
count = 10;                    count = 5;
printf("%d", count);           printf("%d", count);
```

Because **count** is declared as **static** in FILE #2, no name conflicts arise. The **printf( )** statement in FILE #1 displays **10** and the **printf( )** statement in FILE #2 displays **5** because the two **count**s are different variables.

Examples

1. To get an idea about how much faster access to a **register** variable is, try the following program. It makes use of another of C's standard library functions called **clock( )**, which returns the number of system clock ticks since the program began execution. It has the prototype

   clock_t clock(void);

   It uses the TIME.H header. TIME.H also defines the **clock_t** type, which is more or less the same as **long**. To time an event using **clock( )**, call it immediately before the event you wish to time and save the value. Next, call it a second time after the event finishes and subtract the starting value from the ending value. This is the approach used by the program to time how long it takes two loops to execute. One set of loops is controlled by a **register** variable, the other is controlled by a non-**register** variable.

   ```
   #include "stdio.h"
   #include "time.h"

   int i;  /* this will not be transformed into a
              register variable because it is global */

   void main(void)
   {
     register int j;
   ```

```
    int k;
    clock_t start, finish;

    start = clock( );
    for(k=0; k<10; k++)
      for(i=0; i<32000; i++) ;
    finish = clock( );
    printf("non-register loop: %ld ticks\n", finish -
start);

    start = clock( );
    for(k=0; k<10; k++)
      for(j=0; j<32000; j++) ;
    finish = clock( );
    printf("register loop: %ld ticks\n", finish - start);
}
```

For most compilers, the **register**-controlled loop will execute about twice as fast as the non-**register** controlled loop.

The non-**register** variable is global because when feasible, many compilers will automatically convert local variables not specified as **register** types into **register** types as an automatic optimization.

2. As you know, the compiler can optimize access speed for only a limited number of **register** variables in any one function (usually, just two). However, this does not mean that your program can only have a few **register** variables. Because of the way a C program executes, each function may utilize **register** variables. For example, for the average compiler, all the variables shown in the next program will be optimized for speed.

```
#include "stdio.h"

void f2(void);
void f(void);

void main(void)
```

```
{
  register int a, b;
  .
  .
  .
}

void f(void)
{
  register int i, j;
  .
  .
  .
}

void f2(void)
{
  register int j, k;
  .
  .
  .
}
```

3. Local **static** variables have several uses. One is to allow a function to perform various initializations only once, when it is first called. For example, consider the function

```
myfunc(void)
{
  static int first = 1;

  if(first) { /* initialize the system */
    rewind(fp);
    a = 0;
    loc = 0;
    fprintf("system initialized");
    first = 0;
  }
  .
  .
  .
}
```

Because **first** is **static**, it will hold its value between calls. Thus, the initialization code will only be executed the first time the function is called.

4. Another interesting use for a local **static** variable is to control a recursive function. For example, this program prints the numbers **1** through **9** on the screen.

```
#include "stdio.h"

void f(void);

void main(void)
{
  f( );
}

void f(void)
{
  static int stop=0;

  stop++;

  if(stop==10) return;
  printf("%d ", stop);
  f( ); /* recursive call */
}
```

Notice how **stop** is used to prevent a recursive call to **f( )** when it equals 10.

5. Here is another example of using **extern** to allow global data to be accessed by two files.

```
FILE #1:

#include "stdio.h"

char str[80];
```

```
void getname(void);

void main(void)
{
  getname( );
  printf("Hello %s", str);
}


FILE #2:

#include "stdio.h"

extern char str[80];

void getname(void)
{
  printf("Enter your first name: ");
  gets(str);
}
```

Exercises

1. Assume that your compiler will actually optimize access time of only two **register** variables per function. In this program, which two variables are the best ones to be made into **register** variables?

```
#include "stdio.h"
#include "conio.h"

void main(void)
{
  int i, j, k, m;

  do {
    printf("Enter a value: ");
    scanf("%d", &i);
```

```
    m = 0;
    for(j=0; j<i; j++)
      for(k=0; k<100; k++)
        m = k + m;
  } while(i>0);
}
```

2. Write a program that contains a function call **sum_it( )** that has this prototype:

   void sum_it(int value);

   Have this function use a local **static** integer variable to maintain and display a running total of the values of the parameters it is called with. For example, if **sum_it( )** is called three times with the values 3, 6, 4, then **sum_it( )** will display 3, 9, and 13.

3. Try the program descibed in Example 5. Be sure to actually use two files. If you are unsure how to compile and link a program consisting of two files, check your user manual.

4. What is wrong with this fragment?

   ```
   register int i;
   int *p;

   p = &i;
   ```

11.2 USE THE ACCESS MODIFIERS

C includes two type modifiers that affect the way variables are accessed by both your program and the compiler. These modifiers are **const** and **volatile**. This section examines these type modifiers.

If you precede a variable's type with **const**, you prevent that variable from being modified by your program. The variable may be given an initial value, however, through the use of an initialization when it is declared. The compiler is free to locate **const** variables in ROM (read-only memory) in environments that support it. A **const** variable may also have its value changed by hardware-dependent means.

The **const** modifier has a second use. It can prevent a function from modifying the object that a parameter points to. That is, when a pointer parameter is preceded by **const**, no statement in the function can modify the variable pointed to by that parameter.

When you precede a variable's type with **volatile**, you are telling the compiler that the value of the variable may be changed in ways not explicitly defined in the program. For example, a variable's address might be given to an interrupt service routine, and its value changed each time an interrupt occurs. The reason that **volatile** is important is that most C compilers apply complex and sophisticated optimizations to your program to create faster and more efficient executable programs. If the compiler does not know that the contents of a variable may change in ways not explicitly specified by the program, it may not actually examine the contents of the variable each time it is referenced. (Unless it occurs on the left side of an assignment statement, of course.)

Examples

1. The following short program shows how a **const** variable can be given an initial value and used in the

program, as long as it is not on the right side of an assignment statement.

```
#include "stdio.h"

void main(void)
{
  const int i = 10;

  printf("%d", i);
}
```

The following program tries to assign i another value. This program will not compile because i cannot be modified by the program.

```
#include "stdio.h"

void main(void)
{
  const int i = 10;

  i = 20;  /* this line is wrong */

  printf("%d", i);

}
```

2. The next program shows how a pointer parameter can be declared as **const** to prevent the object it points to from being modified.

```
#include "stdio.h"

void pr_str(const char *p);

void main(void)
{
  char str[80];

  printf("Enter a string: ");
  gets(str);
```

```
   pr_str(str);
}

void pr_str(const char *p)
{
   while(*p) putchar(*p++);
}
```

   If you change the program as shown here, it will not compile because this version attempts to alter the string pointed to by **p**.

```
#include "stdio.h"
#include "ctype.h"

void pr_str(const char *p);

void main(void)
{
   char str[80];

   printf("Enter a string: ");
   gets(str);
   pr_str(str);
}

void pr_str(const char *p)
{
   while(*p) {
     *p = toupper(*p);   /* this will not compile */
     putchar(*p++);
   }
}
```

3. Perhaps the most important feature of **const** pointer parameters is that they guarantee that many standard library functions do not modify variables pointed to by their parameters. For example, here is the actual prototype to **strlen( )** specified by the ANSI standard:

    int strlen(const char *p);

4. While short examples of **volatile** are hard to find, the following fragment gives you the flavor of its use.

```
volatile unsigned u;

give_address_to_some_interrupt(&u);

for(;;) { /* watch value of u */
  printf("%d", u);
  .
  .
  .
```

In this example, if **u** had not been declared as **volatile**, the compiler could have optimized the repeated calls to **printf( )** in such a way that **u** was not reexamined each time. The use of **volatile** forces the compiler to actually obtain the value of **u** each time.

Exercises

1. One good time to use **const** is when you want to embed a version control number into a program. By using a **const** variable to hold the version, you prevent it from accidentally being changed. Write a short program that illustrates how this can be done. Use 6.01 as the version number.

2. Write your own version of **strcpy( )** called **mystrcpy( )**, which has the prototype

   char *mystrcpy(char *to, const char *from);

   The function returns a pointer to to. Demonstrate your version of **mystrcpy( )** in a program.

3. On your own, see if you can think of any ways to use **volatile**.

11.3 DEFINE ENUMERATIONS

In C you can define a list of named integer constants called an *enumeration*. These constants can then be used any place an integer can. To define an enumeration, use the general form

enum *tag-name* {*enumeration list*} *variable-list*;

Either the *tag-name* or the *variable-list* is optional. The *tag-name* is essentially the type name of the enumeration. Enumeration variables may only contain values that are defined in the enumeration. For example, in the statement

```
enum color_type {red, green, yellow} color;
```

the variable **color** may be assigned only the values **red, green,** or **yellow**.

By default, the compiler assigns integer values to the constants, beginning with 0 at the far left side of the list. Each constant to the right is one greater than the constant that precedes it. Therefore, in the color enumeration, **red** is 0, **green** is 1, and **yellow** is 2. However, you can override the compiler's default values by explicitly giving a constant a value. For example, in this statement

```
enum color_type {red, green=9, yellow} color;
```

red is still 0, but **green** is 9, and **yellow** is 10.

Once you have defined an enumeration, you can use its tag name to declare enumeration variables at other points in the program. For example, assuming the **color_type** enumeration, this statement is perfectly valid and declares **mycolor** as a **color_type** variable.

```
enum color_type mycolor;
```

The main purposes of an enumeration are to help provide self-documenting code and to clarify the structure of your program.

Examples

1. This short program creates an enumeration consisting of the parts of a computer. It assigns **comp** the value **CPU** and then displays its value (which is 1). Notice how the enumeration tag name is used to declare **comp** as an enumeration variable separately from the actual declaration of **computer**.

    ```
    #include "stdio.h"

    enum computer {keyboard, CPU, screen, printer};

    void main(void)
    {
       enum computer comp;

       comp = CPU;

       printf("%d", comp);
    }
    ```

2. It takes a little work to display the string equivalent of an enumerated constant. Remember, enumerated constants are not strings; they are named integer constants. The following program uses a **switch** statement to output the string equivalent of an enumerated value. The program uses C's random-number generator to choose a means of transportation.

It then displays the means on the screen. (This program is for people who can't make up their minds!)

```c
#include "stdio.h"
#include "stdlib.h"
#include "conio.h"

enum transport {car, train, airplane, bus} tp;

void main(void)
{
  printf("Press a key to select transport: ");

  /* generate a new random number each time
     the program is run
  */
  while(!kbhit( )) rand( );
  getch( );  /* read and discard character */

  tp = rand( ) % 4;
  switch(tp) {
    case car: printf("car");
      break;
    case train: printf("train");
      break;
    case airplane: printf("airplane");
      break;
    case bus: printf("bus");
  }
}
```

In some cases, there is an easier way to obtain a string equivalent of an enumerated value. As long as you do not initialize any of the constants, you can create a two-dimensional string array that contains the string equivalents of the enumerated values in the same order as the constants appear in the enumeration. Then you can simply index the array using an enumeration variable to obtain the string. The following version of the transportation-choosing program, for example, uses this approach.

```c
#include "stdio.h"
#include "stdlib.h"
#include "conio.h"

enum transport {car, train, airplane, bus} tp;

char trans[][20] = {
  "car", "train", "airplane", "bus"
} ;

void main(void)
{
  printf("Press a key to select transport: ");

  /* generate a new random number each time
     the program is run
  */
  while(!kbhit( )) rand( );
  getch( );  /* read and discard character */

  tp = rand( ) % 4;
  printf("%s", trans[tp]);
}
```

3. Remember, the names of enumerated constants are known only to the program, not to any library functions. For example, given the fragment

```c
enum numbers {zero, one, two, three} num;

printf("Enter a number: ");
scanf("%d", &num);
```

you cannot respond to **scanf( )** by entering **one**.

Exercises

1. Compile and run the example programs.

2. Create an enumeration of the coins of the U.S. from penny to dollar.

3. Is this fragment correct? If not, why not?

```
enum cars {Ford, Chrysler, GM} make;

make = GM;
printf("car is %s", make);
```

11.4 UNDERSTAND typedef

In C you can create a new name for an existing type using **typedef**. The general form of **typedef** is

typedef *old-name new-name*;

This new name can be used to declare variables. For example, in the following program, **smallint** is a new name for a **signed char** and is used to declare **i**.

```
#include "stdio.h"

typedef signed char smallint;

void main(void)
{
  smallint i;

  for(i=0; i<10; i++)
    printf("%d ", i);
}
```

Keep two points firmly in mind: First, a **typedef** does not cause the original name to be deactivated. For example, in the program, **signed char** is still a valid type. Second, you can use several **typedef** statements to create many different, new names for the same type.

There are basically two reasons to use **typedef**. The first is to create portable programs. For example, if you know that you will be writing a program that will be executed on computers using 16-bit integers as well as on computers using 32-bit integers, and you want to ensure that certain variables are 16 bits long, no matter which machine is executing, you might want to use a **typedef** when compiling the program for the 16-bit machines as follows:

```
typedef int myint;
```

Then, before compiling the code for a 32-bit computer, you can change the **typedef** statement like this:

```
typedef short int myint;
```

This works because on computers using 32-bit integers, a **short int** will be 16 bits long. Assuming that you used **myint** to declare all integer values that you wanted to be 16 bits long, you need change only one statement to change the type of all variables declared using **myint**.

The second reason you might want to use **typedef** is to help provide self-documenting code. For example, if you are writing an inventory program, you might use this **typedef** statement

```
typedef double subtotal;
```

Now, when anyone reading your program sees a variable declared as **subtotal**, he or she will know that it is used to hold a subtotal.

Examples

1. The new name created by one **typedef** can be used in a subsequent **typedef** to create another name. For example, consider this fragment.

```
typedef int height;
typedef height length;
typedef length depth;

depth d;
```

Here, **d** is still an integer.

2. You can use **typedef** on a complex type as well as the basic types. For example, the following is perfectly valid.

```
enum e_type { one, two, three } ;

typedef e_type mynums;

mynums num;   /* declare a variable */
```

Here, **num** is a variable of type **e_type**.

Exercises

1. Show how to make **UL** a new name for **unsigned long**. Show that it works by writting a short program that declares a variable using **UL**, assigns it a value, and displays the value on the screen.

2. What is wrong with this fragment?

```
typedef balance float;
```

11.5 USE C'S BITWISE OPERATORS

C contains three special operators that perform their operations on a bit-by-bit level. These operators are

    &   bitwise AND
    | bitwise OR
    ^   bitwise XOR (eXclusive OR)
    ~   1's complement

These operators work with character and integer types; they cannot be used with floating-point types.

The AND, OR, and XOR operators produce a result based upon a comparison of corresponding bits in each operand. The AND operator sets a bit if both bits being compared are set. The OR sets a bit if either of the bits being compared are set. The XOR operation sets a bit when either of the two bits involved are 1, but not when both are 1 or both are 0. For example, here is an example of a bitwise AND.

```
  1010 0110
& 0011 1011
  ---------
  0010 0010
```

Notice how the resulting bit is set, based on the outcome of the operation being applied to the corresponding bits in each operand.

The 1's complement operator is a unary operator that reverses the state of each bit within an integer or character.

Examples

1. The XOR operation has one interesting property. When the outcome of an XOR operation is XORed with the same value a second time, the initial value is produced. For example, this output.

```
initial value of i: 100
i after first XOR: 21895
i after second XOR: 100
```

   is produced by the following program:

```c
#include "stdio.h"

void main(void)
{
  int i;

  i = 100;
  printf("initial value of i: %d\n", i);

  i = i ^ 21987;
  printf("i after first XOR: %d\n", i);

  i = i ^ 21987;
  printf("i after second XOR: %d\n", i);
}
```

2. The following program uses a bitwise AND to display, in binary, the ASCII value of a character typed at the keyboard.

```c
#include "stdio.h"
#include "conio.h"

void main(void)
{
  char ch;
  int i;
```

```
   printf("Enter a character: ");
   ch = getche( );
   printf("\n");

   /* display binary representation */
   for(i=128; i>0; i=i/2)
     if(i & ch) printf("1 ");
     else printf("0 ");
}
```

The program works by adjusting the value of **i** so that only one bit is set each time a comparison is made. Since the high-order bit in a byte represents 128, this value is used as a starting point. Each time through the loop, **i** is halved. This causes the next bit position to be set and all others cleared. Thus, each time through the loop, a bit in **ch** is tested. If it is 1, the comparison produces a true result and a **1** is output. Otherwise a **0** is displayed. This process continues until all bits have been tested.

3. By modifying the program from Example 2, it can be used to show the effect of the 1's complement operator.

```
#include "stdio.h"
#include "conio.h"

void main(void)
{
   char ch;
   int i;

   ch = 'a';

   /* display binary representation */
   for(i=128; i>0; i=i/2)
     if(i & ch) printf("1 ");
     else printf("0 ");

   /* reverse bit pattern */
```

```
ch = ~ch;
printf("\n");

/* display binary representation */
for(i=128; i>0; i=i/2)
  if(i & ch) printf("1 ");
  else printf("0 ");
}
```

When you run this program, you will see that the state of bits in **ch** are reversed after the ~ operation has occurred.

4. The following program shows how to use the & operator to determine if a signed integer is positive or negative. (The program assumes 16-bit integers.) Since negative numbers are represented with their high-order bits set, the comparison will only be true if **i** is negative. (The value 32768 is the value of an unsigned integer when only its high-order bit is set. This value is 1000 0000 in binary.)

```
#include "stdio.h"

void main(void)
{
  int i;

  printf("Enter a number: ");
  scanf("%d", &i);

  if(i & 32768) printf("number is negative");
}
```

5. The following program makes **i** into a negative number by setting its high-order bit.

```
#include "studio.h"

void main(void)
{
  int i;
```

```
   i = 1;
   i = i | 32768;
   printf("%d", i);
}
```

It displays **–32,767**.

Exercises

1. One very easy way to encode a file is to reverse the state of each bit using the ~ operator. Write a program that encodes a file using this method. (To decode the file, simply run the program a second time.) Have the user specify the name of the file on the command line.

2. A better method of coding a file uses the XOR operation combined with a user-defined key. Write a program that encodes a file using this method. Have the user specify the file to code as well as a single character key on the command line. (To decode the file, run the program a second time using the same key.)

3. What is the outcome of these operations?

   a. 1010 0011 & 0101 1101

   b. 0101 1101 | 1111 1011

   c. 0101 0110 ^ 1010 1011

4. Sometimes, the high-order bit of a byte is used as a *parity bit* by modem programs. It is used to verify the integrity of each byte transferred. There are two types of parity: even and odd. If even parity is used, the parity bit is used to ensure that each byte has an

even number of 1 bits. If odd parity is used, the parity bit is used to ensure that each byte has an odd number of 1 bits. Since the parity bit is not part of the information being transferred, show how you can clear the high-order bit of a character value.

11.6 MASTER THE SHIFT OPERATORS

C includes two operators not commonly found in other computer languages: the left and right bit-shift operators. The left shift operator is <<, and the right shift operator is >>. These operators may be applied only to character or integer operands. They take these general forms.

variable << integer-expression
variable >> integer-expression

The value of the integer expression determines how many places to the left or right the bits within the variable are shifted. Each left-shift causes all bits within the specified variable to be shifted left one position and a zero is brought in on the right. A right-shift shifts all bits to the right one position and brings a zero in on the left. When bits are shifted off and end, they are lost.

A right shift is equivalent to dividing a number by 2, and a left shift is the same as multiplying the number by 2. However, because of the internal operation of virtually all CPUs, shift operations are faster than their equivalent arithmetic operations.

Examples

1. This program demonstrates the right and left shift operators.

```
#include "stdio.h"

void show_binary(unsigned u);

void main(void)
{
  unsigned u;

  u = 45678;

  show_binary(u);
  u = u << 1;
  show_binary(u);
  u = u >> 1;
  show_binary(u);
}

void show_binary(unsigned u)
{
  unsigned long l;

  for(l=32768; l>0; l=l/2)
    if(u & l) printf("1 ");
    else printf("0 ");

  printf("\n");
}
```

The output from this program is

```
1 0 1 1 0 0 1 0 0 1 1 0 1 1 1 0
0 1 1 0 0 1 0 0 1 1 0 1 1 1 0 0
0 0 1 1 0 0 1 0 0 1 1 0 1 1 1 0
```

Notice that after the left shift, a bit of information has been lost. When the right shift occurs, a zero is brought in. As stated earlier, bits that are shifted off one end are lost.

2. Since a right shift is the same as a division by two, but faster, the **show_binary( )** function can be made more efficient as shown here.

```
void show_binary(unsigned u)
{
  unsigned l;

  for(l=32768; l; l=l>>1)
    if(u & l) printf("1 ");
    else printf("0 ");

  printf("\n");
}
```

Exercises

1. Write a program that uses the shift operators to multiply and divide an integer. Have the user enter the initial value. Display the result of each operation.

2. C does not have a rotate operator. A *rotate* is similar to a shift, except that the bit shifted off one end is inserted onto the other. For example, 1010 0000 shifted left one place is 0100 0001. Write a function called **rotate( )** that rotates a byte left one position each time it is called. (Hint, you will need to use a **union** so that you can have access to the bit shifted off the end of the byte.) Demonstrate the function in a program.

11.7 UNDERSTAND THE ? OPERATOR

C contains one ternary operator: the **?**. A *ternary operator* requires three operands. The **?** operator is used to replace statements such as

```
if(condition) var = exp1;
else var = exp2;
```

The general form of the **?** operator is

var = condition ? exp1: exp2;

Here, *condition* is an expression that evaluates to true or false. If it is true, *var* is assigned the value of *exp1*. If it is false, *var* is assigned the value of *exp2*. The reason for the **?** operator is that a C compiler can produce more efficient code using it instead of the equivalent **if/else** statement.

Examples

1. The following program illustrates the **?** operator. It inputs a number and then converts the number into 1 if the number is positive and −1 if it is negative.

    ```c
    #include "stdio.h"

    void main(void)
    {
      int i;

      printf("Enter a number: ");
      scanf("%d", &i);

      i = i>0 ? 1: -1;

      printf("%d", i);
    }
    ```

2. The next program is a computerized coin toss. It waits for you to press a key and then prints either **heads** or **tails**.

    ```c
    #include "stdio.h"
    #include "stdlib.h"
    ```

```
#include "conio.h"

void main(void)
{
   int i;

   while(!kbhit( )) rand( );

   i = rand( )%2 ? 1: 0;

   if(i) printf("heads");
   else printf("tails");
}
```

The coin-toss program can be written in a more efficient way. There is no technical reason that the **?** operator need assign its value to any variable. Therefore, the coin toss program can be written as

```
#include "stdio.h"
#include "stdlib.h"
#include "conio.h"

void main(void)
{
   while(!kbhit( )) rand( );

   rand( )%2 ? printf("heads"): printf("tails");
}
```

Remember, since a call to a function is a valid C expression, it is perfectly valid to call **printf( )** in the **?** statement.

Exercises

1. One particularly good use for the **?** operator is to provide a means of preventing a division-by-zero error. Write a program that inputs two integers from the user and displays the result of dividing the first by the second. Use **?** to avoid division by zero.

2. Convert the following statement into its equivalent **?** statement.

```
if(a>b) count = 100;
else count = 0;
```

11.8 DO MORE WITH THE ASSIGNMENT OPERATOR

The assignment operator is more powerful in C than in most other computer languages. In this section, you will learn some new things about assignments.

You can assign several variables the same value using the general form

$$var1 = var2 = var3 =...= varN = value;$$

For example, this statement

```
i = j = k = 100;
```

assigns **i**, **j**, and **k** the value 100. In professionally written C code, it is common to see such multiple-variable assignments.

Another variation on the assignment statement is sometimes called C *shorthand*. In C, you can transform a statement like

```
a = a + 3;
```

into a statement like

```
a += 3;
```

In general, any time you have a statement of the form

var = var *op* expression;

You can write it in shorthand form as

var *op*= expression;

Here, *op* is one of the following operators.

```
+
-
*
/
%
<<
>>
&
|
^
```

There must be no space between the operator and the equal sign. The reason you will want to use the shorthand form is not that it saves you a little typing effort, but because the C compiler can create more efficient executable code.

Examples

1. The following program illustrates the multiple-assignment statement.

```
#include "stdio.h"

void main(void)
{
  int i, j, k;

  i = j = k = 99;

  printf("%d %d %d", i, j, k);
}
```

2. The next program counts to 98 by twos. Notice that it uses C shorthand to increment the loop-control variable by two each iteration.

```
#include "stdio.h"

void main(void)
{
  int i;

  /* count by 2s */
  for(i=0; i<100; i+=2)
    printf("%d ", i);
}
```

3. The following program uses the left-shift operator in shorthand form to multiply the value of **i** by 2, three times. (The resulting value is 8.)

```
#include "stdio.h"

void main(void)
{
  int i = 1;

  i <<= 3;  /* multiply by 2, 3 times */

  printf("%d", i);
}
```

Exercises

1. Compile and run the program in Example 1 to prove to yourself that the multiple-assignment statement works.

2. How is the following statement written using C shorthand?

   ```
   x = x & y;
   ```

3. Write a program that displays all the even multiples of 17 from 17 to 1000. Use C shorthand.

11.9 UNDERSTAND THE COMMA OPERATOR

The last operator we will examine is the comma. It has a very unique function: it tells the compiler to "do this and this and this." That is, the comma is used to string together several operations. The most common use of the comma is in the **for** loop. In the following loop, the comma is used in the initialization portion to initialize two loop-control variables, and in the increment portion to increment **i** and decrement **j**.

```
for(i=0, j=0; i+j<count; i++, j++) . . .
```

The value of a comma-separated list of expressions is the rightmost expression. For example, the following statement assigns 100 to **value**.

```
value = (count, 99, 33, 100);
```

The parentheses are necessary because the comma operator is lower in precedence than the assignment operator.

Examples

1. This program displays the numbers 0 through 49. It uses the comma operator to maintain two loop-control variables.

    ```c
    #include "stdio.h"

    void main(void)
    {
      int i, j;

      /* count to 49 */
      for(i=0, j=100; i<j; i++, j--)
        printf("%d ", i);
    }
    ```

2. In many places in C, it is actually syntactically correct to use the comma in place of the semicolon. For example, examine the following short program.

    ```c
    #include "stdio.h"
    #include "conio.h"

    void main(void)
    {
      char ch;

      ch = getch( ),   /* notice the comma here */
      putchar(ch+1);
    }
    ```

Because the comma tells the compiler to "do this and this," the program runs the same with the comma after **getch( )** as it would had a semicolon been used. Using a comma in this way is considered extremely bad form, however. It is possible that an unwanted side effect could occur. (This use of the comma operator *does* make interesting coffee-break conversion, however! Many C programmers are not aware of this interesting twist in the C syntax.)

Exercises

1. Write a program that uses the comma operator to maintain three **for** loop-control variables. Have one variable run from 0 to 99, the second run from –50 to 49, and have the third set to the sum of the first two, both initially and each time the loop iterates. Have the loop stop when the first variable reaches 100. Have the program display the value of the third variable each time the loop repeats.

2. What is the value of **i** after the following statement executes?

    ```
    i = (1, 2, 3);
    ```

11.10 KNOW THE PRECEDENCE SUMMARY

The following table shows the precedence of all the C operators.

Highest   ( ) [] -> .

            ! ~ ++ -- - (type cast) * & sizeof

            * / %

            + -

            << >>

            < <= > >=

            == !=

            &

            ^

            |

            &&

            ||

            ?

            = += -= *= /=

Lowest   ,

EXERCISES

At this point you should be able to answer these questions and perform these exercises.

MASTERY
SKILLS CHECK

√

1. What does the **register** specifier do?

2. What do the **const** and **volatile** modifiers do?

3. Write a program that sums the numbers 1 to 100. Make the program execute as fast as possible.

4. Is this statement valid? If so, what does it do?

    ```
    typedef long double bigfloat;
    ```

5. Write a program that inputs two characters and compares corresponding bits. Have the program display the number of each bit in which a match occurs. For example, if the two integers are

    1001 0110
    1110 1010

the program will report that bits 7, 1, and 0 match. (Use the bitwise operators to solve this problem.)

6. What do the << and >> operators do?

7. Show how this statement can be rewritten.

```
c = c + 10;
```

8. Rewrite this statement using the **?** operator.

```
if(!done) count = 100;
else count = 0;
```

9. What is an enumeration? Show an example that enumerates the planets.

EXERCISES

This section checks how well you have integrated the material in this chapter with that from earlier chapters.

INTEGRATING NEW SKILLS CHECK

1. Write a program that swaps the low-order four bits of a byte with the high-order four bits. Demonstrate that your routine works by displaying the contents of the byte before and after, using the **show_binary( )** function developed earlier. (Change **show_binary( )** so that it works on an eight-bit quantity, however.)

2. Earlier you wrote a program that encoded files using the 1s complement operator. Write a program that reads a text file encoded using this method and displays its decoded contents. Leave the actual file encoded, however.

3. Is this fragment correct?

```
register FILE *fp;
```

4. Using the program you developed for Chapter 10, Section 10.3, Exercise 1, optimize the program by selecting appropriate local variables to become **register** types.

CHAPTER OBJECTIVES

12.1 Learn more about **#define** and **#include**

12.2 Understand conditonal compilation

12.3 Learn about **#error**, **#undef**, **#line**, and **#pragma**

12.4 Examine C's built-in macros

12.5 Use the # and ## operators

12.6 Understand function pointers

12.7 Master dynamic allocation

·12·

The C Preprocessor and Some Advanced Topics

Congratulations! If you have worked your way through all the preceding chapters, you can definitely call yourself a C programmer. This chapter examines three topics: the C preprocessor, pointers to functions, and C's dynamic allocation system. All of the features discussed in this chapter are important, and you need to be aware of their existence. However, you won't use many of them right away. This is not because any of the features discussed in this chapter are particularly difficult, but because some features are more applicable to large programming efforts and the management of sophisticated systems. As your proficiency in C increases, however, you will begin to make use of them.

EXERCISES

Before proceeding you should be able to answer these questions and perform these exercises.

1. What is the major advantage gained when a variable is declared using **register**?

2. What is wrong with this function?

```
void myfunc(const *i)
{
   *i = *i / 2;
}
```

3. What is the outcome of these operations?

   a. 1101 1101 & 1110 0110

   b. 1101 1101 | 1110 0110

   c. 1101 1101 ^ 1110 0110

4. Write a program that uses the left and right shift operators to double and halve a number entered by the user.

5. How can these statements be written differently?

```
a = 1;
b = 1;
c = 1;

if(a<b) max = 100;
else max = 0;

i = i * 2;
```

6. What is the **extern** type specifier for?

12.1 LEARN MORE ABOUT #define AND #include

Although you have been using **#define** and **#include** for some time, both have more features than you currently know. This section covers these features.

In addition to using **#define** to simply define a macro name that will be substituted by the string associated with that macro, you can use **#define** to create *function-like macros*. In a function-like macro, arguments can be passed to the macro when it is expanded by the preprocessor. For example, consider this program.

```
#include "stdio.h"

#define SUM(i, j) i+j

void main(void)
{
  int sum;

  sum = SUM(10, 20);
  printf("%d", sum);
}
```

The line

```
sum = SUM(10, 20);
```

is transformed into

```
sum = 10+20;
```

by the preprocessor. As you can see, the values 10 and 20 are automatically substituted for the parameters **i** and **j** by the preprocessor.

A more practical example is **RANGE( )**, illustrated in the following simple program. It is used to confirm that parameter **i** is within the range specified by parameters **min** and **max**. You can imagine how useful a macro like **RANGE** can be in programs that must perform several range checks. This program uses it to display random numbers between 1 and 100.

```
#include "stdio.h"
#include "conio.h"
#include "stdlib.h"

#define RANGE(i, min, max)  (i<min) || (i>max) ? 1 : 0

void main(void)
{
  int r;

  /* print random numbers between 1 and 100 */
  do {
    do {
      r = rand( );
    } while(RANGE(r, 1, 100));
    printf("%d ", r);
  } while(!kbhit( ));
}
```

The advantage to using function-like macros instead of functions is that in-line code is generated by the macro, thus avoiding the time it takes to call and return from a function. Of course, only relatively simple operations can be made into function-like macros. Also, because code is duplicated, the resulting program will usually be longer than it would be if a function were used.

The **#include** directive actually has these two general forms

#include *"filename"*
#include *<filename>*

So far, all the example programs have used the first form. The reason for this will become apparent after you read the following descriptions.

If you specify the file name between angle brackets, you are instructing the compiler to search for the file in some implementation-defined manner. For most compilers, this means searching a special directory devoted to header files. If you enclose the file name between quotes, the compiler searches for the file in another implementation-defined manner. If that search fails, the search is restarted as if you had specified the file name between angle brackets. For the majority of compilers, enclosing the name between quotes causes the current working directory to be searched first.

The examples in this book have used quotes because there is a greater likelihood of finding the header file with this form. Often beginning C programmers do not configure their C compiler the way the compiler expects. Using quotes, therefore, helps make sure that the header files are found. If you know that you have correctly configured your system, feel free to use the angle brackets, because this form may speed up compile times slightly.

Examples

1. Here is a program that uses the function-like macro **MAX** to compute which argument is larger. Pay close attention to the last **printf( )** statement.

```
#include "stdio.h"

#define MAX(i, j) i>j ? i: j

void main(void)
{
  printf("%d\n", MAX(1, 2));
  printf("%d\n", MAX(1, -1));

  /* this statement does not work correctly */
  printf("%d\n", MAX(100 || -1, 0));
}
```

When the preprocessor expands the final **printf( )** statement, the **MAX** macro is transformed into the expression

```
100 || -1 > 0 ? 100 || -1 : 0
```

Because of C's precedence rules, however, this expression is executed as if these parentheses

```
100 || (-1 > 0) ? 100 || -1 : 0
```

had been added. As you can see, this causes the wrong answer to be computed. To fix this problem, the macro needs to be rewritten as

```
#define MAX(i, j) ((i)>(j)) ? (i) : (j)
```

Now the macro works in all possible situations. In general, you will need to fully parenthesize all parameters to a function-like macro.

Note: The **RANGE( )** macro discussed earlier will need similar parenthesization as well if it is to work in all possible situations. This is left as an exercise.

2. The next program uses angle brackets in the **#include** directive.

```
#include <stdio.h>

void main(void)
```

```
{
  printf("This is a test");
}
```

3. It is permissible to use both forms of the **#include** directive in the same program. For example,

```
#include <stdio.h>
#include "stdlib.h"

void main(void)
{
  printf("This is a random number: %d", rand( ));
}
```

Exercises

1. Correct the **RANGE( )** macro by adding parentheses in the proper locations.

2. Write a program that uses a parameterized macro to compute the absolute value of an integer. Demonstrate its use in a program.

3. Compile Example 2. If your compiler does not find STDIO.H, recheck the installation instructions that came with your compiler.

12.2 UNDERSTAND CONDITIONAL COMPILATION

The C preprocessor includes several directives that allow parts of the source code of a program to be selectively compiled. This is called *conditional compilation*. These directives are

#if
#else
#elif
#endif
#ifdef
#ifndef

This section examines these directives.

The general form of **#if** is shown here

#if *constant-expression*
    statement-sequence
#endif

If the value of the *constant-expression* is true, the statement or statements between **#if** and **#endif** are compiled. If the *constant-expression* is false, the compiler skips the statement or statements. Keep in mind that the preprocessing stage is the first stage of compilation, so the *constant-expression* means exactly that. No variables may be used.

You can use the **#else** to form an alternative to the **#if**. Its general form is shown here.

#if *constant-expression*
    statement-sequence
#else
    statement-sequence
#endif

Notice that there is only one **#endif**. The **#else** automatically terminates the **#if** block of statements. If the *constant-expression* is false, the statement or statements associated with the **#else** are compiled.

You can create an if-else-if ladder using the **#elif** directive, as shown here.

```
#if constant-expression-1
    statement-sequence
#elif constant-expression-2
    statement-sequence
#elif constant-expression-3
    statement-sequence
    .
    .
    .
#endif
```

As soon as the first expression is true, the lines of code associated with that expression are compiled, and the rest of the code is skipped.

Another approach to conditional compilation is the **#ifdef** directive. It has the general form

```
#ifdef macro-name
    statement-sequence
#endif
```

If the *macro-name* is currently defined, then the *statement-sequence* associated with the **#ifdef** directive will be compiled. Otherwise, it is skipped. The **#else** may also be used with **#ifdef** to provide an alternative. However, **#elif** may not be used.

The complement of **#ifdef** is **#ifndef**. It has the same general form as **#ifdef**. The only difference is that the statement sequence associated with an **#ifndef** directive is compiled only if the *macro-name* is *not* defined.

Examples

1. Sometimes you will want a program's behavior to depend on a parameter in the program. Although examples that are both short and meaningful are hard to find, the following program gives the flavor of it. This program can be compiled to display either the ASCII character set by itself, or the full extended set, depending on the value of **CHAR_SET**. As you know, the ASCII character set defines characters for the values 0 through 127. However, most computers reserve the values 128 through 255 for foreign-language characters and mathematical and other special symbols. (You might want to try this program with **CHAR_SET** set to 256. You will see some very interesting characters!)

```c
#include "stdio.h"

/* define CHAR_SET as either 256 or 128 */
#define CHAR_SET 256

void main(void)
{
  int i;
#if CHAR_SET == 256
  printf("displaying full ASCII character set plus
    extensions");
#else
  printf("displaying only ASCII character set");
#endif

  printf("\n");
  for(i=0; i<CHAR_SET; i++)
    printf("%c", i);
}
```

2. A good use of **#ifdef** is for imbedding debugging information into your programs. For example, here

is a program that copies the contents of one file into another.

```c
/* Copy a file. */
#include "stdio.h"
#include "stdlib.h"

#define DEBUG

void main(int argc, char *argv[])
{
  FILE *from, *to;
  char ch;

  /* see if correct number of command line
     arguments
  */
  if(argc!=3) {
    printf("Usage: copy <source> <destination>\n");
    exit(1);
  }

  /* open source file */
  if((from = fopen(argv[1], "rb"))==NULL) {
    printf("Cannot open source file\n");
    exit(1);
  }

  /* open destination file */
  if((to = fopen(argv[2], "wb"))==NULL) {
    printf("Cannot open file\n");
    exit(1);
  }

  /* copy the file */
  while(!feof(from)) {
    ch = fgetc(from);
    if(ferror(from)) {
      printf("error reading source file\n");
      exit(1);
    }
    if(!feof(from)) {
```

```
        fputc(ch, to);
#ifdef DEBUG
        putchar(ch);
#endif
    }
    if(ferror(to)) {
        printf("error writing destination file\n");
        exit(1);
    }
  }
  fclose(from);
  fclose(to);
}
```

If **DEBUG** is defined, the program displays each byte as it is transferred. This can be helpful during the development phase. Once the program is finished, the statement defining **DEBUG** is removed, and the output is not displayed. However, if the program ever misbehaves in the future, **DEBUG** can be defined again, and output will be shown on the screen. While this might seem like a lot of work for such a simple program, in actual practice programs may have many debugging statements, and this procedure can greatly facilitate the development and testing cycle.

Note: As shown in this program, to simply define a macro name, you do not have to associate any string with it.

3. Continuing with the debugging theme, it is possible to use the **#if** to allow several levels of debugging code to be easily managed. For example, here is one of the encryption programs from the answers to Chapter 11 that supports three debugging levels.

```
#include "stdio.h"
#include "stdlib.h"

/* DEBUG levels:
```

```
          0: no debug
          1: display byte read from source file
          2: display byte written to destination file
          3: display bytes read and bytes written
*/
#define DEBUG 2

void main(int argc, char *argv[])
{
  FILE *in, *out;
  unsigned char ch;

  if(argc!=4) {
    printf("Usage: code <in> <out> <key>");
    exit(1);
  }

  if((in = fopen(argv[1], "rb"))==NULL) {
    printf("cannot open input file");
    exit(1);
  }

  if((out = fopen(argv[2], "wb"))==NULL) {
    printf("cannot open output file");
    exit(1);
  }

  while(!feof(in)) {
    ch = fgetc(in);
#if DEBUG == 1 || DEBUG == 3
    putchar(ch);
#endif
    ch = *argv[3] ^ ch;
#if DEBUG >= 2
    putchar(ch);
#endif
    if(!feof(in)) fputc(ch, out);
  }

  fclose(in);
  fclose(out);
}
```

4. The following fragment illustrates the **#elif**. It displays **NUM is 2** on the screen.

```
#define NUM 2

    .

    .

    .


#if NUM == 1
   printf("NUM is 1");
#elif NUM == 2
   printf("NUM is 2");
#elif NUM == 3
   printf("NUM is 3");
#else NUM == 4
   printf("NUM is 4");
#endif
```

Exercises

1. Write a program that defines three macros called **INT, FLOAT,** and **PWR_TYPE**. Define **INT** as 0, **FLOAT** as 1, and **PWR_TYPE** as either **INT** or **FLOAT**. Have the program request two numbers from the user and display the result of the first number raised to the second number. Using **#if** and depending upon the value of **PWR_TYPE**, have both numbers be integers, or allow the first number to be a **double**.

2. Is this fragment correct? If not, show one way to fix it.

```
#define MIKE

#ifdef !MIKE
    .

    .

    .
#endif
```

12.3 LEARN ABOUT #error, #undef, #line, AND #pragma

C's preprocessor supports four seldom-used directives: **#error**, **#undef**, **#line**, and **#pragma**. Each will be examined in turn here.

The **#error** directive has the general form

#error *error-message*

It causes the compiler to stop compilation and issue the *error-message* along with other implementation-specific information, which will generally include the number of the line the **#error** directive is in and the name of the file. Note that the *error-message* is not enclosed between quotes. The principle use of the **#error** directive is in debugging.

The **#undef** directive undefines a *macro-name*. Its general form is

#undef *macro-name*

If the *macro-name* is currently undefined, **#undef** has no effect. The principal use for **#undef** is to localize macro-names.

When a C compiler compiles a source file, it maintains two pieces of information: the number of the line currently being compiled and the name of the source file currently being compiled. The **#line** directive is used to change these values. Its general form is

#line *line-num* "*filename*"

Here, *line-num* becomes the number of the next line of source code, and *filename* becomes the name the compiler will associate with the source file. The value of *line-num* must be between 1 and 32,767. The *filename* may be a string consisting of any valid file name. The principle use for **#line** is for debugging and for managing large projects.

The **#pragma** directive allows a compiler's implementor to define other preprocessing instructions to be given to the compiler. It has the general form

#pragma instructions

If a compiler encounters a **#pragma** statement that it does not recognize, it ignores it. Whether your compiler supports any **#pragmas** depends on how your compiler was implemented.

Examples

1. This program demonstrates the **#error** directive.

    ```
    #include "stdio.h"

    void main(void)
    {
      int i;

      i = 10;
    #error this is an error message
      printf("%d", i);  /* this line will not be compiled */
    }
    ```

    As soon as the **#error** directive is encountered, compilation stops.

2. The next program demonstrates the **#undef** directive. As the program states, only the first **printf( )** statement is compiled.

```
#include "stdio.h"

#define DOG

void main(void)
{
#ifdef DOG
  printf("DOG is defined");
#endif

#undef DOG

#ifdef DOG
  printf("this line is not compiled");
#endif
}
```

3. The following program demonstrates the **#line** directive. Since virtually all implementations of **#error** display the line number and name of the file, it is used here to verify that **#line** did, in fact, perform its function correctly. (In the next section, you will see how a C program can directly access the line number and file name).

```
#include "stdio.h"

void main(void)
{
  int i;

/* reset line number to 1000 and file name to
   myprog.c
*/
#line 1000 "myprog.c"
#error check the line number and file name
}
```

4. Although the ANSI standard does not specify any **#pragma** directives, on your own check your compiler's user manual and learn about any supported by your system.

Exercises

1. Try the example programs. See how these directives work on your system.

12.4 EXAMINE C's BUILT-IN MACROS

If your C compiler complies with the ANSI C standard, it will have at least five predefined macro names that your program may use. They are

```
_ _LINE_ _
_ _FILE_ _
_ _DATE_ _
_ _TIME_ _
_ _STDC_ _
```

Each of these is examined here.

The _ _LINE_ _ macro contains an integer value that is equivalent to the line number of the source line currently being compiled.

The _ _FILE_ _ macro defines a string that is the name of the file currently being compiled.

The _ _DATE_ _ macro defines a string that holds the current system date. The string has the general form

month / day / year

The _ _TIME_ _ macro defines a string that contains the time the compilation of a program began. The string has the general form

hours:minutes:seconds

The _ _STDC_ _ is defined as the value 1 if the compiler conforms to the ANSI standard.

Note: You may not undefine a predifined macro using **#undef**.

Examples

1. This program demonstrates the macros _ _LINE_ _, _ _FILE_ _, _ _DATE_ _, and _ _TIME_ _.

```
#include "stdio.h"

void main(void)
{
  printf("Compiling %s, line: %d, on %s, at %s",
         _ _FILE_ _, _ _LINE_ _, _ _DATE_ _, _ _TIME_ _);
}
```

It is important to understand that the values of the macros are fixed at compile time. For example, if the following program is called T.C, and it is compiled on July 3, 1995, at 10 A.M., it will always display this output no matter when the program is run.

```
Compiling T.C, line: 6, on Jul 3 1995, at 10:00:00
```

The main use of of these macros is to create a *time and date stamp*, which shows when the program was compiled.

2. As you learned in the previous section, you can use the **#line** directive to change the number of the current line of source code and the name of the file. When you do this, you are actually changing the values of _ _LINE_ _ and _ _FILE_ _. For example, this program sets _ _LINE_ _ to 100 and _ _FILE_ _ to **myprog.c**.

```
#include "stdio.h"

void main(void)
{
#line 100 "myprog.c"
  printf("Compiling %s, line: %d, on %s, at %s",
          _ _FILE_ _, _ _LINE_ _, _ _DATE_ _, _ _TIME_ _);
}
```

The program displays the following output, assuming it was compiled on July 3, 1995, at 10 A.M.

```
Compiling myprog.c, line: 101, on Jul 3 1995, at 10:00:00
```

Exercise

1. Compile and run the example programs.

12.5 USE THE # AND ## OPERATORS

The C preprocessor contains two little-used but potentially valuable operators: # and ##. The # operator turns the argument of a function-like macro into a quoted string. The ## operator concatenates two identifiers.

Examples

1. This program demonstrates the # operator.

    ```
    #include "stdio.h"

    #define MKSTRING(str)  # str

    void main(void)
    ```

```
{
  int value;

  value = 10;

  printf("%s is %d", MKSTRING(value), value);
}
```

The program displays **value is 10**. This output occurs because **MKSTRING( )** causes the identifier **value** to be made into a quoted string.

2. The following program demonstrates the **##** operator. It creates the **output( )** macro, which translates into a call to **printf( )**. The value of two variables, which end in 1 or 2, is displayed.

```
#include "stdio.h"

#define output(i)  printf("%d %d\n", i ## 1, i ## 2)
void main(void)
{
  int count1, count2;
  int i1, i2;

  count1 = 10;
  count2 = 20;
  i1 = 99;
  i2 = -10;

  output(count);
  output(i);
}
```

The program displays **10 20 99 –1**. In the calls to **output( )**, **count** and **i** are concatenated with 1 and 2 to form the variable names **count1**, **count2**, **i1**, and **i2** in the **printf( )** statement.

Exercises

1. Compile and run the example programs.

2. What does this program display?

   ```
   #include "stdio.h"

   #define JOIN(a, b) a ## b

   void main(void)
   {
     printf(JOIN("one ", "two"));
   }
   ```

3. On your own, experiment with the # and ## operators. Try to think of ways they can be useful to you in your own programming projects.

12.6 UNDERSTAND FUNCTION POINTERS

This section introduces one of C's most important advanced features: the function pointer. Although it is beyond the scope of this book to discuss all the nuances and implications of function pointers, this section will cover the main points.

A *function pointer* is a variable that contains the address of the entry point of a function. As you probably know, when the compiler compiles your program, it creates an entry point to each function in the program. After the program is linked, this entry point has a physical address, which is called each time a function is referenced. Since this is an address, it is possible to have a pointer variable point to it. Once you have a pointer to a function, it is possible to actually call that function using the pointer. You will see shortly why you might want to do this.

To create a variable that can point to a function, declare the pointer as having the same type as the return type of the function, followed by any parameters. For example, the following declares **p** as a pointer to a function that returns an integer and has two integer parameters, **a** and **b**.

```
int (*p)(int a, int b);
```

The parentheses surrounding ***p** are necessary because of C's precedence rules.

To assign the address of a function to a function pointer, simply use its name without any parentheses. For example, assuming that **sum( )** has the prototype

```
int sum(int a, int b);
```

the assignment statement

```
p = sum;
```

is correct. Once this has been done, you can call **sum( )** indirectly through **p** using a statement like

```
result = (*p)(10, 20);
```

Again, because of C's precedence rules, the parentheses are necessary around ***p**.

Examples

1. As a first example, this program fills in the details and demonstrates the function pointer that was just described.

```
#include "stdio.h"

int sum(int a, int b);

void main(void)
{
   int (*p)(int a, int b);
   int result;

   p = sum;  /* get address of sum( ) */

   result = (*p)(10, 20);
   printf("%d", result);
}

sum(int a, int b)
{
   return a+b;
}
```

The program prompts the user for two numbers, calls **sum( )** indirectly using **p**, and displays the result.

2. Although the program in Example 1 illustrates the mechanics of using function pointers, it does not even hint at their power. The following example, however, will give you a taste.

One of the most important uses of function pointers occurs when a function-pointer array is created. Each element in the array can point to a different function. To call any specific function, the array is simply indexed. A function pointer array allows very efficient code to be written when a variety of different functions need to be called under differing circumstances. Function-pointer arrays are typically used when writing systems software, such as compilers, assemblers, and interpreters. However, they are not limited to these applications.

Although meaningful, short examples of function-pointer arrays are difficult to find, the program shown here hints at their power. Like the program in Example 1, this program prompts the user for two numbers. Next, it asks the user to enter the number of the operation to perform. This number is then used directly to index the function-pointer array to execute the proper function. Finally, the result is displayed.

```c
#include "stdio.h"

int sum(int a, int b);
int subtract(int a, int b);
int mul(int a, int b);
int div(int a, int b);

int (*p[4])(int a, int b);

void main(void)
{
  int result;
  int i, j, op;

  p[0] = sum;  /* get address of sum( ) */
  p[1] = subtract; /* get address of subtract( ) */
  p[2] = mul;  /* get address of mul( ) */
  p[3] = div;  /* get address of div( ) */

  printf("Enter two numbers: ");
  scanf("%d%d", &i, &j);
  printf("0: Add, 1: Subtract, 2: Multiply, 3: Divide\n");
  do {
    printf("Enter number of operation: ");
    scanf("%d", &op);
```

```
  } while(op<0 || op>3);

  result = (*p[op])(i, j);
  printf("%d", result);
}

sum(int a, int b)
{
  return a+b;
}

subtract(int a, int b)
{
  return a-b;
}

mul(int a, int b)
{
  return a*b;
}

div(int a, int b)
{
  if(b) return a/b;
  else return 0;
}
```

When you study this code, it becomes clear that using a function-pointer array to call the appropriate function is more efficient than using a **switch()** statement.

Before leaving this example, we can use it to illustrate one more point: function-pointer arrays can be initialized, just like any other array. The following version of the program illustrates this.

```
#include "stdio.h"

int sum(int a, int b);
int subtract(int a, int b);
```

```c
int mul(int a, int b);

int div(int a, int b);

/* initialize the pointer array */
int (*p[4])(int a, int b) = {
  sum, subtract, mul, div
} ;

void main(void)
{
  int result;
  int i, j, op;

  printf("Enter two numbers: ");
  scanf("%d%d", &i, &j);
  printf("0: Add, 1: Subtract, 2: Multiply, 3: Divide\n");
  do {
    printf("Enter number of operation: ");
    scanf("%d", &op);
  } while(op<0 || op>3);

  result = (*p[op])(i, j);
  printf("%d", result);
}

sum(int a, int b)
{
  return a+b;
}

subtract(int a, int b)
{
  return a-b;
}

mul(int a, int b)
{
  return a*b;
}

div(int a, int b)
```

```
{
  if(b) return a/b;
  else return 0;
}
```

3. One of the most common uses of a function pointer occurs when utilizing another of C's standard library functions, **qsort( )**. The **qsort( )** function is a generic sort routine that can sort any type of singly dimensioned array, using the Quicksort algorithm. Its prototype is

    void qsort(void *array, size_t number, size_t size,
                int (*comp)(const void *a, const void *b));

    Here, *array* is a pointer to the first element in the array to be sorted. The number of elements in the array is specified by *number,* and the size of each element of the array is specified by *size.* (Remember, **size_t** is defined by the C compiler and is loosely the same as **unsigned**.) The final parameter is a pointer to a function (which you create) that compares two elements of the array and returns the following results.

    *a < *b   returns a negative value
    *a == *b   returns a zero
    *a > *b   returns a positive value

    The **qsort( )** has no return value.

        The following program loads a 100-element integer array with random numbers, sorts it, and displays the sorted form.

```
#include "stdio.h"
#include "stdlib.h"

int comp(int *i, int *j);

void main(void)
{
```

```
    int sort[100], i;

    for(i=0; i<100; i++)
       sort[i] = rand( );
    qsort(sort, 100, sizeof(int), comp);

    for(i=0; i<100; i++)
       printf("%d\n", sort[i]);
}

comp(int *i, int *j)
{
    return *i - *j;
}
```

Exercises

1. Compile and run all of the Example programs. Experiment with them, making minor changes.

2. Another of C's standard library functions is called **bsearch( )**. This function is used to search a sorted array, given a key. It returns a pointer to the first entry in the array that matches the key. If no match is found, a null pointer is returned. Its prototype is

   void *bsearch(const void *key, const void *array,
   $\qquad$ size_t number, size_t size,
   $\qquad$ int (*comp)(const void *a, const void *b));

   All the parameters to **bsearch( )** are the same as for **qsort( )** except the first, which is a pointer to key, the object being sought. The **comp( )** function operates the same for **bsearch( )** as it does for **qsort( )**.

   Modify the program in Example 3 so that after the array is sorted, the user is prompted to enter a number. Next, using **bsearch( )**, search the sorted array and report if a match is found.

3. Add a function called **modulus( )** to the final version of the arithmetic program in Example 2. Have the function return the result of **a % b**. Add this option to the menu and fully integrate it into the program.

12.7 MASTER DYNAMIC ALLOCATION

This final section of the book introduces you to C's dynamic-allocation system. *Dynamic allocation* is the process by which memory is allocated as needed during runtime. This allocated memory can be used for a variety of purposes. Most commonly, memory is allocated by applications that need to take full advantage of all the memory in the computer. For example, a word processor will want to let the user edit documents that are as large as possible. However, if the word processor uses a normal character array, it must fix its size at compile time. Thus, it would have to be compiled to run in computers with the minimum amount of memory, not allowing users with more memory to edit larger documents. If memory is allocated dynamically (as needed until memory is exhausted), however, any user may make full use of the memory in the system. Other uses for dynamic allocation include linked lists and binary trees.

The core of C's dynamic-allocation functions are **malloc( )**, which allocates memory, and **free( )**, which releases previously allocated memory. Their prototypes are

void *malloc(size_t *numbytes*);
void free(void *ptr*);

Here, *numbytes* is the number of bytes of memory you wish to allocate. The **malloc( )** function returns a pointer to the start of the allocated piece of memory. If **malloc( )** cannot fulfill the memory request—for example, there may be insufficient memory available—it returns a null pointer. To free memory, call **free( )** with a pointer to the start of the block of memory (previously allocated using **malloc( )**) you wish to free. Both functions use the header file STDLIB.H.

Memory is allocated from a region called the *heap*. Although the actual physical layout of memory may differ, conceptually the heap lies between your program and the stack. Since this is a finite area, an allocation request can fail when memory is exhausted.

When a program terminates, all allocated memory is automatically released.

Examples

1. You must confirm that a call to **malloc( )** is successful before you use the pointer it returns. If you perform an operation on a null pointer, you could crash your program and maybe even the entire computer. The easiest way to check for a valid pointer is shown in this fragment.

    ```
    p = malloc(SIZE);

    if(!p) {
      printf("Allocation Error");
      exit(1);
    }
    ```

2. The following program allocates 80 bytes and assigns a character pointer to it. This creates a dynamic character array. It then uses the allocated memory to input a string using **gets( )**. Finally, the string is

redisplayed and the pointer is freed. (As stated earlier, all memory is freed when the program ends, so the call to **free( )** is included in this program simply to demonstrate its use.)

```c
#include "stdio.h"
#include "stdlib.h"

void main(void)
{
  char *p;

  p = malloc(80);

  if(!p) {
    printf("allocation failed");
    exit(1);
  }

  printf("Enter a string: ");
  gets(p);
  printf(p);
  free(p);
}
```

3. The next program tells you approximately how much free memory is available to your program.

```c
#include "stdio.h"
#include "stdlib.h"

void main(void)
{
  char *p;
  long l;

  l = 0;
  do {
```

```
    p = malloc(1000);
    if(p) l += 1000;
  } while(p);

  printf("Approximately %ld bytes of free memory", l);
}
```

The program works by allocating 1000-byte-long chunks of memory until an allocation request fails. When **malloc( )** returns null, the heap is exhausted. Hence, the value of **l** represents (within 1000 bytes) the amount of free memory available to the program.

4. One good use for dynamic allocation is to create buffers for file I/O when you are using **fread( )** and/or **fwrite( )**. Often, you only need a buffer for a short period of time, so it makes sense to allocate it when needed and free it when done. The following program shows how dynamic allocation can be used to create a buffer. The program allocates enough space to hold ten floating-point values. It then assigns ten random numbers to the allocated memory, indexing the pointer as an array. Next, it writes the values to disk and frees the memory. Finally, it reallocates memory, reads the file and displays the random numbers. Although there is no need to free and then reallocate the memory that serves as a file buffer in this short example, it illustrates the basic idea.

```
#include "stdio.h"
#include "stdlib.h"

void main(void)
{
```

```
int i;
double *p;
FILE *fp;

/* get memory */
p = malloc(10 * sizeof (double));
if(!p) {
  printf("Allocation Error");
  exit(1);
}

/* generate 10 random numbers */
for(i=0; i<10; i++)
  p[i] = (double) rand( );

if((fp = fopen("myfile", "wb"))==NULL) {
  printf("cannot open file");
  exit(1);
}

/* write the entire array in one step */
if(fwrite(p, 10*sizeof(double), 1, fp)!=1) {
    printf("write error");
    exit(1);
  }
fclose(fp);

free(p);  /* memory not needed now */

/*
  imagine something transpires here
  .
  .
  .
*/

/* get memory again */
p = malloc(10 * sizeof (double));
if(!p) {
```

```
    printf("Allocation Error");
    exit(1);
  }

  if((fp = fopen("myfile", "rb"))==NULL) {
    printf("cannot open file");
    exit(1);
  }
  /* read the entire array in one step */
  if(fread(p, 10*sizeof(double), 1, fp)!=1) {
      printf("read error");
      exit(1);
  }
  fclose(fp);

  /* display the array */
  for(i=0; i<10; i++) printf("%lf ", p[i]);
  free(p);
}
```

5. Just as array boundaries can be overrun, so can the boundaries of allocated memory. For example, this fragment is syntactically valid, but wrong.

```
p = malloc(10);

for(i=0; i<100; i) p[i] = i;
```

Exercises

1. Compile and run the example programs.

2. Write a program that creates a ten-element dynamic integer array. Assign the pointer to the dynamic array to an integer pointer. Next, using pointer arithmetic or array indexing, assign the value 1 through 10 to the integers that comprise the array. Finally, display the values and free the memory.

3. What's wrong with this fragment?

```
char *p;

*p = malloc(10);

gets(p);
```

EXERCISES

At this point you should be able to answer these questions and perform these exercises.

1. What is the difference between using quotes and angle brackets with the **#include** directive?

2. Using an **#ifdef**, show how to conditionally compile this fragment of code based upon whether **DEBUG** is defined or not.

```
if(!(j%2)) {
   printf("j = %d\n", j);
   j = 0;
}
```

3. Using the fragment from Exercise 3, show how you can conditionally compile the code when **DEBUG** is defined as 1. (Hint: Use **#if**).

4. How do you undefine a macro?

5. What is __FILE__ and what does it represent?

6. What do the # and ## preprocessor operators do?

7. Write a program that sorts the string "this is a test of qsort". Display the sorted output.

8. Write a program that dynamically allocates memory for one **double**. Have the program assign that loca-

tion the value 99.01, display the value, and then free the memory.

EXERCISES

This section checks how well you have integrated the material in this chapter with that from earlier chapters.

1. Section 10.1, Example 3, presents a computerized card-catalog program that uses an array of structures to hold information on books. Change this program so that only an array of structure pointers is created, and use dynamically allocated memory to actually hold the information for each book as it is entered. This way, less memory is used when information on only a few books is stored.

2. Show the macro equivalent of the function

```
char code_it(char c)
{
    return ~c;
}
```

Demonstrate that your macro version works in a program.

3. On your own, look over the programs that you have written in the course of working through this book. Try to find places where you can

   • Use conditional compilation

   • Replace a short function with a function-like macro

   • Replace statically allocated arrays with dynamic arrays

- Use function pointers

4. On your own, study the user's manual for your C compiler, paying special attention to the description of its standard library functions. The C standard library contains several hundred library functions that can make your programming tasks easier. Also, Appendix A in this book discusses some of the most common library functions.

5. Now that you have finished this book, go back and skim through each chapter, thinking about how each aspect of C relates to the rest of it. As you will see, C is a highly integrated language, in which one feature complements another. The connection between pointers and arrays, for example, is pure elegance.

6. C is a language best learned by doing! Continue to write programs in C and to study other programmers' programs. You will be surprised at how quickly C will become second nature!

Some Common C
Library Functions

This appendix discusses a number of the more important ANSI C library functions. If you have looked
through the library section in your C compiler's manual, you are no doubt aware that there are a great many
library functions. It is far beyond the scope of this book
to cover each one. However, the ones you will most
commonly need are discussed here.

The library functions can be grouped into the following categories.

- I/O functions

- String and character functions

- Mathematics functions

- Time and date functions

- Dynamic allocation functions

- Miscellaneous functions

The I/O functions were thoroughly covered in Chapters 8 and 9 and will not be expanded upon here.

Each function's description begins with the header file required by the function followed by its prototype. The prototype provides you with a quick way of knowing what types of arguments and how many of them the function takes and what type of value it returns.

Keep in mind that ANSI C specifies many data types, which are defined in the header files used by the functions. New type names will be discussed as they are introduced.

STRING AND CHARACTER FUNCTIONS

The C standard library has a rich and varied set of string- and character-handling functions. In C, a string is a null-terminated array of characters. The declarations for the string functions are found in the header file

STRING.H. The character functions use CTYPE.H as their header file.

Because C has no bounds-checking on array operations, it is the programmer's responsibility to prevent an array overflow.

The character functions are declared to take an integer argument. While this is true, only the low-order byte is used by the function. Generally, you are free to use a character argument because it will automatically be elevated to **int** at the time of the call.

#include "ctype.h"
int isalnum(int ch);

DESCRIPTION   The **isalnum( )** function returns a non-0 if its argument is either a letter or a digit. If the character is not alphanumeric, then 0 is returned.

EXAMPLE   This program checks each character read from **stdin** and reports all alphanumeric ones.

```
#include "ctype.h"
#include "stdio.h"
#include "conio.h"

main( )
{
  char ch;

  for(;;) {
    ch = getche( );
    if(ch==' ') break;
    if(isalnum(ch)) printf("%c is alphanumeric\n", ch);
  }
}
```

#include "ctype.h"
int isalpha(int ch);

DESCRIPTION   The **isalpha( )** function returns a non-0 if *ch* is a letter of the alphabet; otherwise 0 is returned.

EXAMPLE   This program checks each character read from **stdin** and reports all those that are letters of the alphabet.

```
#include "ctype.h"
#include "stdio.h"
#include "conio.h"

main( )
{
  char ch;

  for(;;) {
    ch = getche( );
    if(ch==' ') break;
    if(isalpha(ch)) printf("%c is a letter\n", ch);
  }
}
```

#include "ctype.h"
int iscntrl(int ch);

DESCRIPTION   The **iscntrl( )** function returns non-0 if *ch* is between 0 and 0x1F or is equal to 0x7F (DEL); otherwise 0 is returned.

EXAMPLE   This program checks each character read from **stdin** and reports all control characters.

```
#include "ctype.h"
#include "stdio.h"
#include "conio.h"

main( )
{
  char ch;

  for(;;) {
    ch = getche( );
    if(ch==' ') break;
    if(iscntrl(ch))
       printf("%c is a control character\n", ch);
  }
}
```

#include "ctype.h"
int isdigit(int ch);

DESCRIPTION   The **isdigit( )** function returns a non-0 if *ch* is a digit (0 through 9); otherwise 0 is returned.

EXAMPLE   This program checks each character read from **stdin** and reports all those that are digits.

```
#include "ctype.h"
#include "stdio.h"
#include "conio.h"

main( )
{
  char ch;

  for(;;) {
    ch = getche( );
    if(ch==' ') break;
    if(isdigit(ch)) printf("%c is a digit\n", ch);
```

```
    }
}
```

#include "ctype.h"
int isgraph(int ch);

DESCRIPTION The **isgraph( )** function returns non-0 if *ch* is any printable character other than a space; otherwise 0 is returned. Printable characters are in the range 0x21 through 0x7E.

EXAMPLE This program checks each character read from **stdin** and reports all printing characters.

```
#include "ctype.h"
#include "stdio.h"

main( )
{
  char ch;

  for(;;) {
    ch = getche( );
    if(ch==' ') break;
    if(isgraph(ch))
        printf("%c is a printing character\n",ch);
  }
}
```

#include "ctype.h"
int islower(int ch);

DESCRIPTION The **islower( )** function returns non-0 if *ch* is a lowercase letter (a through z); otherwise 0 is returned.

EXAMPLE   This program checks each character read from **stdin** and reports all those that are lowercase letters.

```c
#include "ctype.h"
#include "stdio.h"
#include "conio.h"

main( )
{
  char ch;

  for(;;) {
    ch = getche( );
    if(ch==' ') break;
    if(islower(ch)) printf("%c is lowercase\n", ch);
  }
}
```

#include "ctype.h"
int isprint(int ch);

DESCRIPTION   The **isprint( )** function returns non-0 if *ch* is a printable character, including a space; otherwise 0 is returned. Printable characters are often in the range 0x20 through 0x7E.

EXAMPLE   This program checks each character read from **stdin** and reports all those that are printable.

```c
#include "ctype.h"
#include "stdio.h"
#include "conio.h"
```

```
main( )
{
  char ch;

  for(;;) {
    ch = getche( );
    if(ch==' ') break;
    if(isprint(ch)) printf("%c is printable\n", ch);
  }
}
```

#include "ctype.h"
int ispunct(int ch);

DESCRIPTION   The **ispunct( )** function returns non-0 if *ch* is a punctuation character, excluding the space; otherwise 0 is returned. The term "punctuation," as defined by this function, includes all printing characters that are neither alphanumeric nor a space.

EXAMPLE   This program checks each character read from **stdin** and reports all those that are punctuation.

```
#include "ctype.h"
#include "stdio.h"
#include "conio.h"

main( )
{
  char ch;
```

```
for(;;) {
  ch = getche( );
  if(ch==' ') break;
  if(ispunct(ch)) printf("%c is punctuation\n", ch);
  }
}
```

#include "ctype.h"
int isspace(int ch);

DESCRIPTION   The **isspace( )** function returns non-0 if *ch* is either a space, tab, vertical tab, form feed, carriage return, or newline character; otherwise 0 is returned.

EXAMPLE   This program checks each character read from **stdin** and reports all those that are whitespace characters.

```
#include "ctype.h"
#include "stdio.h"
#include "conio.h"

main( )
{
  char ch;

  for(;;) {
    ch = getche( );
    if(isspace(ch)) printf("%c is whitespace\n", ch);
    if(ch==' ') break;
  }
}
```

#include "ctype.h"
int isupper(int ch);

DESCRIPTION   The **isupper( )** function returns non-0 if *ch* is an uppercase letter (A through Z); otherwise 0 is returned.

EXAMPLE   This program checks each character read from **stdin** and reports all those that are uppercase letters.

```
#include "ctype.h"
#include "stdio.h"
#include "conio.h"

main( )
{
  char ch;

  for(;;) {
    ch = getche( );
    if(ch==' ') break;
    if(isupper(ch)) printf("%c is uppercase\n", ch);
  }
}
```

#include "ctype.h"
int isxdigit(int ch);

DESCRIPTION   The **isxdigit( )** function returns non-0 if *ch* is a hexadecimal digit; otherwise 0 is returned. A hexadecimal digit will be in one of these ranges: **A** through **F, a** through **f,** or **0** through **9**.

EXAMPLE   This program checks each character read from **stdin** and reports all those that are hexadecimal digits.

```
#include "ctype.h"
#include "stdio.h"
#include "conio.h"

main( )
{
  char ch;

  for(;;) {
    ch = getche( );
    if(ch==' ') break;
    if(isxdigit(ch)) printf("%c is hexadecimal \n", ch);
  }
}
```

#include "string.h"
char *strcat(char *str1, const char *str2);

DESCRIPTION   The **strcat( )** function concatenates a copy of *str2* to *str1* and terminates *str1* with a null. The null terminator originally ending *str1* is overwritten by the first character of *str2*. The string *str2* is untouched by the operation. The **strcat( )** function returns *str1*.

REMEMBER: No bounds-checking takes place, so it is the programmer's responsibility to ensure that *str1* is large enough to hold both its original contents and those of *str2*.

EXAMPLE   This program appends the first string read from **stdin** to the second. For example, assuming the user enters **hello** and **there**, the program will print **therehello**.

```
#include "string.h"
#include "stdio.h"

main ( )
{
  char s1[80], s2[80];

  printf("enter two strings: ");
  gets(s1);
  gets(s2);

  strcat(s2, s1);
  printf(s2);
}
```

#include "string.h"
char *strchr(const char *str, int ch);

DESCRIPTION　The **strchr( )** function returns a pointer to the first occurrence of the low-order byte of **ch** in the string pointed to by *str*. If no match is found, a null pointer is returned.

EXAMPLE　This program prints the string **this is a test**.

```
#include "string.h"
#include "stdio.h"

main ( )
{
  char *p;
```

```
   p = strchr("this is a test", (int) ' ');
   printf(p);
}
```

#include "string.h"
int strcmp(const char *str1, const char* str2);

DESCRIPTION A **strcmp( )** function lexicographically compares two null-terminated strings and returns an integer based on the outcome, as shown here.

Value	Meaning
less than 0	str1 is less than str2
0	str1 is equal to str2
greater than 0	str1 is greater than str2

EXAMPLE The following function can be used as a password verification routine. It will return 0 on failure and 1 on success.

```
#include "string.h"

password( )
{
  char s[80];

  printf("enter password: ");
  gets(s);

  if(strcmp(s,"pass")) {
    printf("invalid password\n");
    return 0;
  }
  return 1;
}
```

#include "string.h"
char *strcpy(char *str1, const char *str2);

DESCRIPTION   The **strcpy( )** function is used to copy the contents of *str2* into *str1*; *str2* must be a pointer to a null-terminated string. The **strcpy( )** function returns a pointer to *str1*.

If *str1* and *str2* overlap, the behavior of **strcpy( )** is undefined.

EXAMPLE   The following code fragment will copy "hello" into string **str**.

```
char str[80];
strcpy(str, "hello");
```

#include "string.h"
size_t strlen(const char *str);

DESCRIPTION   The **strlen( )** function returns the length of the null-terminated string pointed to by *str*. The null is not counted. The **size_t** type is specified by ANSI and is defined in STRING.H.

EXAMPLE   The following code fragment will print **5** on the screen.

```
strcpy(s, "hello");
printf("%d", strlen(s));
```

#include "stdio.h"
char *strstr(const char *str1, const char *str2);

DESCRIPTION The **strstr( )** function returns a pointer to the first occurrence of the string pointed to by *str2* in the string pointed to by *str1* (except *str2's* null terminator). It returns a null pointer if no match is found.

EXAMPLE This program displays the message **is is a test**.

```
#include "string.h"
#include "stdio.h"

main( )
{
  char *p;

  p = strstr("this is a test","is");
  printf(p);
}
```

#include "string.h"
char *strtok(char *str1, const char *str2);

DESCRIPTION The **strtok( )** function returns a pointer to the next token in the string pointed to by *str1*. The characters making up the string pointed to by *str2* are the delimiters that determine the token. A null pointer is returned when there is no token to return.

The first time **strtok( )** is called, *str1* is actually used in the call. Subsequent calls use a null pointer for the first argument. In this way the entire string can be reduced to its tokens.

It is important to understand that the **strtok( )** function modifies the string pointed to by *str1*. Each time a token is found, a null is placed where the delimiter was found. In this way **strtok( )** can continue to advance through the string.

It is possible to use a different set of delimiters for each call to **strtok( )**.

EXAMPLE   This program tokenizes the string "The summer soldier, the sunshine partriot" with spaces and commas as the delimiters. The output will be **The | summer | soldier | the | sunshine | patriot**.

```
#include "string.h"
#include "stdio.h"

main( )
{
  char *p;

  p = strtok("The summer soldier, the sunshine patriot",
             " ,");
  printf(p);
  do {
    p = strtok('\0', ", ");
    if(p) printf("|%s", p);
  } while(p);
}
```

```
#include "ctype.h"
int tolower(int ch);
```

DESCRIPTION   The **tolower( )** function returns the lowercase equivalent of *ch* if *ch* is a letter; otherwise *ch* is returned unchanged.

EXAMPLE   This fragment displays 'q.'

```
putchar(tolower('Q'));
```

```
#include "ctype.h"
int toupper(int ch);
```

DESCRIPTION   The **toupper( )** function returns the uppercase equivalent of *ch* if *ch* is a letter; otherwise *ch* is returned unchanged.

EXAMPLE   This displays 'A.'

```
putchar(toupper('a'));
```

THE MATHEMATICS FUNCTIONS

ANSI C defines several mathematics functions that take **double** arguments and return **double** values. These functions fall into the following categories:

- Trigonometric functions

- Hyperbolic functions

- Exponential and logarithmic functions

- Miscellaneous functions

All the math functions require that the header MATH.H be included in any program that uses them. In addition to declaring the math functions, this header defines a macro called **HUGE_VAL**. If an operation produces a result that is too large to be represented by a **double**, an overflow occurs, which causes the routine to return **HUGE_VAL**. This is called a *range error*. For all the mathematics functions, if the input value is not in the domain for which the function is defined, a *domain error* occurs.

#include "math.h"
double acos(double arg);

DESCRIPTION   The **acos( )** function returns the arc cosine of *arg*. The argument to **acos( )** must be in the range −1 through 1; otherwise a domain error will occur.

EXAMPLE   This program prints the arc cosines, in one-tenth increments, of the values −1 through 1.

```
#include "math.h"
#include "stdio.h"

main( )
{
  double val = -1.0;
```

```
  do {
    printf("arc cosine of %f is %f\n", val, acos(val));
    val += 0.1;
  } while(val<=1.0);
}
```

#include "math.h"
double asin(double arg);

DESCRIPTION   The **asin( )** function returns the arc sine of *arg*. The argument to **asin( )** must be in the range −1 through 1; otherwise a domain error will occur.

EXAMPLE   This program prints the arc sines, in one-tenth increments, of the values −1 through 1.

```
#include "math.h"
#include "stdio.h"

main( )
{
  double val=-1.0;

  do {
    printf("arc sine of %f is %f\n", val, asin(val));
    val += 0.1;
  } while(val<=1.0);
}
```

#include "math.h"
double atan(double arg);

DESCRIPTION   The **atan( )** function returns the arc tangent of *arg*.

EXAMPLE   This program prints the arc tangents, in one-tenth increments, of the values −1 through 1.

```
#include "math.h"
#include "stdio.h"

main( )
{
  double val=-1.0;

  do {
    printf("arc tangent of %f is %f\n", val, atan(val));
    val += 0.1;
  } while(val<=1.0);
}
```

#include "math.h"
double atan2(double y, double x);

DESCRIPTION   The **atan2( )** function returns the arc tangent of *y/x*. It uses the signs of its arguments to compute the quadrant of the return value.

EXAMPLE   This program prints the arc tangents, in one-tenth increments of *y*, from −1 through 1.

```
#include "math.h"
#include "stdio.h"

main( )
{
  double y=-1.0;

  do {
    printf("atan2 of %f is %f\n", y, atan2(y, 1.0));
    y += 0.1;
  } while(y<=1.0);
}
```

#include "math.h"
double ceil(double num);

DESCRIPTION   The **ceil( )** function returns the
smallest integer (represented as a **double**) that is not
less than *num*. For example, given 1.02, **ceil( )** would
return 2.0; given −1.02, **ceil( )** would return −1.

EXAMPLE   This fragment prints **10** on the screen.

```
printf("%f", ceil(9.9));
```

#include "math.h"
double cos(double arg);

DESCRIPTION   The **cos( )** function returns the cosine of *arg*. The value of *arg* must be in radians.

EXAMPLE   This program prints the cosines, in one-
tenth increments, of the values −1 through 1.

```
#include "math.h"
#include "stdio.h"

main( )
{
  double val=-1.0;

  do {
    printf("cosine of %f is %f\n", val, cos(val));
    val += 0.1;
  } while(val<=1.0);
}
```

#include "math.h"
double cosh(double arg);

DESCRIPTION   The **cosh( )** function returns the hyperbolic cosine of *arg*. The value of *arg* must be in radians.

EXAMPLE   This program prints the hyperbolic cosines, in one-tenth increments, of the values −1 through 1.

```
#include "math.h"
#include "stdio.h"

main( )
{
  double val=-1.0;

  do {
    printf("hyperbolic cosine of %f is %f\n", val, cosh(val));
    val += 0.1;
  } while(val<=1.0);
}
```

#include "math.h"
double exp(double arg);

DESCRIPTION   The **exp( )** function returns the natural logarithm *e* raised to the *arg* power.

EXAMPLE   This fragment displays the value of *e* (rounded to 2.718282).

```
printf("value of e to the first: %f", exp(1.0));
```

#include "math.h"
double fabs(double num);

DESCRIPTION   The **fabs( )** function returns the absolute value of *num*.

EXAMPLE   This program prints the numbers **1.0 1.0** on the screen.

```
#include "math.h"
#include "stdio.h"

main( )
{
  printf("%1.1f %1.1f", fabs(1.0), fabs(-1.0));
}
```

#include "math.h"
double floor(double num);

DESCRIPTION   The **floor( )** function returns the largest integer (represented as a **double**) not greater than *num*. For example, given 1.02, **floor( )** would return 1.0; given –1.02, **floor( )** would return –2.0.

EXAMPLE   This fragment prints **10** on the screen.

```
printf("%f", floor(10.9));
```

#include "math.h"
double log(double num);

DESCRIPTION   The **log( )** function returns the natural logarithm for *num*. A domain error occurs if *num* is negative and a range error occurs if the argument is 0.

EXAMPLE   This program prints the natural logarithms for the numbers 1 through 10.

```
#include "math.h"
#include "stdio.h"

main( )
{
  double val=1.0;

  do {
    printf("%f %f\n", val, log(val));
    val++;
  } while (val<11.0);
}
```

#include "math.h"
double log10(double num);

DESCRIPTION   The **log10( )** function returns the base 10 logarithm for the variable *num*. A domain error occurs if *num* is negative and a range error occurs if the argument is 0.

EXAMPLE   This program prints the base 10 logarithms for the numbers 1 through 10.

```
#include "math.h"
#include "stdio.h"

main( )
{
  double val=1.0;

  do {
    printf("%f %f\n", val, log10(val));
    val++;
  } while (val<11.0);
}
```

#include "math.h"
double pow(double base, double exp);

DESCRIPTION   The **pow( )** function returns *base* raised to the *exp* power (*base* ^{exp}). A domain error occurs if *base* is 0 and *exp* is less than or equal to 0. This may also happen if *base* is negative and *exp* is not an integer. An overflow produces a range error.

EXAMPLE   This program prints the first ten powers of 10.

```
#include "math.h"
#include "stdio.h"

main( )
{
  double x=10.0, y=0.0;

  do {
    printf("%f",pow(x, y));
```

```
    y++;
  } while(y<11);
}
```

#include "math.h"
double sin(double arg);

DESCRIPTION   The **sin( )** function returns the sine of *arg*. The value of *arg* must be in radians.

EXAMPLE   This program prints the sines, in one-tenth increments, of the values −1 through 1.

```
#include "math.h"
#include "stdio.h"

main( )
{
  double val=-1.0;

  do {
    printf("sine of %f is %f\n", val, sin(val));
    val += 0.1;
  } while(val<=1.0);
}
```

#include "math.h"
double sinh(double arg);

DESCRIPTION   The **sinh( )** function returns the hyperbolic sine of *arg*. The value of *arg* must be in radians.

EXAMPLE   The following program prints the hyperbolic sines, in one-tenth increments, of the values −1 through 1.

```
#include "math.h"
#include "stdio.h"

main( )
{
  double val=-1.0;

  do {
    printf("hyperbolic sine of %f is %f\n", val, sinh(val));
    val += 0.1;
  } while(val<=1.0);
}
```

#include "math.h"
double sqrt(double num);

DESCRIPTION   The **sqrt( )** function returns the
square root of *num*. If called with a negative argument,
a domain error will occur.

EXAMPLE   This fragment prints **4** on the screen.

```
printf("%f", sqrt(16.0));
```

#include "math.h"
double tan(double arg);

DESCRIPTION   The **tan( )** function returns the tangent of *arg*. The value of *arg* must be in radians.

EXAMPLE   This program prints the tangents, in one-tenth increments, of the values −1 through 1.

```
#include "math.h"
#include "stdio.h"

main ( )
{
  double val=-1.0;

  do {
    printf("tangent of %f is %f\n", val, tan(val));
    val += 0.1;
  } while(val<=1.0);
}
```

#include "math.h"
double tanh(double arg);

DESCRIPTION   The **tanh( )** function returns the hyperbolic tangent of *arg*. The value of *arg* must be in radians.

EXAMPLE   This program prints the hyperbolic tangents, in one-tenth increments, of the values −1 through 1.

```
#include "math.h"
#include "stdio.h"

main ( )
{
  double val=-1.0;

  do {
    printf("tanh tangent of %f is %f\n", val, tanh(val));
    val += 0.1;
```

```
    } while(val<=1.0);
}
```

TIME AND DATE FUNCTIONS

The time and date functions require the header TIME.H
for their prototypes. It also defines four types and two
macros. The type **time_t** is able to represent the system
time and date as a **long** integer. This is called the *calendar
time*. The structure type **tm** holds date and time broken
down into its elements. The **tm** structure is defined as
shown here.

```
struct tm {
    int tm_sec;  /* seconds, 0-59 */
    int tm_min;  /* minutes, 0-59 */
    int tm_hour; /* hours, 0-23 */
    int tm_mday; /* day of the month, 1-31 */
    int tm_mon;  /* months since Jan, 0-11 */
    int tm_year; /* years from 1900 */
    int tm_wday; /* days since Sunday, 0-6 */
    int tm_yday; /* days since Jan 1, 0-365 */
    int tm_isdst /* Daylight Savings Time indicator */
}
```

The value of **tm_isdst** will be positive if Daylight Savings Time is in effect, 0 if it is not in effect, and negative
if there is no information available. When the date and
time are represented in this way, they are referred to as
broken-down time.

   The type **clock_t** is defined the same as **time_t**. The
header file also defines **size_t**.

   The macros defined are **NULL** and **CLK_TCK**.

#include "time.h"
char *asctime(const struct tm *ptr);

DESCRIPTION   The **asctime( )** function returns a pointer to a string that converts the information stored in the structure pointed to by *ptr* into the following form.

day month date hours:minutes:seconds year\n\0

For example:

Wed Jun 19 12:05:34 1999

The structure pointer passed to **asctime( )** is generally obtained from either **localtime( )** or **gmtime( )**.

The buffer used by **asctime( )** to hold the formatted output string is a statically allocated character array and is overwritten each time the function is called. If you want to save the contents of the string, you need to copy it elsewhere.

EXAMPLE   This program displays the local time defined by the system.

```
#include "time.h"
#include "stdio.h"

main( )
{
  struct tm *ptr;
  time_t lt;
```

```
lt = time(NULL);
ptr = localtime(&lt);
printf(asctime(ptr));
}
```

#include "time.h"
clock_t clock(void);

DESCRIPTION   The **clock( )** function returns the number of system clock cycles that have occurred since the program began execution. To compute the number of seconds, divide this value by the **CLK_TCK** macro.

EXAMPLE   The following program displays the number of system clock cycles occurring since it began.

```
#include "stdio.h"
#include "time.h"

main( )
{
  int i;

  for(i=0; i<100; i++) ;

  printf("%u", clock( ));
}
```

#include "time.h"
char *ctime(const time_t *time);

DESCRIPTION   The **ctime( )** function returns a pointer to a string of the form day month date hours:minutes:seconds year\n\0

given a pointer to the calendar time. The calendar time is generally obtained through a call to **time( )**. The **ctime( )** function is equivalent to

```
asctime(localtime(time))
```

The buffer used by **ctime( )** to hold the formatted output string is a statically allocated character array and is overwritten each time the function is called. If you wish to save the contents of the string, you need to copy it elsewhere.

EXAMPLE   This program displays the local time defined by the system.

```
#include "time.h"
#include "stdio.h"

main( )
{
  time_t lt;

  lt = time(NULL);
  printf(ctime(&lt));
}
```

#include "time.h"
double difftime(time_t time2, time_t time1);

DESCRIPTION   The **difftime( )** function returns the difference, in seconds, between *time1* and *time2*. That is, *time2– time1*.

EXAMPLE   This program times the number of seconds that it takes for the empty **for** loop to go from 0 to 500000.

```
#include "time.h"
#include "stdio.h"

main( )
{
  time_t start,end;
  long unsigned int t;

  start = time(NULL);
  for(t=0; t<500000L; t++);
  end = time(NULL);
  printf("loop required %f seconds\n", difftime(end, start));
}
```

#include "time.h"
struct tm *gmtime(const time_t *time);

DESCRIPTION   The **gmtime( )** function returns a pointer to the broken-down form of *time* in the form of a **tm** structure. The time is represented in Greenwich mean time. The *time* value is generally obtained through a call to **time( )**.

The structure used by **gmtime( )** to hold the broken-down time is statically allocated and is overwritten each time the function is called. If you wish to save the contents of the structure, you need to copy it elsewhere.

EXAMPLE   This program prints both the local time and the Greenwich mean time of the system.

```
#include "time.h"
#include "stdio.h"
```

```
/* print local and GM time */
main( )
{
  struct tm *local, *gm;
  time_t t;

  t = time(NULL);
  local = localtime(&t);
  printf("Local time and date: %s", asctime(local));
  gm = gmtime(&t);
  printf("Greenwich mean time and date: %s", asctime(gm));
}
```

#include "time.h"
struct tm *localtime(const time_t *time);

DESCRIPTION   The **localtime( )** function returns a pointer to the broken-down form of *time* in the form of a **tm** structure. The time is represented in local time. The *time* value is generally obtained through a call to the **time( )** function.

The structure used by **localtime( )** to hold the broken-down time is statically allocated and is overwritten each time the function is called. If you wish to save the contents of the structure, you need to copy it elsewhere.

EXAMPLE   This program prints both the local time and the Greenwich mean time of the system.

```
#include "time.h"
#include "stdio.h"

/* print local and Greenwich mean time */
main( )
{
```

```
   struct tm *local;
   time_t t;

   t = time(NULL);
   local = localtime(&t);
   printf("Local time and date: %s", asctime(local));
   local = gmtime(&t);
   printf("Greenwich mean time and date: %s", asctime(local));
}
```

#include "time.h"
time_t time(time_t *time);

DESCRIPTION   The **time( )** function returns the current calendar time of the system. If the system has no time-keeping mechanism, then −1 is returned.

The **time( )** function can be called either with a null pointer or with a pointer to a variable of type **time_t**. If the latter is used, then the argument will also be assigned the calendar time.

EXAMPLE   This program displays the local time defined by the system.

```
#include "time.h"
#include "stdio.h"

main( )
{
  struct tm *ptr;
  time_t lt;

  lt = time(NULL);
  ptr = localtime(&lt);
  printf(asctime(ptr));
}
```

DYNAMIC ALLOCATION

There are two primary ways a C program can store information in the main memory of the computer. The first uses global and local variables—including arrays and structures. In the case of global and static local variables, the storage is fixed throughout the run time of your program. For dynamic local variables, storage is allocated from the stack space of the computer. Although these variables are efficiently implemented in C, they require the programmer to know in advance the amount of storage needed for every situation. The second way information can be stored is with C's dynamic allocation system. In this method, storage for information is allocated from the free memory area as it is needed.

The ANSI standard specifies that the header information necessary to the dynamic allocation system is in STDLIB. In this file, the type **size_t** is defined. This type is used extensively by the allocation functions and is essentially the equivalent of **unsigned**.

#include "stdlib.h"
void *calloc(size_t num, size_t size);

DESCRIPTION   The **calloc( )** function returns a pointer to the allocated memory. The amount of memory allocated is equal to *num * size*. That is, **calloc( )** allocates sufficient memory for an array of *num* objects of size *size*.

The **calloc( )** function returns a pointer to the first byte of the allocated region. If there is not enough memory to satisfy the request, a null pointer is returned.

It is always important to verify that the return value is not a null pointer before attempting to use it.

EXAMPLE   This function returns a pointer to a dynamically allocated array of 100 **float**s.

```
#include "stdlib.h"
#include "stdio.h"

float *get_mem( )
{
  float *p;

  p = (float *) calloc(100, sizeof(float));
  if(!p) {
    printf("allocation failure - aborting");
    exit(1);
  }
  return p;
}
```

#include "stdlib.h"
void free(void *ptr);

DESCRIPTION   The **free( )** function deallocates the memory pointed to by *ptr*. This makes the memory available for future allocation.

It is imperative that the **free( )** function be called only with a pointer that was previously allocated using one of the dynamic allocation system's functions, such as **malloc( )** or **calloc( )**. Using an invalid pointer in the call will probably destroy the memory management mechanism and cause a system crash.

EXAMPLE   This program first allocates room for the user-entered strings and then frees them.

```
#include "stdlib.h"
#include "stdio.h"

main( )
{
  char *str[100];
  int i;

  for(i=0; i<100; i++) {
    if((str[i] = (char *)malloc(128))==NULL) {
        printf("allocation error - aborting");
        exit(0);
    }
    gets(str[i]);
  }

  /* now free the memory */
  for(i=0; i<100; i++) free(str[i]);
}
```

#include "stdlib.h"
void *malloc(size_t size);

DESCRIPTION   The **malloc( )** function returns a pointer to the first byte of a region of memory of size *size* that has been allocated from the heap. (Remember, the heap is a region of free memory managed by C's dynamic allocation subsystem.) If there is insufficient memory in the heap to satisfy the request, **malloc( )** returns a null pointer. It is always important to verify that the return value is not a null pointer before attempting to use it. Attempting to use a null pointer will usually result in a system crash.

EXAMPLE   This function allocates sufficient memory to hold structures of type **addr**.

```
#include "stdlib.h"
#include "stdio.h"

struct addr {
  char name[40];
  char street[40];
  char city[40];
  char state[3];
  char zip[10];
};
.
.
.

struct addr *get_struct(void)
{
  struct addr *p;

  if((p=(struct addr *)malloc(sizeof(struct addr)))==NULL)
{
    printf("allocation error - aborting");
    exit(0);
  }
  return p;
}
```

#include "stdlib.h"
void *realloc(void *ptr, size_t size);

DESCRIPTION   The **realloc( )** function changes the size of the allocated memory pointed to by *ptr* to that specified by *size*. The value of *size* may be greater or less than the original. A pointer to the memory block is returned since it may be necessary for **realloc( )** to move the block to increase its size. If this occurs, the contents of the old block are copied into the new block—no information is lost.

 If there is not enough free memory in the heap to allocate *size* bytes, a null pointer is returned and the original block is freed (lost). This means it is important to verify the success of a call to **realloc( )**.

EXAMPLE   This program first allocates 17 characters, copies the string "this is 16 chars" into the space, and then uses **realloc( )** to increase the size to 18 in order to place a period at the end.

```c
#include "stdlib.h"
#include "stdio.h"
#include "string.h"

main ( )
{
  char *p;

  p = (char *) malloc(17);
  if(!p) {
    printf("allocation error - aborting");
    exit(1);
  }

  strcpy(p,"this is 16 chars");

  p = realloc(p,18);
  if(!p) {
    printf("allocation error - aborting");
    exit(1);
  }

  strcat(p, ".");

  printf(p);

  free(p);
}
```

MISCELLANEOUS FUNCTIONS

The functions discussed in this section are all standard functions that don't easily fit in any other category.

#include "stdlib.h"
void abort(void);

DESCRIPTION   The **abort( )** function causes immediate termination of a program. Whether it closes any open files is defined by the implementation, but generally it won't.

EXAMPLE   In this program, if the user enters **A**, the program will terminate.

```
#include "stdlib.h"
#include "stdio.h"
#include "conio.h"

main( )
{
  for(;;)
    if(getche( )=='A') abort( );
}
```

#include "stdlib.h"
int abs(int num);

DESCRIPTION   The **abs( )** function returns the absolute value of the integer *num*.

EXAMPLE   This function converts the user-entered numbers into their absolute values.

```
#include "stdlib.h"
#include "stdio.h"

get_abs(void)
{
  char num[80];

  gets(num)

  return abs(atoi(num));
}
```

#include "stdlib.h"
double atof(const char *str);

DESCRIPTION   The **atof( )** function converts the string pointed to by *str* into a **double** value. The string must contain a valid floating-point number. If this is not the case, the returned value is 0.

The number may be terminated by any character that cannot be part of a valid floating-point number. This includes whitespace characters, punctuation (other than periods), and characters other than 'E' or 'e.' Thus, if **atof( )** is called with "100.00HELLO", the value 100.00 will be returned.

EXAMPLE   This program reads two floating-point numbers and displays their sum.

```
#include "stdlib.h"
#include "stdio.h"

main( )
{
```

```
   char num1[80], num2[80];

   printf("enter first: ");
   gets(num1);
   printf("enter second: ");
   gets(num2);
   printf("the sum is: %f",atof(num1)+atof(num2));
```

#include "stdlib.h"
int atoi(const char *str);

DESCRIPTION   The **atoi( )** function converts the
string pointed to by *str* into an **int** value. The string must
contain a valid integer number. If this is not the case,
the returned value is 0.

The number may be terminated by any character
that cannot be part of an integer number. This includes
whitespace characters, punctuation, and other characters. Thus, if **atoi( )** is called with 123.23, the integer
value 123 will be returned, and the 0.23 ignored.

EXAMPLE   This program reads two integer numbers
and displays their sum.

```
#include "stdlib.h"
#include "stdio.h"

main( )
{
  char num1[80], num2[80];

  printf("enter first: ");
  gets(num1);
  printf("enter second: ");
  gets(num2);
  printf("the sum is: %d",atoi(num1)+atoi(num2));
}
```

#include "stdlib.h"
int atol(const char *str);

DESCRIPTION   The **atol( )** function converts the string pointed to by *str* into a **long int** value. The string must contain a valid long integer number. If this is not the case, the returned value is 0.

The number may be terminated by any character that cannot be part of an integer number. This includes whitespace characters, punctuation, and other characters. Thus, if **atol( )** is called with 123.23, the integer value 123 will be returned, and the 0.23 ignored.

EXAMPLE   This program reads two long integer numbers and displays their sum.

```
#include "stdlib.h"
#include "stdio.h"

main( )
{
  char num1[80], num2[80];

  printf("enter first: ");
  gets(num1);
  printf("enter second: ");
  gets(num2);
  printf("the sum is: %ld",atol(num1)+atol(num2));
}
```

```
#include "stdlib.h"
void *bsearch(const void *key, const
              void*base, size_t num, size_t
              size,int(*compare
              (const void *,const void *));
```

DESCRIPTION   The **bsearch( )** function performs a binary search on the sorted array pointed to by *base* and returns a pointer to the first member that matches the key pointed to by *key*. The number of elements in the array is specified by *num* and the size (in bytes) of each element is described by *size*. (The **size_t** type is defined in STDLIB.H and is essentially the equivalent of **unsigned**.)

The function pointed to by *compare* is used to compare an element of the array with the key. The form of *compare* must be

function_name (const void *arg1*, const void *arg2*)

It must return the following values:

If *arg1* is less than *arg2* then return less than 0.
If *arg1* is equal to *arg2* then return 0.
If *arg1* is greater than *arg2* then return greater than 0.

The array must be sorted in ascending order, with the lowest address containing the lowest element.

If the array does not contain the key, then a null pointer is returned.

EXAMPLE   This program reads characters entered at the keyboard (assuming buffered keyboard I/O) and determines whether they belong to the alphabet.

```
#include "stdlib.h"
#include "ctype.h"
#include "stdio.h"
int comp( );

char *alpha="abcdefghijklmnopqrstuvwxyz";

comp(const char *ch, const char *s);

main( )
{
  char ch;
  char *p;
  int comp( );

  do {
    printf("enter a character: ");
    scanf("%c%*c",&ch);
    ch = tolower(ch);
    p = (char *) bsearch(&ch,alpha, 26, 1, comp);
    if(p) printf("is in alphabet\n");
    else printf("is not in alphabet\n");
  } while(p);
}

/* compare two characters */
comp(const char *ch, const char *s)
{
  return *ch-*s;
}
```

```
#include "stdlib.h"
void exit(int status);
```

DESCRIPTION   The **exit( )** function causes immediate normal termination of a program.

The value of *status* is passed to the calling process, usually the operating system, if the environment supports it. By convention, if the value of *status* is 0, normal program termination is assumed. A non-0 value may be used to indicate an error.

EXAMPLE   This function performs menu selection for a mailing list program. If **Q** is selected, the program is terminated.

```c
menu(void)
{
  char choice;

  do {
    printf("Enter names (E)\n");
    printf("Delete name (D)\n");
    printf("Print (P)\n");
    printf("Quit (Q)\n");
  } while(!strchr("EDPQ",toupper(ch));
  if(ch=='Q') exit(0);
  return ch;
}
```

```
#include "stdlib.h"
long labs(long num);
```

DESCRIPTION   The **labs( )** function returns the absolute value of the **long int** *num*.

EXAMPLE   This function converts the user-entered numbers into their absolute values.

```
#include "stdlib.h"
#include "stdio.h"

long int get_labs( )
{
  char num[80];

  gets(num)

  return labs(atol(num));
}
```

#include "setjmp.h"
void longjmp(jmp_buf envbuf, int val);

DESCRIPTION   The **longjmp( )** instruction causes program execution to resume at the point of the last call to **setjmp( )**. These two functions are the way ANSI C provides for a jump between functions. Notice that the header SETJUMP.H is required.

The **longjmp( )** function operates by resetting the stack as described in *envbuf,* which must have been set by a prior call to **setjmp( )**. This causes program execution to resume at the statement following the **setjmp( )** invocation—the computer is "tricked" into thinking that it never left the function that called **setjmp( )**. (As a somewhat graphic explanation, the **longjmp( )** function "warps" across time and (memory) space to a previous point in your program, without having to perform the normal function-return process.)

The buffer *envbuf* is of type **jmp_buf**, which is defined in the header SETJMP.H. The buffer must have been set through a call to **setjmp( )** prior to calling **longjmp( )**.

The value of *val* becomes the return value of **setjump( )** and may be interrogated to determine where the long jump came from. The only value not allowed is 0.

It is important to understand that the **longjmp( )** function must be called before the function that called **setjmp( )** returns. If not, the result is technically undefined. In actuality, a crash will almost certainly occur.

By far the most common use of **longjmp( )** is to return from a deeply nested set of routines when a catastrophic error occurs.

EXAMPLE   This program prints **1 2 3**.

```
#include "setjmp.h"
#include "stdio.h"

void f2(void);

jmp_buf ebuf;

main( )
{
  char first=1;
  int i;

  printf("1 ");
  i = setjmp(ebuf);
  if(first) {
    first = !first;
    f2( );
    printf("this will not be printed");
  }
  printf("%d", i);
}
```

```
void f2(void)
{
 printf("2 ");
 longjmp(ebuf, 3);
}
```

#include "stdlib.h"
void qsort(void *base, size_t num, size_t size,
int (*compare)(const *void, const *void));

DESCRIPTION   The **qsort( )** function sorts the array pointed to by *base* using a Quicksort (which was developed by C. A. R. Hoare). The Quicksort is generally considered the best general-purpose sorting algorithm. Upon termination, the array will be sorted. The number of elements in the array is specified by *num* and the size (in bytes) of each element is described by *size*. (The **size_t** type is defined in STDLIB.H and is essentially the equivalent of **unsigned**.)

The function pointed to by *compare* is used to compare an element of the array with the key. The form of *compare* must be

function_name (const void *arg1*, const void *arg2*)

It must return the following values.

If *arg1* is less than *arg2* then return less than 0.
If *arg1* is equal to *arg2* then return 0.
If *arg1* is greater than *arg2* then return greater than 0.

The array is sorted in ascending order, with the lowest address containing the lowest element.

EXAMPLE   This program sorts a list of integers and displays the result.

```c
#include "stdlib.h"
#include "stdio.h"

int comp( );

int num[10]= {
  1,3,6,5,8,7,9,6,2,0
};

main( )
{
  int i;

  printf("original array: ");
  for(i=0; i<10; i++) printf("%d ", num[i]);

  qsort(num, 10, sizeof(int), comp);

  printf("sorted array: ");
  for(i=0; i<10; i++) printf("%d ", num[i]);
}

/* compare the integers */
comp(const int *i, const int *j)
{
  return *i-*j;
}
```

#include "stdlib.h"
int rand(void);

DESCRIPTION   The **rand( )** function generates a sequence of pseudo-random numbers. Each time it is called, an integer between 0 and **RAND_MAX** is returned. **RAND_MAX** is defined in STDLIB.H. The ANSI standard stipulates that the macro **RAND_MAX** will have a value of at least 32,767.

EXAMPLE   This program displays ten pseudo-random numbers.

```
#include "stdlib.h"
#include "stdio.h"

main( )
{
  int i;

  for(i=0; i<10; i++)
    printf("%d ",rand( ));
}
```

#include "setjmp.h"
void setjmp(jmp_buf envbuf);

DESCRIPTION   The **setjmp()** function saves the contents of the system stack in the buffer *envbuf* for later use by **longjmp()**.

The **setjmp()** function returns 0 upon invocation. However, **longjmp()** passes an argument to **setjmp()** when it executes, and it is this value (always non-0) that will appear to be the value of **setjmp()** after a call to **longjmp()**.

See the **longjmp()** section for more information.

EXAMPLE   This program prints **1 2 3**.

```
#include "setjmp.h"
#include "stdio.h"

void f2(void);

jmp_buf ebuf;

main( )
{
  char first=1;
  int i;

  printf("1 ");
  i = setjmp(ebuf);
  if(first) {
    first = !first;
    f2( );
    printf("this will not be printed");
  }
  printf("%d",i);
}

void f2(void)
{
 printf("2 ");
 longjmp(ebuf, 3);
}
```

#include "stdlib.h"
void srand(unsigned seed);

DESCRIPTION   The **srand( )** function is used to set a starting point for the sequence generated by **rand( )**, which returns pseudo-random numbers.

Generally **srand( )** is used to allow multiple program runs using different sequences of pseudo-random numbers.

EXAMPLE   This program uses the system time to randomly initialize the **rand( )** function using **srand( )**.

```
#include "stdio.h"
#include "stdlib.h"
#include "time.h"

/* Seed rand with the system time
   and display the first 100 numbers.
*/
main( )
{
  int i, utime;
  long  ltime;

  /* get the current calendar time */

  ltime = time(NULL);
  utime = (unsigned int) ltime/2;
  srand(utime);
  for(i=0; i<10; i++) printf("%d ", rand( ));
}
```

·B·
C Keyword Summary

These are the 32 keywords that, combined with the formal C syntax, form the C language as defined by the ANSI standard. These keywords are shown in Table B-1.

All C keywords use lowercase letters. In C, uppercase and lowercase are different; for instance, **else** is a keyword, ELSE is not.

TABLE B-1.   Keyword List

auto	double	int	struct
break	else	long	switch
case	enum	register	typedef
char	extern	return	union
const	float	short	unsigned
continue	for	signed	void
default	goto	sizeof	volatile
do	if	static	while

An alphabetical summary of each of the keywords follows.

auto

auto is used to create temporary variables that are created upon entry into a block and destroyed upon exit. For example:

```
#include "stdio.h"
#include "conio.h"

main( )
{
  for(;;) {
    if(getche( )=='a') {
      auto int t;
      for(t=0; t<'a'; t++)
        printf("%d ", t);
    }
  }
}
```

In this example, the variable **t** is created only if the user strikes an **a**. Outside the **if** block, **t** is completely unknown; and any reference to it would generate a compile-time syntax error. The use of **auto** is completely optional since all local variables are **auto** by default.

break

break is used to exit from a **do**, **for**, or **while** loop, bypassing the normal loop condition. It is also used to exit from a **switch** statement.

An example of **break** in a loop is shown here.

```
while(x<100) {
  x = get_new_x( );
  if(kbhit( )) break;   /* key hit on
                          keyboard */
  process(x);

}
```

Here, if a key is typed, the loop will terminate no matter what the value of **x** is.

A **break** always terminates the innermost **for**, **do**, **while**, or **switch** statement, regardless of any nesting. In a **switch** statement, **break** effectively keeps program execution from "falling through" to the next **case**. (Refer to the **switch** section for details.)

case

case is covered in conjunction with **switch**.

char

char is a data type used to declare character variables. For example, to declare **ch** to be a character type, you would write

```
char ch;
```

In C, a character is one byte long.

const

The **const** modifier is used to tell the compiler the variable that follows cannot be modified. It is also used to prevent a function from modifying the object pointed to by one of its arguments.

continue

continue is used to bypass portions of code in a loop and force the conditional test to be performed. For example, the following **while** loop will simply read characters from the keyboard until an **s** is typed.

```
while(ch=getche( )) {
  if(ch!='s') continue;   /* read another char */
  process(ch);
}
```

The call to **process( )** will not occur until **ch** contains the character 's.'

default

default is used in the **switch** statement to signal a default block of code to be executed if no matches are found in the **switch**. See the **switch** section.

do

The **do** loop is one of three loop constructs available in C. The general form of the **do** loop is

```
do {
    statements block
} while(condition);
```

If only one statement is repeated, the braces are not necessary, but they add clarity to the statement.

The **do** loop is the only loop in C that will always have at least one iteration because the condition is tested at the bottom of the loop.

A common use of the **do** loop is to read disk files. This code will read a file until an EOF is encountered.

```
do {
    ch = getc(fp);
    printf("%c", ch);
} while(!feof(fp));
```

double

double is a data type specifier used to declare double-precision floating-point variables. To declare **d** to be of type **double** you would write the following statement.

```
double d;
```

else

See the **if** section.

enum

The **enum** type specifier is used to create enumeration types. An enumeration is simply a list of objects. Hence, an enumeration type specifies what that list of objects consists of. Further, an enumeration type variable may only be assigned values that are part of the enumeration list. For example, the following code declares an enumeration called **color** and a variable of that type called **c** and performs an assignment and a condition test.

```
#include "stdio.h"

enum color {red, green, yellow};
enum color c;

main( )
{
  c = red;
  if(c==red) printf("is red\n");
}
```

extern

The **extern** data type modifier is used to tell the compiler that a variable is declared elsewhere in the program. This is often used in conjuction with separately compiled files that share the same global data and are linked together. In essence, it notifies the compiler of a variable without redeclaring it.

As an example, if **first** was declared in another file as an integer, the following declaration would be used in subsequent files.

```
extern int first;
```

float

float is a data type specifier used to declare floating-point variables. To declare **f** to be of type **float** you would write

```
float f;
```

for

The **for** loop allows automatic initialization and incrementation of a counter variable. The general form is

for(*initialization; condition; increment*) {
    statement-block
}

If the *statement-block* is only one statement, the braces are not necessary.

Although the **for** allows a number of variations, generally the *initialization* is used to set a counter variable to its starting value. The *condition* is generally a relational statement that checks the counter variable against a termination value, and the *increment* increments (or decrements) the counter value.

The following code will print **hello** ten times.

```
for(t=0; t<10; t++) printf("hello\n");
```

goto

The **goto** causes program execution to jump to the *label* specified in the **goto** statement. The general form of the **goto** is

goto *label*;
.

.

.

label:

All *labels* must end in a colon and must not conflict with keywords or function names. Furthermore, a **goto** can only branch within the current function, and not from one function to another.

The following example will print the message **right** but not the message **wrong**.

```
goto lab1;
  printf("wrong");
lab1:
  printf("right");
```

if

The general form of the **if** statement is

```
if(condition) {
   statement block 1
}
else {
   statement block 2
}
```

If single statements are used, the braces are not needed. The **else** is optional.

The *condition* may be any expression. If that expression evaluates to any value other than 0, then *statement block 1* will be executed; otherwise, if it exists, *statement block 2* will be executed.

The following code fragment can be used for keyboard input and to look for a 'q' which signifies "quit."

```
ch = getche( );
if(ch=='q') {
  printf("program terminated");
  exit(0);
}
else  proceed( );
```

int

int is the type specifier used to declare integer variables. For example, to declare **count** as an integer you would write

```
int count;
```

long

long is a data type modifier used to declare double length integer variables. For example, to declare **count** as a long integer, you would write

```
long int count;
```

register

The **register** modifier is used to request that a variable be stored in the way that allows the fastest possible access. In the case of characters or integers, this usually means a register of the CPU. To declare **i** to be a **register** integer, you would write

```
register int i;
```

return

The **return** statement forces a return from a function and can be used to transfer a value back to the calling routine. For example, the following function returns the product of its two integer arguments.

```
mul(int a, int b)
{
   return(a*b);
}
```

Keep in mind that as soon as a **return** is encountered, the function will return, skipping any other code in the function.

short

short is a data type modifier used to declare small integers. For example, to declare **sh** to be a short integer you would write

```
short int sh;
```

signed

The **signed** type modifier is most commonly used to specify a **signed char** data type.

sizeof

The **sizeof** keyword is a compile-time operator that returns the length of the variable or type it precedes. If it precedes a type, the type must be enclosed in parentheses. For example,

```
printf("%d", sizeof(int));
```

will print **2** for many C implementations.

The **sizeof** statement's principal use is in helping to generate portable code when that code depends on the size of the C built-in data types.

static

The **static** keyword is a data type modifier used to instruct the compiler to create permanent storage for the local variable that it precedes. This enables the specified variable to maintain its value between function calls. For example, to declare **last_time** as a **static** integer, you would write

```
static int last_time;
```

struct

The **struct** statement is used to create complex or conglomerate variables, called structures, that are made up of one or more elements. The general form of a structure is

```
struct struct_name {
    type element1;
    type element2;
    .
    .
    .
    type elementN;
} structure_variable_name;
```

The individual elements are referenced using the dot or arrow operators.

switch

The **switch** statement is C's multi-path branch statement. It is used to route execution in one of several ways. The general form of the statement is

```
switch(variable) {
    case (constant1): statement-set 1;
        break;
    case (constant2): statement-set 2;
        break;

        .

        .

        .

    case (constant N): statement-set N;
        break;
    default: default-statements;
}
```

Each *statement-set* may be one or many statements long. The **default** portion is optional.

The **switch** works by checking the *variable* against all the constants. As soon as a match is found, that set of statements is executed. If the **break** statement is omitted, execution will continue until the end of the **switch**. You can think of the **cases** as labels. Execution will continue until a **break** statement is found or the **switch** ends.

The following example can be used to process a menu selection.

```
ch = getche ( );

switch (ch) {
    case 'e': enter ( );
        break;
    case 'l': list ( );
        break;
```

```
case 's': sort( );
    break;
case 'q': exit(0);
default: printf("unknown command\n");
    printf("try again\n");

}
```

typedef

The **typedef** statement allows you to create a new name for an existing data type. The data type may be one of the built-in types or a structure or union name. The general form of **typedef** is

typedef *type-specifier new-name;*

For example, to use the word "balance" in place of "float," you would write

```
typedef float balance;
```

union

The **union** keyword is used to assign two or more variables to the same memory location. The form of the definition and the way an element is referenced are the same as for **struct**. The general form is

union *union-name* {
  type *element1;*
  type *element2;*
   .
   .
   .
  type *elementN;*
} union *variable-name;*

unsigned

The **unsigned** type modifier tells the compiler to eliminate the sign bit of an integer and to use all bits for arithmetic. This has the effect of doubling the size of the largest integer, but restricts it to only positive numbers. For example, to declare **big** to be an unsigned integer you would write

```
unsigned int big;
```

void

The **void** type specifier is primarily used to explicitly declare functions that return no (meaningful) value. It is also used to create **void** pointers (pointers to **void**) that are generic pointers capable of pointing to any type of object.

volatile

The **volatile** modifier is used to tell the compiler that a variable may have its contents altered in ways not explicitly defined by the program. Variables that are changed by the hardware, such as real-time clocks, interrupts, or other inputs are examples.

while

The **while** loop has the general form

```
while(condition) {
    statement block
}
```

If a single statement is the object of the **while**, the braces may be omitted.

The **while** tests its *condition* at the top of the loop. Therefore, if the *condition* is false to begin with, the loop will not execute at all. The *condition* may be any expression.

An example of a **while** follows. It will read 100 characters from a disk file and store them in a character array.

```
t = 0;

while(t<100) {
  s[t] = getc(fp);
  t++;
}
```

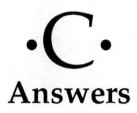

Answers

1.3 EXERCISES

2.
```c
#include "stdio.h"

main( )
{
  int num;

  num = 1000;
  printf("%d is the value of num", num);
}
```

1.4 EXERCISES

2.
```c
#include "stdio.h"

main( )
{
  float a, b;

  printf("Enter two numbers: ");
  scanf("%f", &a);
  scanf("%f", &b);
  printf("their sum is %f", a+b);
}
```

1.5 EXERCISES

1.
```c
#include "stdio.h"

main( )
{
  int len, width, height;

  printf("Enter length: ");
  scanf("%d", &len);
```

```
   printf("Enter width: ");
   scanf("%d", &width);

   printf("Enter height: ");
   scanf("%d", &height);

   printf("volume is %d", len * width * height);
}
```

2.
```
#include "stdio.h"

main( )
{
   printf("number of seconds in a year: ");
   printf("%f", 60.0 * 60.0 * 24.0 * 365.0);
}
```

1.6 EXERCISES

2. Yes, a comment can contain nothing.

3. Yes, you can temporarily remove a line of code from your program by making it into a comment. This is sometimes called "commenting out" a line of code.

1.7 EXERCISES

2.
```
#include "stdio.h"

main( )
{
   one( );
   two( );
}

one( )
{
   printf("The summer soldier, ");
```

```
  }

  two( )
  {
     printf("the sunshine patriot");
  }
```

1.8 EXERCISES

2.
```
#include "stdio.h"

main( )
{
   printf("%d", convert( ));
}

convert( )
{
   int dollars;

   printf("Enter number of dollars: ");
   scanf("%d", &dollars);
   return dollars / 2;
}
```

3. The function **f1( )** returns an integer value, but it is being assigned to a variable of type **double**.

1.9 EXERCISES

1.
```
#include "stdio.h"

main( )
{
```

```
    outnum(10);
}

outnum(int num)
{
    printf("%d", num);
}
```

2. The **sqr_it( )** function requires an integer argument, but it is called with a floating-point value.

MASTERY SKILLS CHECK

1.
```
#include "stdio.h"

main( )
{
    float weight;

    printf("Enter your weight: ");
    scanf("%f", &weight);
    printf("effective moon weight: %f", weight * 0.17);
}
```

2. The comment is not terminated with a */.

3.
```
#include "stdio.h"

main( )
{
    int ounces;
    int cups;

    printf("Enter ounces: ");
    scanf("%d", &ounces);

    cups = o_to_c(ounces);
    printf("%d cups", cups);
}
```

```
o_to_c(int o)
{
   return o / 8;
}
```

4. **char, int, float, double,** and **void**.

5. The variable names are wrong because

    a. A dash may not be used in a variable name.

    b. A dollar sign may not be used in a variable name.

    c. A + sign may not be used in a variable name.

2 SKILLS CHECK

1. All programs must have a **main( )** function. This is the first function called when your program begins executing.

2.
```
#include "stdio.h"

main( )
{
   printf("This is the number %d", 100);
}
```

3. To include a header file, use the **#include** compiler directive. For example,

```
#include "stdio.h"
```

includes the STDIO.H header.

4. The five basic data types are **char, int, float, double,** and **void**.

5. The invalid variable names are b, c, and e.

6. The **scanf( )** function is used to input information from the keyboard.

7.
```c
#include "stdio.h"

main( )
{
   int i;

   printf("Enter a number: ");
   scanf("%d", &i);
   printf("%d", i*i);
}
```

8. Comments must be surrounded by the /* and */ comment symbols. For example, this is a valid C comment.

```c
/* This is a comment. */
```

9. A function returns a value to the calling routine using **return**.

10.
```c
Myfunc(int count, float balance, char ch)
```

2.1 EXERCISES

1. b, d, and e are true.

2.
```c
#include "stdio.h"

main( )
{
   int i;

   printf("enter a number: ");
   scanf("%d", &i);
   if((i%2)==0) printf("even");
   if((i%2)==1) printf("odd");
}
```

2.2 EXERCISES

1.
```c
#include "stdio.h"

main( )
{
  int a, b, op;

  printf("enter first number: ");
  scanf("%d", &a);

  printf("enter second number: ");
  scanf("%d", &b);

  printf("Enter 0 to add, 1 to multiply: ");
  scanf("%d", &op);

  if(op==0) printf("%d", a+b);
  else printf("%d", a*b);
}
```

2.
```c
#include "stdio.h"

main( )
{
  int i;

  printf("enter a number: ");
  scanf("%d", &i);
  if((i%2)==0) printf("even");
  else printf("odd");
}
```

2.3 EXERCISES

1.
```c
#include "stdio.h"

main( )
{
```

```
    int a, b, op;

    printf("Enter 0 to add, 1 to subtract: ");
    scanf("%d", &op);

    if(op==0) { /* add */
      printf("enter first number: ");
      scanf("%d", &a);
      printf("enter second number: ");
      scanf("%d", &b);
      printf("%d", a+b);
    }
    else { /* subtract */
      printf("enter first number: ");
      scanf("%d", &a);
      printf("enter second number: ");
      scanf("%d", &b);
      printf("%d", a-b);
    }
  }
```

2. No, the opening curly brace is missing.

2.4 EXERCISES

1.
```
#include "stdio.h"

main( )
{
  int i;

  for(i=1; i<101; i=i+1) printf("%d ", i);
}
```

2.
```
#include "stdio.h"

main( )
{
  int i;

  for(i=17; i<101; i=i+1)
```

```
     if((i%17)==0) printf("%d ", i);
}
```

3.
```
#include "stdio.h"

main( )
{
  int num, i;

  printf("enter the number to test: ");
  scanf("%d", &num);

  for(i=2; i<(num/2)+1; i=i+1)
    if((num%i)==0) printf("%d ", i);
}
```

2.5 EXERCISES

1.
```
#include "stdio.h"

main( )
{
  int i;

  for(i=1; i<101; i=++) printf("%d ", i);
}
```

```
#include "stdio.h"

main( )
{
  int i;

  for(i=17; i<101; i++)
    if((i%17)==0) printf("%d ", i);
}
```

```
#include "stdio.h"
```

```
main( )
{
  int num, i;

  printf("enter the number to test: ");
  scanf("%d", &num);

  for(i=2; i<num/2; i++) {
    if((num%i)==0) printf("%d ", i);
}
```

2. ```
#include "stdio.h"

main( )
{
  int a, b;

  a = 1;
  a++;
  b = a;
  b--;
  printf("%d %d", a, b);
}
```

# 2.6 EXERCISES

1. ```
#include "stdio.h"

main( )
{
  int i;

  for(i=1; i<11; i++)
    printf("%d %d %d\n", i, i*i, i*i*i);
}
```

2. ```
#include "stdio.h"

main( )
{
  int i, j;
```
```

```
    printf("Enter a number: ");
    scanf("%d", &i);

    for(j=i; j>0; j--) printf("%d ", j);
    printf("\a");
}
```

2.7 EXERCISES

1. The loop prints the numbers **0** through **99**.

2. Yes.

3. No, the first is true, the second is false.

MASTERY SKILLS CHECK

1.
```c
#include "stdio.h"

main( )
{
  int magic;   /* magic number */
  int guess;   /* user's guess */
  int i;

  magic = 1325;


  for(i=0; i<10; i++) {
    printf("Enter your guess: ");
    scanf("%d", &guess);

    if(guess == magic) {
      printf("RIGHT!");
      printf(" %d is the magic number\n", magic);
    }
    else {
      printf("..Sorry, you're wrong..");
```

```
        if(guess > magic)
            printf(" Your guess is too high\n");
        else printf(" your guess is too low\n");
    }
  }
}
```

2.
```
#include "stdio.h"

main( )
{
  int rooms, len, width, total;
  int i;

  printf("Number of rooms? ");
  scanf("%d", &rooms);

  total = 0;
  for(i=rooms; i>0; i--) {
    printf("enter length: ");
    scanf("%d", &len);

    printf("enter width: ");
    scanf("%d", &width);

    total = total + len*width;
  }
  printf("Total square footage: %d", total);
}
```

3. The increment operator increases a variable by one and the decrement operator decreases a variable by one.

4.
```
#include "stdio.h"

main( )
{
  int answer, count;
  int right, wrong;

  right = 0;
  wrong = 0;
```

```
   for(count=1; count < 11; count=count+1) {
     printf("What is %d + %d? ", count, count);
     scanf("%d", &answer);
     if(answer == count+count) {
       printf("Right!  ");
       right++;
     }
     else {
       printf("Sorry, you're wrong ");
       printf("the answer is %d.  ", count+count);
       wrong++;
     }
   }
   printf("You got %d right and %d wrong.", right, wrong);
}
```

5. #include "stdio.h"

```
main( )
{
  int i;

  for(i=1; i<=100; i++) {
    printf("%d\t", i);
    if((i%5)==0) printf("\n");
  }
}
```

3 SKILLS CHECK

1. C's relational and logical operators are <, >, <=, >=, !=, ==, !, &&, and | |.

2. A block of code is a group of logically connected statements. To make a block, surround the statements with curly braces.

3. To output a newline, use the \n backslash character code.

4.
```
#include "stdio.h"

main( )
{
  int i;

  for(i=-100; i<101; i++) printf("%d ", i);
}
```

5.
```
#include "stdio.h"

main( )
{
  int i;

  printf("Enter proverb number: ");
  scanf("%d", &i);

  if(i==1) printf("A bird in the hand...");
  if(i==2) printf("A rolling stone...");
  if(i==3) printf("Once burned, twice shy.");
  if(i==4) printf("Early to bed, early to rise...");
  if(i==5) printf("A penny saved is a penny earned.");
}
```

6.
```
count++;
/* or */
++count;
```

7. In C, true is any non-0 value. False is 0.

3.1 EXERCISES

1.
```
#include "stdio.h"
#include "conio.h"

main( )
{
  int i;
  char ch, smallest;
```

```
    printf("Enter 10 letters\n");

    smallest = 'z'; /* make largest to begin with */

    for(i=0; i<10; i++) {
        ch. = getche( );
        if(ch<smallest) smallest = ch;
    }
    printf("The smallest character is %c.", smallest);
}
```

3.2 EXERCISES

1. The **else** relates to the first **if**; it is not in the same block as the second.

2.
```
#include "stdio.h"
#include "conio.h"

main( )
{
    char ch;
    int s1, s2;
    float radius;

    printf("Compute area of Circle, Square, or Triangle? ");
    ch = getche( );
    printf("\n");

    if(ch=='C') {
        printf("Enter radius of circle: ");
        scanf("%f", &radius);
        printf("Area is: %f", 3.1416*radius*radius);
    }
    else if(ch=='S') {
        printf("Enter length of first side: ");
        scanf("%d", &s1);
        printf("Enter length of second side: ");
        scanf("%d", &s2);
        printf("Area is: %d", s1*s2);
```

```
      }
    else if(ch=='T') {
      printf("Enter length of base: ");
      scanf("%d", &s1);
      printf("Enter height: ");
      scanf("%d", &s2);
      printf("Area is: %d", (s1*s2)/2);
    }
  }
```

3.3 EXERCISES

1.
```
  #include "stdio.h"
  #include "conio.h"

  main( )
  {
    int dist, speed;
    char ch;

    for(ch='Y'; ch=='Y'; ch=getche( )) {
      printf("\nEnter distance: ");
      scanf("%d", &dist);

      printf("Enter average speed: ");
      scanf("%d", &speed);

      printf("Drive time is %d\n", dist/speed);

      printf("Again? (Y/N)");
    }
  }
```

2.
```
  #include "stdio.h"

  main( )
  {
    int i;

    printf("\nEnter a number: ");
```

```
     scanf("%d", &i);

     for( ; i; i--) ;

     printf("\a");
 }
```

3.
```
#include "stdio.h"

main( )
{
    int i;

    for(i=1; i<1001; i=i+i) printf("%d ", i);
}
```

3.4 EXERCISES

1.
```
#include "stdio.h"
#include "conio.h"

main( )
{
    int dist, speed;
    char ch;

    ch = 'Y';
    while(ch=='Y') {
        printf("\nEnter distance: ");
        scanf("%d", &dist);

        printf("Enter average speed: ");
        scanf("%d", &speed);

        printf("Drive time is %d\n", dist/speed);

        printf("Again? (Y/N)");
        ch = getche( );
    }
}
```

2.
```
#include "stdio.h"
#include "conio.h"

main( )
{
  char ch;

  printf("Enter your encoded message.\n");

  ch = getche( );
  while(ch!='\r') {
    printf("%c", ch-1);
    ch = getche( );
  }
}
```

3.5 EXERCISES

1.
```
#include "stdio.h"
#include "conio.h"

main( )
{
  float gallons;
  char ch;

  do {
    printf("\nEnter gallons: ");
    scanf("%f", &gallons);
    printf("Liters: %f\n", gallons*3.7854);

    printf("Again? (Y/N)");
    ch = getche( );
  } while(ch=='Y');
}
```

2.
```
#include "stdio.h"

main( )
{
```

```
      int choice;

      printf("Mailing list menu:\n\n");
      printf("  1. Enter addresses\n");
      printf("  2. Delete address\n");
      printf("  3. Search the list\n");
      printf("  4. Print the list\n");
      printf("  5. Quit\n");

      do {
        printf("Enter the number of the choice (1-5): ");
        scanf("%d", &choice);
      } while(choice<1 || choice>5);
    }
```

3.6 EXERCISES

1.
```
/* This program finds the prime numbers from
     2 to 2000.
*/

#include "stdio.h"

main( )
{
  int i, j, prime;

  for(i=2; i<1000; i++) {
    prime = 1;
    for(j=2; j <= i/2; j++)
      if(!(i%j)) prime=0;
    if(prime) printf("%d is prime\n", i);
  }
}
```

2.
```
#include "stdio.h"
#include "conio.h"

main( )
{
  int i;
```

```
    char ch;

    for(i=0; i<10; i++) {
      printf("\nEnter a letter: ");
      ch = getche( );
      printf("\n");
      for( ; ch; ch--) printf("%c", '.');
    }
}
```

3.7 EXERCISES

2.
```
#include "stdio.h"
#include "conio.h"

main( )
{
  float i;
  char ch;

  printf("Tip computer\n");

  for(i=1.0; i<101.0; i=i+1.0) {
    printf("%f %f %f %f\n", i, i+i*.1, i+i*.15, i+i*.2);
    printf("More? (Y/N) ");
    ch = getche( );
    printf("\n");
    if(ch=='N') break;
  }
}
```

3.8 EXERCISE

1.
```
#include "stdio.h"

main( )
{
  int i;
```

```
   for(i=1; i<101; i++) {
     if(!(i%2)) continue;
     printf("%d ", i);
   }
}
```

3.9 EXERCISES

1. Floating point values may not be used to control **switch**.

2.
```
#include "stdio.h"
#include "conio.h"

main( )
{
  char ch;
  int digit, punc, letter;

  printf("Enter characters, ENTER to stop\n");

  digit = 0;
  punc = 0;
  letter = 0;

  do {
    ch = getche( );
    switch(ch) {
      case '1':
      case '2':
      case '3':
      case '4':
      case '5':
      case '6':
      case '7':
      case '8':
      case '9':
```

```
        case '0':
          digit++;
          break;
        case '.':
        case ',':
        case '?':
        case '!':
        case ':':
        case ';':
          punc++;
          break;
        default:
          letter++;
      }
    } while (ch!='\r');
    printf("\ndigits: %d\n", digit);
    printf("punctuation: %d\n", punc);
    printf("letters: %d\n", letter);
}
```

3.10 EXERCISES

1.
```
#include "stdio.h"

main( )
{
  int i;

  i = 1;

  jump_label:
    if(i>=11) goto done_label;
    printf("%d ", i);
    i++;
    goto jump_label;
  done_label: printf("done");
}
```

MASTERY SKILLS CHECK

1.
```c
#include "stdio.h"
#include "conio.h"

main( )
{
  char ch;

  printf("Enter lowercase letters ");
  printf("(press ENTER to quit)\n");
  do {
    ch = getche( );
    if(ch!='\r') printf("%c", ch-32);
  } while(ch!='\r');
}
```

2.
```c
#include "stdio.h"

main( )
{
  int i;

  printf("Enter a number: ");
  scanf("%d", &i);

  if(!i) printf("zero");
  else if(i<0) printf("negative");
  else printf("positive");
}
```

3. The **for** loop is valid. C allows any of its expressions to be empty.

4.
```c
for( ; ; ) ...
```

5.
```c
/* for */
for(i=1; i<11; i++) printf("%d ", i);

/* do */
i = 1;
do {
```

```
   printf("%d ", i);
   i++;
} while(i<11);

/* while */

i = 1;
while(i<11) {
  printf("%d ", i);
  i++;
}
```

6. The **break** statement causes immediate termination of the loop.

7. Yes.

8. No, the label is missing the colon.

INTEGRATING NEW SKILLS CHECK

1.
```
#include "stdio.h"
#include "conio.h"

main( )
{
  char ch;

  printf("Enter characters (q to quit): \n");
  do {
    ch = getche( );
    switch(ch) {
      case '\t': printf("tab\n");
        break;
      case '\b': printf("backspace\n");
        break;
      case '\r': printf("ENTER\n");
    }
  } while(ch!='q');
}
```

2.
```c
#include "stdio.h"

main( )
{
  int i, j, k;

  for(k=0; k<10; k++) {   /* use increment operator */
    printf("Enter first number: ");
    scanf("%d", &i);

    printf("Enter second number: ");
    scanf("%d", &j);

    if(j) printf("%d\n", i/j);   /* simplify condition */
    else printf("cannot divide by zero\n"); /* use else */
  }
}
```

4 SKILLS CHECK

1.
```c
int i;

for(i=1; i<11; i++) printf("%d ");

i = 1;
do {
  printf("%d ", i);
  i++;
} while(i<11);

i = 1;
while(i<11) {
  printf("%d ", i);
  i++;
}
```

2.
```c
switch(ch) {
  case 'L': load( );
    break;
  case 'S': save( );
```

```
      break;
   case 'E': enter;
      break;
   case 'D': display( );
      break;
   case 'Q': quit( );
      break;
```

3.
```c
#include "stdio.h"
#include "conio.h"

main( )
{
   char ch;

   do {
      ch = getche( );
   } while(ch!='\r');
}
```

4. The **break** statement causes immediate termination of the loop that contains it.

5. The **continue** statement causes the next iteration of a loop to occur.

6.
```c
#include "stdio.h"

main( )
{
   int i;
   float feet, meters, ounces, pounds;

   do {
      printf("Convert\n\n");
      printf("1. feet to meters\n");
      printf("2. meters to feet\n");
      printf("3. ounces to pounds\n");
      printf("4. pounds to ounces\n");
      printf("5. Quit\n\n");
      do {
         printf("Enter the number of your choice: ");
         scanf("%d", &i);
```

```
    } while(i<0 || i>5);

    switch(i) {
      case 1:
        printf("Enter feet: ");
        scanf("%f", &feet);
        printf("Meters: %f\n", feet / 3.28);
        break;
      case 2:
        printf("Enter meters: ");
        scanf("%f", &meters);
        printf("Feet: %f\n", meters * 3.28);
        break;
      case 3:
        printf("Enter ounces: ");
        scanf("%f", &ounces);
        printf("Pounds: %f\n", ounces / 16);
        break;
      case 4:
        printf("Enter pounds: ");
        scanf("%f", &pounds);
        printf("ounces: %f\n", pounds * 16);
        break;
    }
  } while(i!=5);
}
```

4.1 EXERCISES

1. `unsigned short int loc_counter;`

2.
```
#include "stdio.h"

main( )
{
  unsigned long int distance;
  int elapsed_time;

  printf("Enter distance: ");

  scanf("%uld", &distance);
```

```
    printf("%d seconds", distance / 186000);
}
```

3. The statement can be recoded using C's shorthand as follows:

```
short i;
```

4.2 EXERCISES

1. Local variables are known only to the function in which they are declared. Global variables are known to and accessible by all functions. Further, local variables are created when the function is entered and destroyed when the function is exited. Thus they cannot maintain their values between function calls. However, global variables stay in existence during the entire lifetime of the program and maintain their values.

2. Here is the non-generalized version.

```
#include "stdio.h"

int distance;

main( )
{
  printf("Enter distance in feet: ");
  scanf("%d", &distance);
  soundspeed( );
}

soundspeed( )
{
  printf("Travel time: %d", distance / 1129);
}
```

Here is the parameterized version.

```c
#include "stdio.h"

main( )
{
  int distance;

  printf("Enter distance in feet: ");
  scanf("%d", &distance);
  soundspeed(distance);
}

soundspeed(int distance)
{
  printf("Travel time: %d", distance / 1129);
}
```

4.3 EXERCISES

1. To cause a constant to be recognized by the compiler explicitly as a **float**, follow the value with an **F**.

2.
```c
#include "stdio.h"

main( )
{
  long i;

  printf("Enter a number: ");
  scanf("%ld", &i);
  printf("%ld", i);
}
```

3.
```c
#include "stdio.h"

main( )
{
  printf("%s %s %s", "I ", "like ", "C");
}
```

4.4 EXERCISES

1.
```
#include "stdio.h"

main( )
{
    int i=100;

    for( ; i>0; i--) printf("%d ", i);
}
```

2. No. You cannot initialize a variable using another variable.

4.5 EXERCISES

1. The entire expression is **float**.

2. The subexpression is **unsigned long**.

4.6 EXERCISES

1. The program displays **10**.

2. The program displays **3.0**.

4.7 EXERCISE

1.
```
#include "stdio.h"

main( )
{
    float f;
```

```
  for(f=1.0; (int) f<=9; f=f+0.1)
    printf("%f ", f);
}
```

MASTERY SKILLS CHECK

1. The data-type modifiers are

    unsigned
    long
    short
    signed

    They are used to modify the base type so that you can obtain variables that best fit the needs of your program.

2. To define an **unsigned** constant, follow the value with a **U**. To define a **long** constant, follow the value with an **l**. To specify a **long double**, follow the value with an **L**.

3. `float balance = 0.0;`

4. When the C compiler evaluates an expression, it automatically converts all **char**s and **short**s to **int**.

5. A **signed** integer uses the high-order bit as a sign flag. When the bit is set, the number is negative; when it is cleared, the number is positive. An **unsigned** integer uses all bits as part of the number and can represent only positive values.

6. Global variables maintain their values throughout the lifetime of the program. They are also accessible by all functions in the program.

7.
```
#include "stdio.h"

int num = 21;

main( )
{
  int i;

  for(i=0; i<10; i++)
    printf("%d ", series( ));
}

series( )
{
  num = (num*1468) % 467;
  return num;
}
```

8. A type cast temporarily changes the type of a variable. For example, here the **int i** is temporarily changed into a **double**.

```
(double) i
```

INTEGRATING NEW SKILLS CHECK

1. The fragment is not valid because to C, both 'A' and 65 are the same thing, and no two **switch case** constants can be the same.

2. The reason that the return value of **getchar( )** or **getche( )** can be assigned to a **char** is because C automatically removes the high-order byte.

3. No. Because **i** is a signed integer, its maximum value is 32,767. Therefore, it will never exceed 33,000.

5   SKILLS CHECK

1. A local variable is known only to the function in which it is declared. Further, it is created when the function is entered and destroyed when the function returns. A global variable is known throughout the entire program and remains in existence the entire time the program is executing.

2. A C compiler will assign the following types:

   a. int

   b. int

   c. double

   d. long

   e. long

3.
```c
#include "stdio.h"

main( )
{
  long l;
  short s;
  double d;

  printf("Enter a long value: ");
  scanf("%ld", &l);

  printf("Enter a short value: ");
  scanf("%hd", &s);

  printf("Enter a double value: ");
  scanf("%f", &d);
```

```
   printf("%ld\n", l);
   printf("%hd\n", s);
   printf("%f\n", d);
}
```

4. A type cast temporarily changes the type of value.

```
#include "stdio.h"
#include "math.h"

main( )
{
   int i;

   for(i=1; i<11; i++)
     printf("%lf\n", sqrt((double) i));
}
```

5. The **if** is associated with the **if(j)** statement, contrary to what the (incorrect) indentation would have you believe.

6. When **i** is 1, **a** is 2. When **i** is 4, **a** is 5.

5.1 EXERCISES

1. The array **count** is being overrun. It is only 10 elements long, but the program requires one that is 100 elements long.

2.
```
#include "stdio.h"

main( )
{
   int i[10], j, k, match;
```

```
   printf("Enter 10 numbers:\n");
   for(j=0; j<10; j++) scanf("%d", &i[j]);

   /* see if any match */
   for(j=0; j<10; j++) {
     match = i[j];
     for(k=j+1; k<10; k++)
       if(match==i[k])
         printf("%d is duplicated\n", match);
   }
 }
```

3.
```
   #include "stdio.h"
   #include "stdlib.h"

   main( )
   {
     float item[100], t;
     int a, b;
     int count;

     /* read in numbers */
     printf("How many numbers? ");
     scanf("%d", &count);
     for(a=0; a<count; a++) scanf("%f", &item[a]);

     /* now, sort them using a bubble sort */
     for(a=1; a<count; ++a)
       for(b=count-1; b>=a; --b) {
         /* compare adjacent elements */
         if(item[b-1] > item[b]) {
           /* exchange elements */
           t = item[b-1];
           item[b-1] = item[b];
           item[b] = t;
         }
       }

     /* display sorted list */
     for(a=0; a<count; a++) printf("%f ", item[a]);
   }
```

5.2 EXERCISES

1.
```
/* Reverse a string. */
#include "stdio.h"
#include "string.h"

main( )
{
  char str[80];
  int i;

  printf("Enter a string: ");
  gets(str);

  for(i=strlen(str)-1; i>=0; i--)
    printf("%c", str[i]);
}
```

2. The string **str** is not long enough to hold the string "this is a test".

3.
```
#include "stdio.h"
#include "string.h"

main( )
{
  char bigstr[1000]="", str[80];

  for( ; ; ) {
    printf("Enter a string: ");
    gets(str);
    if(!strcmp(str, "quit")) break;
    strcat(str, "\n");
    strcat(bigstr, str);

    /* prevent an array overrun */
    if(strlen (bigstr) + strlen (str) >=1000) break;
  }

  printf(bigstr);
}
```

5.3 EXERCISES

1.
```c
#include "stdio.h"

main( )
{
  int three_d[3][3][3];
  int i, j, k;

  for(i=0; i<3; i++)
    for(j=0; j<3; j++)
      for(k=0; k<3; k++) {
        three_d[i][j][k] = (i+1) * (j+1) * (k+1);
        printf("%d ", three_d[i][j][k]);
      }
}
```

2.
```c
#include "stdio.h"

main( )
{
  int three_d[3][3][3];
  int i, j, k, sum;

  for(i=0; i<3; i++)
    for(j=0; j<3; j++)
      for(k=0; k<3; k++) {
        three_d[i][j][k] = (i+1) * (j+1) * (k+1);
        printf("%d ", three_d[i][j][k]);
      }

  /* sum all elements */
  sum = 0;
  for(i=0; i<3; i++)
    for(j=0; j<3; j++)
      for(k=0; k<3; k++)
        sum = sum + three_d[i][j][k];

  printf("\n%d", sum);
}
```

5.4 EXERCISES

1. No. The list must be enclosed between curly braces.

2. No. The array **name** is only 4 characters long. The attempted call to **strcpy( )** will cause the array to be overrun.

3.
```c
#include "stdio.h"

int cube[10][3] = {
   1,  1,  1,
   2,  4,  8,
   3,  6,  18,
   4,  16,  64,
   5,  25,  75,
   6,  36,  216,
   7,  49,  343,
   8,  64,  512,
   9,  81,  729,
   10,  100,  1000
};

main( )
{
   int num, i;

   printf("Enter cube: ");
   scanf("%d", &num);

   for(i=0; i<10; i++)
     if(cube[i][2]==num) {
       printf("Root: %d\n", cube[i][0]);
       printf("Square: %d", cube[i][1]);
       break;
     }

   if(i==10) printf("Cube not found.\n");
}
```

5.5 EXERCISES

1.
```
#include "stdio.h"
#include "conio.h"

char digits[10][10] = {
  "zero", "one", "two", "three",
  "four", "five", "six", "seven",
  "eight", "nine"
};

main( )
{
  char num;

  printf("Enter number: ");
  num = getche( );
  printf("\n");

  num = num - '0';
  if(num>=0 && num<10) printf("%s", digits[num]);
}
```

MASTERY SKILLS CHECK

1. An array is a list of like-type variables.

2. The statement will not generate an error message because C provides no bounds checking on array operations, but it is wrong because it causes **count** to be overrun.

3.
```
#include "stdio.h"

main( )
{
  int stats[20], i, j;
  int mode, count, oldcount, oldmode;
```

```
      printf("Enter 20 numbers: \n");
      for(i=0; i<20; i++) scanf("%d", &stats[i]);

      oldcount = 0;
      /* find the mode */
      for(i=0; i<20; i++) {
        mode = stats[i];
        count = 1;

        /* count the occurrences of this value */
        for(j=i+1; j<20; j++)
          if(mode==stats[j]) count++;

        /* if count is greater than old count,
           use new mode */
        if(count>oldcount) {
          oldmode = mode;
          oldcount = count;
        }
      }

      printf("The mode is %d\n", oldmode);
   }
```

4. `int items[ ] = {1, 2, 3, 4, 5, 6, 7, 8, 9, 10};`

5.
```
   #include "stdio.h"
   #include "string.h"

   main( )
   {
     char str[80];

     do {
       printf("Enter a string: ");
       gets(str);
     } while(strcmp("quit", str));
   }
```

6.
```
   /* Computerized dictionary program. */

   #include "stdio.h"
   #include "string.h"
```

```
char dict[][2][40] = {
  "house", "a place of dwelling",
  "car", "a vehicle",
  "computer", "a thinking machine",
  "program", "a sequence of instructions",
  "", ""
};

main( )
{
  char word[80];
  int i;

  printf("Enter word: ");
  gets(word);

  /* look up the word */
  i = 0;
  /* search while null string not yet encountered */
  while(strcmp(dict[i][0], "")) {
    if(!strcmp(word, dict[i][0])) {
      printf("meaning: %s", dict[i][1]);
      break;
    }
    i++;
  }
  if(!strcmp(dict[i][0], ""))
    printf("Not in dictionary\n");
}
```

INTEGRATING NEW SKILLS CHECK

1.  ```
    #include "stdio.h"
    #include "string.h"

    main( )
    {
      char str[80];
      int i;

      printf("Enter a string: ");
    ```
    ```

```
    gets(str);

    /* pad the string if necessary */
    for(i=strlen(str); i<79; i++)
      strcat(str, ".");

    printf(str);
  }
```

2.
```
  /* A simple coding program. */

  #include "stdio.h"
  #include "string.h"

  main( )
  {
    char str[80];
    int i, j;

    printf("Enter message: ");
    gets(str);

    /* code it */
    i=0; j = strlen(str) - 1;
    while(i<=j) {
      if(i<j) printf("%c%c", str[i], str[j]);
      else printf("%c", str[i]);
      i++; j--;
    }
  }
```

3.
```
  #include "stdio.h"
  #include "string.h"

  main( )
  {
    char str[80];
    int spaces, periods, commas;
    int i;

    printf("Enter a string: ");
    gets(str);
```

```
    spaces = 0;
    commas = 0;
    periods = 0;

    for(i=0; i<strlen(str)-1; i++)
      switch(str[i]) {
        case '.': periods++;
          break;
        case ',': commas++;
          break;
        case ' ': spaces++;
      }

    printf("spaces: %d\n", spaces);
    printf("commas: %d\n", commas);
    printf("periods: %d", periods);
}
```

4. The **getche( )** function returns a character, not a string. Hence, it cannot be used as shown. You must use **gets( )** to read a string from the keyboard.

5.
```
/* A simple game of Hangman */

#include "stdio.h"
#include "string.h"
#include "conio.h"

char word[] = "concatenation";
char temp[] = "_ _ _ _ _ _ _ _ _ _ _ _ _";

main( )
{
  char ch;
  int i, count;

  count = 0; /* count number of guesses */
  do {
    printf("%s\n", temp);
    printf("Enter your guess: ");
    ch = getche( );
    printf("\n");
```

```
    /* see if letter matches any in word */
    for(i=0; i<strlen(word); i++)
      if(ch==word[i]) temp[i] = ch;

    count++;
  } while(strcmp(temp, word));
  printf("%s\n", temp);
  printf("You guessed the word and used %d guesses",
         count);
}
```

6 SKILLS CHECK

1.
```
#include "stdio.h"

main( )
{
  int num[10], i, even, odd;

  printf("Enter 10 integers: ");

  for(i=0; i<10; i++) scanf("%d", &num[i]);

  even = 0; odd = 0;
  for(i=0; i<10; i++) {
    if(num[i]%2) odd = odd + num[i];
    else even = even + num[i];
  }

  printf("Sum of even numbers: %d\n", even);
  printf("Sum of odd numbers: %d", odd);
}
```

2.
```
#include "stdio.h"
#include "string.h"

main( )
{
  char pw[80];
  int i;
```

```
    for(i=0; i<3; i++) {
      printf("Password: ");
      gets(pw);
      if(!strcmp("Tristan", pw)) break;
    }

    if(i==3) printf("Access denied");
    else printf("Log-on successful");
  }
```

3. The array, **name**, is not big enough to hold the string begin assigned to it.

4. A null string is a string that contains only the null character.

5. The **strcpy( )** function copies the contents of one string into another. The **strcmp( )** function compares two strings and returns less than 0 if the first string is less than the second, 0 if the strings match, or greater than zero if the first string is greater than the second.

6.
```
/* A Simple computerized telelphone book. */

#include "stdio.h"
#include "string.h"

char phone[][2][40] = {
  "Fred", "555-1010",
  "Barney", "555-1234",
  "Ralph", "555-2347",
  "Tom", "555-8396",
  "", ""
};

main( )
{
  char name[80];
  int i;
```

```
   printf("Name? ");
   gets(name);

   for(i=0; phone[i][0][0]; i++)
     if(!strcmp(name, phone[i][0]))
       printf("number: %s", phone[i][1]);
}
```

6.1 EXERCISES

1. A pointer is a variable that contains the address of another variable.

2. The pointer operators are the * and the &. The * operator returns the value of the object pointed to by the pointer it precedes. The & operator returns the address of the variable it precedes.

3. The base type of a pointer is important because all pointer arithmetic is done relative to it.

4.
```
#include "stdio.h"

main( )
{
  int i, *p;

  p = &i;

  for(i=0; i<10; i++) printf("%d ", *p);
}
```

6.2 EXERCISES

1. You cannot multiply a pointer.

2. No, you can only add or subtract integer values.

3. 108

6.3 EXERCISES

1. No, you cannot change the value of a pointer that is generated by using an array name without an index.

2. 8

3.
```
#include "stdio.h"

main( )
{
  char str[80], *p;

  printf("Enter a string: ");
  gets(str);

  p = str;

  /* while not at the end of the string and no
     space has been encountered, increment p to
     point to next character.
  */
  while(*p && *p!=' ') p++;

  printf(p);
}
```

6.4 EXERCISE

1.
```
#include "stdio.h"

char *one = "one";
char *two = "two";
char *three = "three";
```

```
main( )
{

   printf("%s %s %s\n", one, two, three);
   printf("%s %s %s\n", one, three, two);
   printf("%s %s %s\n", two, one, three);
   printf("%s %s %s\n", two, three, one);
   printf("%s %s %s\n", three, one, two);
   printf("%s %s %s\n", three, two, one);
}
```

6.5 EXERCISE

1.
```
#include "stdio.h"
#include "string.h"

char *p[3] = {
  "yes", "no",
  "maybe - rephrase the question"
} ;

main( )
{
  char str[80];

  printf("Enter your question: \n");
  gets(str);

  printf(p[strlen(str) % 3]);
}
```

6.6 EXERCISE

1.
```
#include "stdio.h"

main( )
{
  int i, *p, **mp;
```

```
   p = &i;
   mp = &p;

   **mp = 10;

   printf("%p %p %p", &i, p, mp);
}
```

6.7 EXERCISES

1.
```
#include "stdio.h"
#include "string.h"

main( )
{
  char str[80];

  strcpy(str, "first part");
  mystrcat(str, " second part");
  printf(str);
}

mystrcat(char *to, char *from)
{
  /* find the end of to */
  while(*to) to++;

  /* concatenate the string */
  while(*from) *to++ = *from++;

  /* add the null terminator */
  *to = '\0';
}
```

2.
```
#include "stdio.h"

main( )
{
  int i;

  f(&i);
```

```
   printf("%d", i);
}

f(int *p)
{
   *p = -1;
}
```

MASTERY SKILLS CHECK

1. `double *p;`

2.
```
#include "stdio.h"

main( )
{
   int i, *p;

   p = &i;

   *p = 100;

   printf("%d", i);
}
```

3. No. The pointer **p** has never been initialized to point to a valid piece of memory that can hold a string.

4. Pointers and arrays are basically two ways of looking at the same thing. They are virtually interchangeable.

5. `str[2]`

   `*(str+2)`

6. 108

INTEGRATING NEW SKILLS CHECK

1. Pointers are generally faster than array indexing.

2. To make the program more efficient, use pointers instead of array indexing, as shown here.

```c
#include "stdio.h"

main( )
{
  char str[80], *p;
  int spaces;

  printf("Enter a string: ");
  gets(str);

  spaces = 0;
  p = str;
  while(*p) {
    if(*p==' ') spaces++;
    p++;
  }

  printf("Number of spaces: %d", spaces);
}
```

3. `*(count + (44 * 100) + 8))`

7 SKILLS CHECK

1. The fragment assigns to **i** the value 19 indirectly using a pointer.

2. An array name with no index generates a pointer to the start of the array.

3. Yes, the fragment is correct. It works because the compiler creates a string table entry for the string

"this is a string" and assigns **p** a pointer to the start of it.

4.
```
#include "stdio.h"

main( )
{
  double d, *p;

  p = &d;

  *p = 100.99;

  printf("%lf", d);
}
```

5.
```
#include "stdio.h"

main( )
{
  char str[80];

  printf("Enter a string: ");
  gets(str);

  printf("Length is %d", mystrlen(str));
}

mystrlen(char *p)
{
  int i;

  i = 0;
  while(*p) {
    i++;
    p++;
  }
  return i;
}
```

6. The fragment is correct. It displays **C**.

7.1 EXERCISES

1.
```
#include "stdio.h"

double avg( );

void main( )
{
  printf("%lf", avg( ));
}

double avg( )
{
  int i;
  double sum, num;

  sum = 0.0;
  for(i=0; i<10; i++) {
    printf("Enter next number: ");
    scanf("%lf", &num);
    sum = sum + num;
  }
  return sum / 10.0;
}
```

2. The program is incorrect because **myfunc( )** is declared as returning a **float**, but is defined as returning a **double**.

7.2 EXERCISES

1.
```
#include "stdio.h"

double avg(void);

void main(void)
{
  printf("%lf", avg( ));
}
```

```
double avg(void)
{
  int i;
  double sum, num;

  sum = 0.0;
  for(i=0; i<10; i++) {
    printf("Enter next number: ");
    scanf("%lf", &num);
    sum = sum + num;
  }
  return sum / 10.0;
}
```

2. The program is correct. However, the program would be better if a full function prototype is used when declaring **myfunc( )**.

7.3 EXERCISES

1.
```
#include "stdio.h"

int fact(int i);

void main(void)
{
  printf("5 factorial is %d", fact(5));
}

fact(int i)
{
  if(i==1) return 1;
  else return i * fact(i-1);
}
```

2. The function will call itself repeatedly, until it crashes the program, because there is no condition that prevents a recursive call from occurring.

3.
```c
#include "stdio.h"

display(char *p);

void main(void)
{
  display("this is a test");
}

display(char *p)
{
  if(*p) {
    printf("%c", *p);
    display(p+1);
  }
}
```

7.4 EXERCISES

1. No. The function **myfunc( )** is being called with a pointer to the first parameter instead of the parameter itself.

2.
```c
#include "stdio.h"

void prompt(char *msg, char *str);

void main(void)
{
  char str[80];

  prompt("Enter a string: ", str);
  printf("Your string is: %s", str);
}

void prompt(char *msg, char *p)
{
  printf(msg);
  gets(p);
}
```

7.5 EXERCISES

1.
```
#include "stdio.h"
#include "string.h"
#include "stdlib.h"

void main(int argc, char *argv[])
{
  int i;

  if(argc!=3) {
    printf("You must specify two arguments");
    exit(1);
  }

  i = strcmp(argv[1], argv[2]);
  if(i<0) printf("%s > %s", argv[2], argv[1]);
  else if(i>0) printf("%s > %s", argv[1], argv[2]);
  else printf("They are the same");
}
```

2.
```
#include "stdio.h"
#include "string.h"
#include "stdlib.h"

void main(int argc, char *argv[])
{
  if(argc!=3) {
    printf("You must specify two numbers");
    exit(1);
  }

  printf("%lf", atof(argv[1]) + atof(argv[2]));
}
```

3.
```
#include "stdio.h"
#include "string.h"
#include "stdlib.h"

void main(int argc, char *argv[])
{
  if(argc!=4) {
```

```
        printf("You must specify the operation ");
        printf("followed by two numbers");
        exit(1);
    }

    if(!strcmp("add", argv[1]))
        printf("%lf", atof(argv[2]) + atof(argv[3]));
    else if(!strcmp("subtract", argv[1]))
        printf("%lf", atof(argv[2]) - atof(argv[3]));
    else if(!strcmp("multiply", argv[1]))
        printf("%lf", atof(argv[2]) * atof(argv[3]));
    if(!strcmp("divide", argv[1]))
        printf("%lf", atof(argv[2]) / atof(argv[3]));
}
```

7.6 EXERCISE

1.
```
#include "stdio.h"

double f_to_m( );

void main(void)
{
  double feet;

  printf("Enter feet: ");
  scanf("%lf", &feet);
  printf("Meters: %lf", f_to_m(feet));
}

double f_to_m(f)
double f;
{
  return f / 3.28;
}
```

MASTERY SKILLS CHECK

1. A function that does not return a value is declared as **void**.

2. A function prototype tells the compiler these three things: the return type of the function, the type of its parameters, and the number of its parameters. It is useful because it allows the compiler to find errors if the function is called incorrectly.

3. Command-line arguments are passed to a C program through the **argc** and **argv( )** parameters to **main( )**.

4.
```c
#include "stdio.h"

void alpha(char ch);

void main(void)
{
  alpha('A');
}

void alpha(char ch)
{
  printf("%c", ch);
  if(ch < 'Z') alpha(ch+1);
}
```

5.
```c
#include "stdio.h"
#include "stdlib.h"

void main(int argc, char *argv[])
{
  char *p;
```

```
if(argc!=2) {
  printf("You need to specify a string");
  exit(1);
}

p = argv[1];

while(*p) {
  printf("%c", (*p)+1);
  p++;
}
}
```

6. The prototype is shown here.

```
double myfunc(int x, int y , char ch);
```

7. Using the classic function declaration, the function from Exercise 6 looks like this.

```
double myfunct(x, y, ch)
int x, y;
char ch;
{
  .
  .
  .
}
```

8. The **exit( )** function causes immediate program termination. It also returns a value to the operating system.

9. The **atoi( )** function converts its string argument into its equivalent integer form. The string must represent (in string form) a valid integer.

INTEGRATING NEW SKILLS CHECK

1.
```c
#include "stdio.h"
#include "string.h"
#include "stdlib.h"

void main(int argc, char *argv[])
{
  if(argc!=2) {
    printf("Specify a password");
    exit(1);
  }
  if(!strcmp(argv[1], "password"))
    printf("Access permitted");
  else printf("Access denied");
}
```

2.
```c
#include "stdio.h"
#include "ctype.h"

void string_up(char *p);

void main(void)
{
  char str[] = "this is a test";

  string_up(str);
  printf(str);
}

void string_up(char *p)
{
  while(*p) {
    *p = toupper(*p);
    p++;
  }
}
```

3.
```
#include "stdio.h"

void avg(double *d, int num);

void main(void)
{
    double nums[] = {1.0, 2.0, 3.0, 4.0, 5.0,
                     6.0, 7.0, 8.0, 9.0, 10.0};

    avg(nums, 10);
}

void avg(double *d, int num)
{
    double sum;
    int temp;

    temp = num-1;

    for(sum=0; temp>=0; temp--)
        sum = sum + d[temp];

    printf("Average is %lf", sum / (double) num);
}
```

4. A pointer contains the address of another variable. When a pointer is passed to a function, the function may alter the contents of the object pointed to by the pointer. This is the equivalent of call by reference.

8 SKILLS CHECK

1. You must prototype the function at the top of your program. If your compiler is not ANSI compatible, then you will at least have to declare the function even if you can't use its full prototype.

2. Function prototypes enable the compiler to provide stronger type checking between the arguments used to call a function and the parameters of the function. Also, it lets the compiler confirm that the function is called with the proper number of arguments.

3.
```
#include "stdio.h"
#include "math.h"

double hypot(double s1, double s2);

void main(void)
{
  printf("%lf", hypot(12.2, 19.2));
}

double hypot(double s1, double s2)
{
  double h;

  h = s1*s1 + s2*s2;
  return sqrt(h);
}
```

4. When a function does not return a value, its return type should be specified as **void**. If your compiler is not ANSI compatible, then you will simply have to let the function default to **int**.

5.
```
#include "stdio.h"

int rstrlen(char *p);

void main(void)
{
  printf("%d", rstrlen("hello there"));
}

int rstrlen(char *p)
```

```
{
  if(*p) {
    p++;
    return 1+rstrlen(p);
  }
  else return 0;
}
```

5.
```
#include "stdio.h"

void main(int argc, char *argv[])
{
  printf("there were %d arguments\n", argc);
  printf("the last one is %s", argv[argc-1]);
}
```

7.
```
func(a, ch, d)
int a;
char ch;
double d;
{
```

8.1 EXERCISES

1.
```
#include "stdio.h"

#define MAX 100
#define COUNTBY 3

void main(void)
{
  int i;

  for(i=0; i<MAX; i++)
    if(!(i%COUNTBY)) printf("%d ", i);
}
```

2. No, the fragment is wrong because a macro cannot be defined in terms of another before the second macro is defined. Stated differently, **MIN** is not defined when **MAX** is being defined.

3. As the macro is used, the fragment is wrong. The string needs to be within doubles quotes.

4. Yes.

8.2 EXERCISES

1.
```
#include "stdio.h"

void main (void)
{
  int i;

  do {
    i = getchar( );
    if (i==EOF) {
      printf("error on input");
      break;
    }
    if (putchar('.')==EOF) {
      printf("error on output");
      break;
    }
  } while ((char) i != '\n');
}
```

2. The **putchar( )** function outputs a character. It cannot output a string.

8.3 EXERCISES

1.
```c
#include "conio.h"
#include "stdio.h"

void main(void)
{
  char ch;

  ch = getch( );
  printf("%d", ch);
}
```

2.
```c
#include "stdio.h"
#include "conio.h"

void main(void)
{
  do {
    printf("%c", '.');
  } while(!kbhit( ));
}
```

8.4 EXERCISES

2. No. The program is incorrect because **gets( )** must be called with a pointer to an actual array.

8.5 EXERCISES

1.
```c
#include "stdio.h"

void main(void)
{
  unsigned long i;

  for(i=2; i<=100; i++)
```

```
      printf("%-10lu %-10lu %-10lu\n", i, i*i, i*i*i);
   }
```

2. `printf("Clearance price: 40%% off as marked");`

3. `printf("%.2f", 1023.03);`

8.6 EXERCISES

1.
```
#include "stdio.h"

void main(void)
{
  char first[21], middle[21], last[21];

  printf("Enter your entire name: ");
  scanf("%20s%20s%20s", first, middle, last);
  printf("%s %s %s", first, middle, last);
}
```

2.
```
#include "stdio.h"

void main(void)
{
  char num[80];

  printf("Enter a floating point number: ");
  scanf("%[0-9.]", num);
  printf(num);
}
```

3. No, a character can only have a maximum field length of 1.

4.
```
#include "stdio.h"

void main(void)
{
  char str[80];
  double d;
  int i, num;
```

```
     printf("enter a string, a double, and an integer: ");
     scanf("%s%d%i%n", str, &d, &i, &num);
     printf("%d", num);
   }
```

5.
```
#include "stdio.h"

void main(void)
{
   unsigned u;

   printf("Enter hexadecimal number: ");
   scanf("%x", &u);
   printf("Decimal equivalent: %u", u);
}
```

MASTERY SKILLS CHECK

1. All these functions input a character from the keyboard. The **getchar( )** function is often implemented using line-buffered I/O which makes its use in interactive unacceptable. The **getche( )** is an interactive equivalent to **getchar( )**. The **getch( )** function is the same as **getche( )** except that it does not echo the character typed.

2. The **%e** specifier outputs a number in scientific notation using a lowercase 'e'. The **%E** specifier outputs a number in scientific notation using an 'E'.

3. A scanset is a set of characters that **scanf( )** matches with input. As long as the characters being read are part of the scanset, **scanf( )** continues to input them into the array pointed to by the scanset's corresponding argument.

4. `#include "stdio.h"`

```
void main(void)
{
  char name[80], date[80], phone[80];

  printf("Enter first name, birthdate ");
  printf("and phone number:\n");
  scanf("%s%8s%8s", name, date, phone);
  printf("%s %s %s", name, date, phone);
}
```

5. The **puts( )** function is much smaller and faster than **printf( )**.

6.
```
#include "stdio.h"

#define COUNT 100

void main(void)
{
  int i;

  for(i=0; i<COUNT; i++)
    printf("%d ", i);
}
```

7. **EOF** is a macro that stands for end-of-file. It is defined in STDIO.H.

INTEGRATING NEW SKILLS CHECK

1.
```
#include "stdio.h"

void main(void)
{
  char name[9][80];
  double b_avg[9];
  int i, h, l;

  double high, low, team_avg;
```

```
  for(i=0; i<9; i++) {
    printf("Enter name %d: ", i+1);
    scanf("%s", name[i]);
    printf("Enter batting average: ");
    scanf("%lf", &b_avg[i]);
    printf("\n");
  }

  high = 0.0;
  low = 1000.0;
  team_avg = 0.0;
  for(i=0; i<9; i++) {
    if(b_avg[i]>high) {
      h = i;
      high = b_avg[i];
    }
    if(b_avg[i]<low) {
      l = i;
      low = b_avg[i];
    }
    team_avg = team_avg+b_avg[i];
  }

  printf("The high is %s %lf\n", name[h], b_avg[h]);
  printf("The low is %s %lf\n", name[l], b_avg[l]);
  printf("The team average is %lf", team_avg/9.0);
}
```

2. Note: There are many ways you could have written
    this program. This one is simply representative.

```
/* An electronic card catalog. */
#include "stdio.h"
#include "conio.h"
#include "string.h"

#define MAX 100

int menu(void);
void display(int i);
void author_search(void), title_search(void);
void enter(void);
```

```c
char names[MAX][80];   /* author names */
char titles[MAX][80];   /* titles */
char pubs[MAX][80];    /* publisher */

int top = 0;   /* last location used */

void main(void)
{
  int choice;

  do {
    choice = menu( );
    switch(choice) {
      case 1: enter( ); /* enter books */
        break;
      case 2: author_search( ); /* search by author */
        break;
      case 3: title_search( ); /* search by title */
        break;
    }
  } while(choice!=4);
}

/* Return a menu selection. */
menu(void)
{
  int i;

  printf("Card Catalog:\n");
  printf("  1. Enter\n");
  printf("  2. Search by Author\n");
  printf("  3. Search by Title\n");
  printf("  4. Quit\n");

  do {
    printf("Choose your selection: ");
    i = getche( )-'0';
    printf("\n");
  } while(i<1 || i>4);

  return i;
}
```

```
/* Enter books into database. */
void enter(void)
{
  int i;

  for(i=top; i<MAX; i++) {
    printf("Enter author name (ENTER to quit): ");
    gets(names[i]);
    if(!*names[i]) break;
    printf("Enter title: ");
    gets(titles[i]);
    printf("Enter publisher: ");
    gets(pubs[i]);
  }
  top = i;
}

/* Search by author. */
void author_search(void)
{
  char name[80];
  int i, found;

  printf("Name: ");
  gets(name);

  found = 0;
  for(i=0; i<top; i++)
    if(!strcmp(name, names[i])) {
      display(i);
      found = 1;
      printf("\n");
    }

  if(!found) printf("not found\n");
}

/* Search by title. */
```

```
void title_search(void)
{
  char title[80];
  int i, found;

  printf("Title: ");
  gets(title);

  found = 0;
  for(i=0; i<top; i++)
    if(!strcmp(title, titles[i])) {
      display(i);
      found = 1;
      printf("\n");
    }
  if(!found) printf("not found\n");
}

/* Display catalog entry. */
void display(int i)
{
  printf("%s\n", titles[i]);
  printf("by %s\n", names[i]);
  printf("Published by %s\n", pubs[i]);
}
```

9 SKILLS CHECK

1. The **getchar( )** function is defined by the ANSI standard and is used to input characters from the keyboard. However, in most implementations, it uses line-buffered I/O, which makes it impractical for interactive use. The **getche( )** function is not defined by the ANSI standard, but it is quite common and is essentially an interactive version of **getchar( )**.

2. When **scanf( )** is reading a string, it stops when it encounters the first whitespace character.

3.
```c
#include "stdio.h"

int isprime(int i);

void main(void)
{
  int i, count;

  count = 0;
  for(i=2; i<1001; i++)
   if(isprime(i)) {
     printf("%10d", i);
     count++;
     if(count==3) {
       printf("\n");
       count = 0;
     }
   }
}

isprime(int i)
{
  int j;

  for(j=2; j<=(i/2); j++)
    if(!(i%j)) return 0;
  return 1;
}
```

4.
```c
#include "stdio.h"

void main(void)
{
  double d;
  char ch;
  char str[80];

  printf("Enter a double, a chararacter, and a string\n");
  scanf("%lf%c%20s", &d, &ch, str);
  printf("%lf %c %s", d, ch, str);
}
```

5.
```
#include "stdio.h"

void main(void)
{
  char str[80];

  printf("Enter leading digits followed by a string\n");
  scanf("%*[0-9]%s", str);
  printf("%s", str);
}
```

9.2 EXERCISES

1.
```
#include "stdio.h"
#include "stdlib.h"

void main(int argc, char *argv[])
{
  FILE *fp;
  char ch;

  /* see if filename is specified */
  if(argc!=2) {
    printf("File name missing");
    exit(1);
  }

  if((fp = fopen(argv[1], "r"))==NULL) {
    printf("cannot open file");
    exit(1);
  }

  while((ch=fgetc(fp))!=EOF) putchar(ch);

  fclose(fp);
}
```

2.
```c
#include "stdio.h"
#include "stdlib.h"
#include "ctype.h"

int count[26];

void main(int argc, char *argv[])
{
  FILE *fp;
  char ch;
  int i;

  /* see if file name is specified */
  if(argc!=2) {
    printf("File name missing");
    exit(1);
  }

  if((fp = fopen(argv[1], "r"))==NULL) {
    printf("cannot open file");
    exit(1);
  }

  while((ch=fgetc(fp))!=EOF) {
    ch = toupper(ch);
    if(ch>='A' && ch<='Z') count[ch-'A']++;
  }

  for(i=0; i<26; i++)
    printf("%c occurred %d times\n", i+'A', count[i]);

  fclose(fp);
}
```

3.
```c
/* Copy a file. */
#include "stdio.h"
#include "stdlib.h"
#include "string.h"

void main(int argc, char *argv[])
{
  FILE *from, *to;
  char ch, watch;
```

```
    /* see if correct number of command line
       arguments
    */
    if(argc<3) {
      printf("Usage: copy <source> <destination>\n");
      exit(1);
    }

    /* open source file */
    if((from = fopen(argv[1], "rb"))==NULL) {
      printf("Cannot open source file\n");
      exit(1);
    }

    /* open destination file */
    if((to = fopen(argv[2], "wb"))==NULL) {
      printf("Cannot open file\n");
      exit(1);
    }

    if(argc==4 && !strcmp(argv[3], "watch")) watch = 1;
    else watch = 0;

    /* copy the file */
    while((ch=fgetc(from))!=EOF) {
      fputc(ch, to);
      if(watch) putchar(ch);
    }
    fclose(from);
    fclose(to);
}
```

9.3 EXERCISES

1.
```
#include "stdio.h"
#include "stdlib.h"

void main(int argc, char *argv[])
{
  FILE *fp;
```

```
  unsigned count;

  /* see if file name is specified */
  if(argc!=2) {
    printf("File name missing");
    exit(1);
  }

  if((fp = fopen(argv[1], "rb"))==NULL) {
    printf("cannot open file");
    exit(1);
  }

  count = 0;
  while(!feof(fp)) {
    fgetc(fp);
    if(ferror(fp)) {
      printf("file error");
      exit(1);
    }
    count++;
  }

  printf("file has %u bytes", count);
  fclose(fp);
}
```

2.
```
/* Exchange two files. */
#include "stdio.h"
#include "stdlib.h"
#include "string.h"

void main(int argc, char *argv[])
{
  FILE *f1, *f2, *temp;
  char ch;

  /* see if correct number of command line
     arguments
  */
  if(argc!=3) {
    printf("Usage: exchange <f1> <f2>\n");
    exit(1);
```

```
}

/* open first file */
if((f1 = fopen(argv[1], "rb"))==NULL) {
  printf("Cannot open first file\n");
  exit(1);
}

/* open second file */
if((f2 = fopen(argv[2], "rb"))==NULL) {
  printf("Cannot open second file\n");
  exit(1);
}

/* open temporary file */
if((temp = fopen("temp.tmp", "wb"))==NULL) {
  printf("Cannot open temporary file\n");
  exit(1);
}

/* copy f1 to temp */
while(!feof(f1)) {
  ch = fgetc(f1);
  fputc(ch, temp);
}

fclose(f1);
/* open first file for output */
if((f1 = fopen(argv[1], "wb"))==NULL) {
  printf("Cannot open first file\n");
  exit(1);
}

/* copy f2 to f1 */
while(!feof(f2)) {
  ch = fgetc(f2);
  fputc(ch, f1);
}
fclose(f2);
fclose(temp);

/* open second file for output */
if((f2 = fopen(argv[2], "wb"))==NULL) {
```

```
       printf("Cannot open second file\n");
       exit(1);
    }
    /* open temp file for input */
    if((temp = fopen("temp.tmp", "rb"))==NULL) {
       printf("Cannot open temporary file\n");
       exit(1);
    }

    /* copy temp to f2 */
    while(!feof(temp)) {
       ch = fgetc(temp);
       fputc(ch, f2);
    }

    fclose(f1);
    fclose(f2);
    fclose(temp);
}
```

9.4 EXERCISES

1.
```
/* A simple computerized telelphone book. */

#include "stdio.h"
#include "string.h"
#include "conio.h"
#include "stdlib.h"

char names[100][40];
char numbers[100][40];

int loc=0;

int menu(void);
void enter(void), load(void), save(void);
void find(void);

void main(void)
{
   int choice;
```

```
    do {
      choice = menu( );
      switch(choice) {
        case 1: enter( );
          break;
        case 2: find( );
          break;
        case 3: save( );
          break;
        case 4: load( );
      }
    } while(choice!=5);
}

/* Get menu choice. */
menu(void)
{
  int i;

  printf("1. Enter names and numbers\n");
  printf("2. Find numbers\n");
  printf("3. Save directory to disk\n");
  printf("4. Load directory from disk\n");
  printf("5. Quit\n");

  do {
    printf("Enter your choice: ");
    i = getche( );
    printf("\n");
  } while(i<'1' || i>'5');
  return i-'0';
}


void enter(void)
{

  for(;loc<100;) {
    if(loc<100) {
      printf("enter name and phone number:\n");
      gets(names[loc]);
      if(!*names[loc]) break;
```

```
        gets(numbers[loc]);
        loc++;
      }
    }
}

void find(void)
{
  char name[80];
  int i;

  printf("Enter name: ");
  gets(name);

  for(i=0; i<100; i++)
    if(!strcmp(name, names[i]))
      printf("%s %s\n", names[i], numbers[i]);
}

void load(void)
{
  FILE *fp;

  if((fp = fopen("phone", "r"))==NULL) {
    printf("cannot open file");
    exit(1);
  }

  loc = 0;
  while(!feof(fp)) {
    fscanf(fp, "%s%s", names[loc], numbers[loc]);
    loc++;
  }
  fclose(fp);
}

void save(void)
{
  FILE *fp;
  int i;

  if((fp = fopen("phone", "w"))==NULL) {
    printf("cannot open file");
```

```
      exit(1);
    }

    for(i=0; i<loc; i++) {
      fprintf(fp, "%s %s ", names[i], numbers[i]);
    }
    fclose(fp);
  }
```

2.
```
#include "stdio.h"
#include "stdlib.h"
#include "conio.h"
#include "ctype.h"

void main(int argc, char *argv[])
{
  FILE *fp;
  char ch;
  char str[80];
  int count;

  /* see if correct number of command line
     arguments
  */
  if(argc!=2) {
    printf("Usage: display <file>\n");
    exit(1);
  }

  /* open the file */
  if((fp = fopen(argv[1], "r"))==NULL) {
    printf("Cannot open the file\n");
    exit(1);
  }

  count = 0;
  while(!feof(fp)) {
    fgets(str, 79, fp);
    printf("%s", str);
    count++;

    if(count==23) {
      printf("More? (y/n) ");
```

```
        ch = getche( );
        if(toupper(ch)=='N') break;
        count = 0;
      }
   }

   fclose(fp);
}
```

3.
```
/* Copy a file. */
#include "stdio.h"
#include "stdlib.h"
#include "string.h"

void main(int argc, char *argv[])
{
  FILE *from, *to;
  char str[128];

  /* see if correct number of command line
     arguments
  */
  if(argc<3) {
    printf("Usage: copy <source> <destination>\n");
    exit(1);
  }

  /* open source file */
  if((from = fopen(argv[1], "r"))==NULL) {
    printf("Cannot open source file\n");
    exit(1);
  }

  /* open destination file */
  if((to = fopen(argv[2], "w"))==NULL) {
    printf("Cannot open file\n");
    exit(1);
  }

  /* copy the file */
  while(!feof(from)) {
    fgets(str, 127, from);
    if(ferror(from)) {
```

```
      printf("error on input");
      break;
    }
    if(!feof(from)) fputs(str, to);
    if(ferror(to)) {
      printf("error on output");
      break;
    }
  }
  fclose(from);
  fclose(to);
}
```

9.5 EXERCISES

1.
```
#include "stdio.h"
#include "stdlib.h"

void main(void)
{
  FILE *fp1, *fp2;
  double d;
  int i;

  if((fp1 = fopen("values", "wb"))==NULL) {
    printf("cannot open file");
    exit(1);
  }

  if((fp2 = fopen("count", "wb"))==NULL) {
    printf("cannot open file");
    exit(1);
  }

  d = 1.0;
  for(i=0; d!=0.0 && i<32766; i++) {
    printf("Enter a number (0 to quit): ");
    scanf("%lf", &d);
    fwrite(&d, sizeof d, 1, fp1);
  }
```

```
    fwrite(&i, sizeof i, 1, fp2);

  fclose(fp1);
  fclose(fp2);
}
```

2.
```
#include "stdio.h"
#include "stdlib.h"

void main(void)
{
  FILE *fp1, *fp2;
  double d;
  int i;

  if((fp1 = fopen("values", "rb"))==NULL) {
    printf("cannot open file");
    exit(1);
  }

  if((fp2 = fopen("count", "rb"))==NULL) {
    printf("cannot open file");
    exit(1);
  }

  fread(&i, sizeof i, 1, fp2); /* get count */

  for(; i>0; i--) {
    fread(&d, sizeof d, 1, fp1);
    printf("%lf\n", d);
  }

  fclose(fp1);
  fclose(fp2);
}
```

9.6 EXERCISES

1.
```
#include "stdio.h"
#include "stdlib.h"

void main(int argc, char *argv[])
{
  FILE *fp;
  char ch;
  long l;

  if(argc!=2) {
    printf("You must specify the file");
    exit(1);
  }

  if((fp = fopen(argv[1], "rb"))==NULL) {
    printf("cannot open file");
    exit(1);
  }

  fseek(fp, 0, SEEK_END); /* find end of file */
  l = ftell(fp);

  /* go back to the start of the file */
  fseek(fp, 0, SEEK_SET);
  for( ; l>=0; l = l - 2L) {
    ch = fgetc(fp);
    putchar(ch);
    fseek(fp, 2L, SEEK_CUR); /* advance two bytes from
                                current location */
  }

  fclose(fp);
}
```

2.
```c
#include "stdio.h"
#include "stdlib.h"

void main(int argc, char *argv[])
{
  FILE *fp;
  unsigned char ch, val;

  if(argc!=3) {
    printf("Usage: find <filename> <value>");
    exit(1);
  }

  if((fp = fopen(argv[1], "rb"))==NULL) {
    printf("cannot open file");
    exit(1);
  }

  val = atoi(argv[2]);

  while(!feof(fp)) {
    ch = fgetc(fp);
    if(ch == val)
      printf("found value at %ld\n", ftell(fp));
  }

  fclose(fp);
}
```

9.7 EXERCISES

1.
```c
#include "stdio.h"
#include "stdlib.h"
#include "conio.h"
#include "ctype.h"

void main(void)
{
  char fname[80];
```

```
   printf("Enter name of file to erase: ");
   gets(fname);
   printf("Are you sure? (Y/N) ");
   if(toupper(getche( ))=='Y')
     if(remove(fname))
       printf("\nFile not found or write protected");
}
```

9.8 EXERCISE

1.
```
/* Copy using redirection.

   Execute like this:

   C>NAME < in > out

*/

#include "stdio.h"

void main(void)
{
  char ch;

  while(!feof(stdin)) {
    scanf("%c", &ch);
    printf("%c", ch);
  }
}
```

MASTERY SKILLS CHECK

1.
```
#include "stdio.h"
#include "stdlib.h"
#include "ctype.h"
#include "conio.h"
```

```
void main(int argc, char *argv[])
{
  FILE *fp;
  char str[80];

  /* see if file name is specified */
  if(argc!=2) {
    printf("File name missing");
    exit(1);
  }

  if((fp = fopen(argv[1], "r"))==NULL) {
    printf("cannot open file");
    exit(1);
  }

  while(!feof(fp)) {
    fgets(str, 79, fp);
    if(!feof(fp)) printf("%s", str);
    printf("...More? (y/n) ");
    if(toupper(getche( ))=='N') break;
    printf("\n");
  }

  fclose(fp);
}
```

2.
```
/* Copy a file and convert to uppercase. */
#include "stdio.h"
#include "stdlib.h"
#include "ctype.h"

void main(int argc, char *argv[])
{
  FILE *from, *to;
  char ch;

  /* see if correct number of command line
     arguments
  */
  if(argc!=3) {
```

```
   printf("Usage: copy <source> <destination>\n");
   exit(1);
 }

 /* open source file */
 if((from = fopen(argv[1], "r"))==NULL) {
   printf("Cannot open source file\n");
   exit(1);
 }

 /* open destination file */
 if((to = fopen(argv[2], "w"))==NULL) {
   printf("Cannot open file\n");
   exit(1);
 }

 /* copy the file */
 while(!feof(from)) {
   ch = fgetc(from);
   fputc(toupper(ch), to);
 }
 fclose(from);
 fclose(to);
}
```

3. The **fprintf( )** and **fscanf( )** functions operate exactly like **printf( )** and **scanf( )**, except that they work with files.

4.
```
#include "stdio.h"
#include "stdlib.h"

void main(void)
{
  FILE *fp;
  int i, num;

  if((fp = fopen("rand", "wb"))==NULL) {
    printf("cannot open file");
    exit(1);
  }
```

```
    for(i=0; i<100; i++) {
      num = rand( );
      fwrite(&num, sizeof num, 1, fp);
    }

    fclose(fp);
  }
```

5.
```
  #include "stdio.h"
  #include "stdlib.h"

  void main(void)
  {
    FILE *fp;
    int i, num;

    if((fp = fopen("rand", "rb"))==NULL) {
      printf("cannot open file");
      exit(1);
    }

    for(i=0; i<100; i++) {
      fread(&num, sizeof num, 1, fp);
      printf("%d\n", num);
    }

    fclose(fp);
  }
```

6.
```
  #include "stdio.h"
  #include "stdlib.h"

  void main(void)
  {
    FILE *fp;
    long i;
    int num;

    if((fp = fopen("rand", "rb"))==NULL) {
      printf("cannot open file");
      exit(1);
    }
```

```
     printf("Which number (0-99)? ");
     scanf("%ld", &i);
     fseek(fp, i * sizeof(int), SEEK_SET);
     fread(&num, sizeof num, 1, fp);
     printf("%d\n", num);

     fclose(fp);
   }
```

INTEGRATING NEW SKILLS CHECK

1.
```
   /* An electronic card catalog. */
   #include "stdio.h"
   #include "conio.h"
   #include "string.h"
   #include "stdlib.h"

   #define MAX 100

   int menu(void);
   void display(int i);
   void author_search(void), title_search(void);
   void enter(void), save(void), load(void);

   char names[MAX][80];  /* author names */
   char titles[MAX][80];  /* titles */
   char pubs[MAX][80];    /* publisher */

   int top = 0;  /* last location used */

   void main(void)
   {
     int choice;

     load( ); /* read in catalog */

     do {
       choice = menu( );
       switch(choice) {
         case 1: enter( ); /* enter books */
           break;
```

```
        case 2: author_search( ); /* search by author */
          break;
        case 3: title_search( ); /* search by title */
          break;
        case 4: save( );
      }
  } while(choice!=5);
}

/* Return a menu selection. */
menu(void)
{
  int i;

  printf("Card Catalog:\n");
  printf("  1. Enter\n");
  printf("  2. Search by Author\n");
  printf("  3. Search by Title\n");
  printf("  4. Save catalog\n");
  printf("  5. Quit\n");

  do {
    printf("Choose your selection: ");
    i = getche( )-'0';
    printf("\n");
  } while(i<1 || i>5);

  return i;
}

/* Enter books into database. */
void enter(void)
{
  int i;

  for(i=top; i<MAX; i++) {
    printf("Enter author name (ENTER to quit): ");
    gets(names[i]);
    if(!*names[i]) break;
    printf("Enter title: ");
    gets(titles[i]);
    printf("Enter publisher: ");
    gets(pubs[i]);
```

```
  }
  top = i;
}

/* Search by author. */
void author_search(void)
{
  char name[80];
  int i, found;

  printf("Name: ");
  gets(name);

  found = 0;
  for(i=0; i<top; i++)
    if(!strcmp(name, names[i])) {
      display(i);
      found = 1;
      printf("\n");
    }

  if(!found) printf("not found\n");
}

/* Search by title. */
void title_search(void)
{
  char title[80];
  int i, found;

  printf("Title: ");
  gets(title);

  found = 0;
  for(i=0; i<top; i++)
    if(!strcmp(title, titles[i])) {
      display(i);
      found = 1;
      printf("\n");
    }
  if(!found) printf("not found\n");
}
```

```
/* Display catalog entry. */
void display(int i)
{
  printf("%s\n", titles[i]);
  printf("by %s\n", names[i]);
  printf("Published by %s\n", pubs[i]);
}

/* Load the catalog file. */
void load(void)
{
  FILE *fp;

  if((fp = fopen("catalog", "r"))==NULL) {
    printf("Catalog file not on disk\n");
    return;
  }

  fread(&top, sizeof top, 1, fp); /* read count */
  fread(names, sizeof names, 1, fp);
  fread(titles, sizeof titles, 1, fp);
  fread(pubs, sizeof pubs, 1, fp);

  fclose(fp);
}

/* save the catalog file. */
void save(void)
{
  FILE *fp;

  if((fp = fopen("catalog", "w"))==NULL) {
    printf("Cannot open catalog file\n");
    exit(1);
  }

  fwrite(&top, sizeof top, 1, fp);
  fwrite(names, sizeof names, 1, fp);
  fwrite(titles, sizeof titles, 1, fp);
  fwrite(pubs, sizeof pubs, 1, fp);

  fclose(fp);
}
```

```
2.  /* Copy a file and remove tabs. */
    #include "stdio.h"
    #include "stdlib.h"
    #include "string.h"

    void main(int argc, char *argv[])
    {
      FILE *from, *to;
      char ch;
      int tab, count;

      /* see if correct number of command line
         arguments
      */
      if(argc!=3) {
        printf("Usage: copy <source> <destination>\n");
        exit(1);
      }

      /* open source file */
      if((from = fopen(argv[1], "r"))==NULL) {
        printf("Cannot open source file\n");
        exit(1);
      }

      /* open destination file */
      if((to = fopen(argv[2], "w"))==NULL) {
        printf("Cannot open file\n");
        exit(1);
      }
      /* copy the file */
      count = 0;
      while(!feof(from)) {
        ch = fgetc(from);
        if(ch=='\t') {
          for(tab = count; tab<8; tab++)
            fputc(' ', to);
          count = 0;
        }
        else {
          fputc(ch, to);
          count++;
          if(count==8 || ch=='\n') count = 0;
```

```
    }
  }
  fclose(from);
  fclose(to);
}
```

10 SKILLS CHECK

1.
```
/* Copy a file. */
#include "stdio.h"
#include "stdlib.h"

void main(int argc, char *argv[])
{
FILE *from, *to;
  char ch;

  /* see if correct number of command line
     arguments
  */
  if(argc!=3) {
    printf("Usage: copy <source> <destination>\n");
    exit(1);
  }

  /* open source file */
  if((from = fopen(argv[1], "rb"))==NULL) {
    printf("Cannot open source file\n");
    exit(1);
  }

  /* open destination file */
  if((to = fopen(argv[2], "wb"))==NULL) {
    printf("Cannot open file\n");
    exit(1);
  }

  /* copy the file */

  while(!feof(from)) {
    ch = fgetc(from);
```

```
      if(ferror(from)) {
        printf("Error on input");
        break;
      }
      fputc(ch, to);
      if(ferror(to)) {
        printf("Error on output");
        break;
      }
    }
    fclose(from);
    fclose(to);
  }
```

2.
```
  #include "stdio.h"
  #include "stdlib.h"

  void main( )
  {
    FILE *fp;

    /* open file */
    if((fp = fopen("myfile", "w"))==NULL) {
      printf("Cannot open file\n");
      exit(1);
    }

    fprintf(fp, "%s %.2lf %X %c", "this is a string",
            1230.23,0x1FFF, 'A';

    fclose(fp);
  }
```

3.
```
  #include "stdio.h"
  #include "stdlib.h"

  void main( )
  {
    FILE *fp;
    int count[20], i;

    /* open file */
    if((fp = fopen("TEMP", "wb"))==NULL) {
```

```
        printf("Cannot open file\n");
        exit(1);
    }

    for(i=0; i<20; i++) count[i] = i+1;

    fwrite(count, sizeof count, 1, fp);

    fclose(fp);
}
```

4.  ```
    #include "stdio.h"
    #include "stdlib.h"

    void main( )
    {
      FILE *fp;
      int count[20], i;

      /* open file */
      if((fp = fopen("TEMP", "rb"))==NULL) {
        printf("Cannot open file\n");
        exit(1);
      }

      fread(count, sizeof count, 1, fp);

      for(i=0; i<20; i++) printf("%d ", count[i]);

      fclose(fp);
    }
    ```

5. **Stdin**, **stdout**, and **stderr** are three streams that are opened automatically when your C program begins executing. By default they refer to the console, but in operating systems that support I/O redirection, they can be redirected to other devices.

6. The **printf( )** and **scanf( )** functions are part of the C file system. They are simply special case functions that automatically use **stdin** and **stdout**.
    ```

10.1 EXERCISES

1. ```c
/* A simple computerized telelphone book. */

#include "stdio.h"
#include "string.h"
#include "conio.h"
#include "stdlib.h"

#define MAX 100

struct phone_type {
  char name[40];
  int areacode;
  char number[9];
} phone[MAX];

int loc=0;

int menu(void);
void enter(void), load(void), save(void);
void find(void);

void main(void)
{
  int choice;

  do {
    choice = menu( );
    switch(choice) {
      case 1: enter( );
        break;
      case 2: find( );
        break;
```
```

```
        case 3: save( );
          break;
        case 4: load( );
      }
  } while(choice!=5);
}

/* Get menu choice. */
menu(void)
{
  int i;

  printf("1. Enter names and numbers\n");
  printf("2. Find numbers\n");
  printf("3. Save directory to disk\n");
  printf("4. Load directory from disk\n");
  printf("5. Quit\n");

  do {
    printf("Enter your choice: ");
    i = getche( );
    printf("\n");
  } while(i<'1' || i>'5');
  return i-'0';
}


void enter(void)
{
  char temp[80];

  for(;loc<100;) {
    if(loc<100) {
      printf("Enter name: ");
      gets(phone[loc].name);
      if(!*phone[loc].name) break;
      printf("Enter area code: ");
      gets(temp);
      phone[loc].areacode = atoi(temp);
      printf("Enter number: ");
      gets(phone[loc].number);
      loc++;
    }
```

```
    }
}

void find(void)
{
  char name[80];
  int i;

  printf("Enter name: ");
  gets(name);
  if(!*name) return;

  for(i=0; i<100; i++)
    if(!strcmp(name, phone[i].name))
      printf("%s (%d) %s\n", phone[i].name,
             phone[i].areacode,phone[i].number);
}

void load(void)
{
  FILE *fp;

  if((fp = fopen("phone", "r"))==NULL) {
    printf("cannot open file");
    exit(1);
  }

  loc = 0;
  while(!feof(fp)) {
    fscanf(fp, "%s%d%s", phone[loc].name,
           &phone[loc].areacode, phone[loc].number);
    loc++;
  }
  fclose(fp);
}

void save(void)
{
  FILE *fp;
  int i;

  if((fp = fopen("phone", "w"))==NULL) {
    printf("cannot open file");
```

```
    exit(1);
  }

  for(i=0; i<loc; i++) {
    fprintf(fp, "%s %d %s ", phone[i].name,
            phone[i].areacode,phone[i].number);
  }
  fclose(fp);
}
```

2. The variable **i** is an element of structure **s**. Therefore, it cannot be used by itself. Instead, it must be accessed using **s** and the dot operator, as shown here.

```
s.i = 10;
```

10.2 EXERCISES

1. No. Since **p** is a pointer to a structure, you must use the arrow operator, not the dot operator, to access a structure element.

2.
```
#include "stdio.h"
#include "time.h"

void main(void)
{
  struct tm *systime, *gmt;
  time_t t;

  t = time(NULL);
  systime = localtime(&t);

  printf("Time is %.2d:%.2d:%.2d\n", systime->tm_hour,
         systime->tm_min, systime->tm_sec);
  gmt = gmtime(&t);
  printf("GM time is %.2d:%.2d:%.2d\n", gmt->tm_hour,
         gmt->tm_min, gmt->tm_sec);
  printf("Date: %.2d/%.2d/%.2d", systime->tm_mon+1,
```

```
        systime->tm_mday, systime->tm_year);
}
```

10.3 EXERCISES

1.  ```
    /* A simple computerized telelphone book. */

    #include "stdio.h"
    #include "string.h"
    #include "conio.h"
    #include "stdlib.h"

    #define MAX 100

    struct address {
      char street[40];
      char city[40];
      char state[3];
      char zip[12];
    };

    struct phone_type {
      char name[40];
      int areacode;
      char number[9];
      struct address addr;
    } phone[MAX];

    int loc=0;

    int menu(void);
    void enter(void), load(void), save(void);
    void find(void);

    void main(void)
    {
      int choice;

      do {
        choice = menu( );
        switch(choice) {
    ```
    ```

```
      case 1: enter( );
        break;
      case 2: find( );
        break;
      case 3: save( );
        break;
      case 4: load( );
    }
  } while(choice!=5);
}

/* Get menu choice. */
menu(void)
{
  int i;

  printf("1. Enter names and numbers\n");
  printf("2. Find numbers\n");
  printf("3. Save directory to disk\n");
  printf("4. Load directory from disk\n");
  printf("5. Quit\n");

  do {
    printf("Enter your choice: ");
    i = getche( );
    printf("\n");
  } while(i<'1' || i>'5');
  return i-'0';
}


void enter(void)
{
  char temp[80];

  for(;loc<100;) {
    if(loc<100) {
      printf("Enter name: ");
      gets(phone[loc].name);
      if(!*phone[loc].name) break;
      printf("Enter area code: ");
      gets(temp);
      phone[loc].areacode = atoi(temp);
```

```c
        printf("Enter number: ");
        gets(phone[loc].number);

        /* input address info */
        printf("Enter street address: ");
        gets(phone[loc].addr.street);
        printf("Enter city: ");
        gets(phone[loc].addr.city);
        printf("Enter State: ");
        gets(phone[loc].addr.state);
        printf("Enter zip code: ");
        gets(phone[loc].addr.zip);
        loc++;
      }
    }
}

void find(void)
{
  char name[80];
  int i;

  printf("Enter name: ");
  gets(name);
  if(!*name) return;

  for(i=0; i<100; i++)
    if(!strcmp(name, phone[i].name)) {
      printf("%s (%d) %s\n", phone[i].name,
             phone[i].areacode, phone[i].number);
      printf("%s\n%s %s %s\n", phone[i].addr.street,
             phone[i].addr.city, phone[i].addr.state,
             phone[i].addr.zip);
    }
}

void load(void)
{
  FILE *fp;

  if((fp = fopen("phone", "rb"))==NULL) {
    printf("cannot open file");
    exit(1);
```

```
  }
  loc = 0;
  while(!feof(fp)) {
    fread(&phone[loc], sizeof phone[loc], 1, fp);
    loc++;
  }
  fclose(fp);
}

void save(void)
{
  FILE *fp;
  int i;

  if((fp = fopen("phone", "wb"))==NULL) {
    printf("cannot open file");
    exit(1);
  }

  for(i=0; i<loc; i++) {
    fwrite(&phone[i], sizeof phone[i], 1, fp);
  }
  fclose(fp);
}
```

10.4 EXERCISES

1.
```
#include "stdio.h"

void main(void)
{
  struct b_type {
    int a: 3;
    int b: 3;
    int c: 2;
  } bvar;

  bvar.a = -1;
  bvar.b = 3;
  bvar.c = 1;
```

```
      printf("%d %d %d", bvar.a, bvar.b, bvar.c);
}
```

10.5 EXERCISES

1.
```
#include "stdio.h"
#include "stdlib.h"

union u_type {
  double d;
  unsigned char c[8];
} ;

double uread(FILE *fp);
void uwrite(double num, FILE *fp);

void main(void)
{
  FILE *fp;
  double d;

  if((fp = fopen("myfile", "wb+"))==NULL) {
    printf("Cannot open file");
    exit(1);
  }

  uwrite(100.23, fp);
  d = uread(fp);
  printf("%lf", d);
}

void uwrite(double num, FILE *fp)
{
  int i;
  union u_type var;

  var.d = num;
  for(i=0; i<8; i++) fputc(var.c[i],fp);
}

double uread(FILE *fp)
```

```
{
  int i;
  union u_type var;

  rewind(fp);
  for(i=0; i<8; i++) var.c[i] = fgetc(fp);

  return var.d;
}
```

2.
```
#include "stdio.h"

void main(void)
{
  union t_type {
    long l;
    int i;
  } uvar;

  uvar.l = 0L; /* clear l */
  uvar.i = 100;

  printf("%ld", uvar.l);
}
```

MASTERY SKILLS CHECK

1. A structure is a named group of related variables. A **union** defines a memory location shared by two or more variables of different types.

2.
```
struct s_type {
   char ch;
   float d;
   int i;
   char str[80];
   double balance;
} s_var;
```

3. Because **p** is a pointer to a structure, you must use the arrow operator to reference an element, not the dot operator.

4.
```
#include "stdio.h"
#include "stdlib.h"

struct s_type {
  char name[40];
  char phone[14];
  int hours;
  double wage;
} emp[10];

void main(void)
{
  FILE *fp;
  int i;
  char temp[80];

  if((fp = fopen("emp", "wb"))==NULL) {
    printf("Cannot open EMP file");
    exit(1);
  }

  for(i=0; i<10; i++) {
    printf("Enter name: ");
    gets(emp[i].name);
```

```
        printf("Enter telephone number: ");
        gets(emp[i].phone);
        printf("Enter hours worked: ");
        gets(temp);
        emp[i].hours = atoi(temp);
        printf("Enter hourly wage: ");
        gets(temp);
        emp[i].wage = atof(temp);
    }

    fwrite(emp, sizeof emp, 1, fp);
    fclose(fp);
}
```

5.
```
#include "stdio.h"
#include "stdlib.h"

struct s_type {
  char name[40];
  char phone[14];
  int hours;
  double wage;
} emp[10];

void main(void)
{
  FILE *fp;
  int i;

  if((fp = fopen("emp", "rb"))==NULL) {
    printf("Cannot open EMP file");
    exit(1);
  }

  fread(emp, sizeof emp, 1, fp);
  for(i=0; i<10; i++) {
    printf("%s %s\n", emp[i].name, emp[i].phone);
    printf("%d %lf\n\n", emp[i].hours, emp[i].wage);
  }

  fclose(fp);
}
```

6. A bit-field is a structure element that specifies its
    length in bits;

7.
```
#include "stdio.h"

void main(void)
{
  union u_type {
    int i;
    unsigned char c[2];
  } uvar;

  uvar.i = 99;

  printf("High order byte: %u\n", uvar.c[1]);
  printf("Low order byte: %u\n", uvar.c[0]);
}
```

INTEGRATING NEW SKILLS CHECK

1.
```
#include "stdio.h"

struct s_type {
  int i;
  char ch;
  double d;
} var1, var2;

void struct_swap(struct s_type *i, struct s_type *j);

void main(void)
{
  var1.i = 100;
  var2.i =  99;
  var1.ch = 'a';
  var2.ch = 'b';
  var1.d = 1.0;
  var2.d = 2.0;
```

```
  struct_swap(&var1, &var2);

  printf("var1: %d %c %lf\n", var1.i, var1.ch, var1.d);
  printf("var2: %d %c %lf", var2.i, var2.ch, var2.d);
}

void struct_swap(struct s_type *i, struct s_type *j)
{
  struct s_type temp;

  temp = *i;
  *i = *j;
  *j = temp;
}
```

2.
```
/* Copy a file. */
#include "stdio.h"
#include "stdlib.h"

void main(int argc, char *argv[])
{
  FILE *from, *to;
  union u_type {
    int i;
    char ch;
  } uvar;

  /* see if correct number of command line
     arguments
  */
  if(argc!=3) {
    printf("Usage: copy <source> <destination>\n");
    exit(1);
  }

  /* open source file */
  if((from = fopen(argv[1], "rb"))==NULL) {
    printf("Cannot open source file\n");
    exit(1);
  }

  /* open destination file */
  if((to = fopen(argv[2], "wb"))==NULL) {
```

```
      printf("Cannot open file\n");
      exit(1);
    }

  /* copy the file */
  for(;;) {
    uvar.i = fgetc(from);
    if(uvar.i==EOF) break;

    fputc(uvar.ch, to);
  }
  fclose(from);
  fclose(to);
}
```

3. You cannot use a structure as an argument to **scanf( )**. However, you can use a structure element as an argument, as shown here.

```
scanf("%d", &var.a);
```

4.
```
#include "string.h"
#include "stdio.h"

struct s_type {
  char str[80];
} var;

void f(struct s_type i);

void main(void)
{
  strcpy(var.str, "this is original string");
  f(var);
  printf("%s", var.str);
}

void f(struct s_type i)
{
  strcpy(i.str, "new string");
  printf("%s\n", i.str);
}
```

11 SKILLS CHECK

1.
```c
#include "stdio.h"

struct num_type {
  int i;
  int sqr;
  int cube;
} nums[10];

void main(void)
{
  int i;

  for(i=1; i<11; i++) {
    nums[i].i = i;
    nums[i].sqr = i*i;
    nums[i].cube = i*i*i;
  }

  for(i=1; i<11; i++) {
    printf("%d ", nums[i].i);
    printf("%d ", nums[i].sqr);
    printf("%d\n", nums[i].cube);
  }
}
```

2.
```c
#include "stdio.h"

union i_to_c {
  char c[2];
  int i;
} ic;

void main(void)
{
  printf("Enter an integer: ");
  scanf("%d", &ic.i);
  printf("character represention of each byte: %c %c",
         ic.c[0], ic.c[1]);
}
```

3. The fragment displays **8**, the size of the largest element of the union.

4. To access a structure element when actually using a structure variable, you must use the dot operator. The arrow operator is used when accessing an element using a pointer to a structure.

5. A bit-field is a structure element whose size is specified in bits.

11.1 EXERCISES

1. The best variables to make into **register** types are **k** and **m**, because they are accessed most frequently.

2.
```
#include "stdio.h"

void sum_it(int value);

void main(void)
{
  sum_it(10);
  sum_it(20);
  sum_it(30);
  sum_it(40);
}

void sum_it(int value)
{
  static int sum=0;

  sum = sum + value;
  printf("current value: %d\n", sum);
}
```

4. You cannot obtain the address of a **register** variable.

11.2 EXERCISES

1.
```
#include "stdio.h"

const double version = 6.01;

void main(void)
{
  printf("Version %.2lf", version);
}
```

2.
```
#include "stdio.h"

char *mystrcpy(char *to, const char *from);

void main(void)
{
  char *p, str[80];

  p = mystrcpy(str, "testing");

  printf("%s %s", p, str);
}

char *mystrcpy(char *to, const char *from)
{
  char *temp;

  temp = to;

  while(*from) *to++ = *from++;
  *to = '\0'; /* null terminator */

  return temp;
}
```

11.3 EXERCISES

2. enum money {penny, nickel, quarter, half_dollar, dollar};

3. No, you cannot output an enumeration constant as a string as is attempted in the **printf( )** statement.

11.4 EXERCISES

1.
```
#include "stdio.h"

typedef unsigned long UL;

void main(void)
{
  UL count;

  count = 312323;

  printf("%lu", count);
}
```

2. The **typedef** statement is out of order. The correct form of **typedef** is

typedef *oldname newname;*

11.5 EXERCISES

1.
```
#include "stdio.h"
#include "stdlib.h"
```

```
void main(int argc, char *argv[])
{
  FILE *in, *out;
  unsigned char ch;

  if(argc!=3) {
    printf("Usage: code <in> <out>");
    exit(1);
  }

  if((in = fopen(argv[1], "rb"))==NULL) {
    printf("cannot open input file");
    exit(1);
  }

  if((out = fopen(argv[2], "wb"))==NULL) {
    printf("cannot open output file");
    exit(1);
  }

  while(!feof(in)) {
    ch = fgetc(in);
    if(!feof(in)) fputc(~ch, out);
  }

  fclose(in);
  fclose(out);
}
```

2.
```
#include "stdio.h"
#include "stdlib.h"

void main(int argc, char *argv[])
{
  FILE *in, *out;
  unsigned char ch;

  if(argc!=4) {
    printf("Usage: code <in> <out> <key>");
```

```
        exit(1);
    }

    if((in = fopen(argv[1], "rb"))==NULL) {
      printf("cannot open input file");
      exit(1);
    }

    if((out = fopen(argv[2], "wb"))==NULL) {
      printf("cannot open output file");
      exit(1);
    }

    while(!feof(in)) {
      ch = fgetc(in);
      ch = *argv[3] ^ ch;
      if(!feof(in)) fputc(ch, out);
    }

    fclose(in);
    fclose(out);
}
```

3. **a.** 0000 0001
    b. 1111 1111
    c. 1111 1101

4.
```
char ch;
    .
    .
    .
/* To zero high order bit, AND with 127, which
   in binary is 0111 1111.  This causes the high-
   order bit to be zeroed and all other bits left
   untouched.
*/
ch = ch & 127;
```

11.6 EXERCISES

1.
```c
#include "stdio.h"

void main(void)
{
  int i, j, k;

  printf("Enter a number: ");
  scanf("%d", &i);

  j = i << 1;
  k = i >> 1;
  printf("%d doubled: %d\n", i, j);
  printf("%d halved: %d", i, k);
}
```

2.
```c
#include "stdio.h"

void rotate(unsigned char *c);

void main(void)
{
  unsigned char ch;
  int i;

  ch = 1;

  for(i=0; i<16; i++) {
    rotate(&ch);
    printf("%u\n", ch);
  }
}

void rotate(unsigned char *c)
{
  union {
    unsigned char ch[2];
    unsigned u;
```

```
} rot;

rot.u = 0; /* clear 16 bits */

rot.ch[0] = *c;

/* shift integer left */
rot.u = rot.u << 1;

/* See if a bit got shifted into c[1].
   If so, OR it back onto the other end. */
if(rot.ch[1]) rot.ch[0] = rot.ch[0] | 1;

*c = rot.ch[0];
}
```

11.7 EXERCISES

1.
```
#include "stdio.h"

void main(void)
{
  int i, j, answer;

  printf("Enter two integers: ");
  scanf("%d%d", &i, &j);

  answer = j ? i/j: 0;
  printf("%d", answer);
}
```

2. `count = a>b ? 100: 0;`

11.8 EXERCISES

2. `x &= y;`

3.
```c
#include "stdio.h"

void main(void)
{
  int i;

  for(i=17; i<=1000; i+=17)
    printf("%d\n", i);
}
```

11.9 EXERCISES

1.
```c
#include "stdio.h"

void main(void)
{
  int i, j, k;

  for(i=0, j=-50, k=i+j; i<100; i++, j++, k=i+j)
    printf("k = %d\n", k);
}
```

2. 3

MASTERY SKILLS CHECK

1. The **register** specifier causes the C compiler to pro-vides the fastest access possible for the variable it precedes.

2. The **const** specifier tells the C compiler that no state-ment in the program may modify a variable de-clared as **const**. Also, a **const** pointer parameter may not be used to modify the object pointed to by the pointer. The **volatile** specifier tells the compiler that

any variable it precedes may have its value changed
in ways not explicitly specified by the program.

3. `#include "stdio.h"`

```
void main(void)
{
  register int i, sum;

  sum = 0;
  for(i=1; i<101; i++)
    sum = sum + i;

  printf("%d", sum);
}
```

4. Yes, the statement is valid. It creates another name
for the type **long double**.

5. `#include "stdio.h"`
`#include "conio.h"`

```
void main(void)
{
  char ch1, ch2;
  char mask, i;

  printf("Enter two chracters: ");
  ch1 = getche( );
  ch2 = getche( );
  printf("\n");

  mask = 1;
  for(i=0; i<8; i++) {
    if((mask & ch1) && (mask & ch2))
      printf("bits %d the same\n", i);
    mask <<= 1;
  }
}
```

6. The **<<** and **>>** are the left and right shift operators,
respectively.

7. `c += 10;`

8. `count = done ? 0: 100;`

9. An enumeration is a list of named integer constants. Here is one that enumerates the planets.

```
enum planets {Mercury, Venus, Earth, Mars,
              Jupiter, Saturn, Neptune, Uranus,
              Pluto} ;
```

INTEGRATING NEW SKILLS CHECK

1.
```
#include "stdio.h"

void show_binary(unsigned u);

void main(void)
{
  unsigned char ch, t1, t2;

  ch = 100;
  show_binary(ch);

  t1 = ch;
  t2 = ch;

  t1 <<= 4;
  t2 >>= 4;

  ch = t1 | t2;

  show_binary(ch);
}

void show_binary(unsigned u)
{
  unsigned l;
```

```
    for(l=128; l>0; l=l/2)
      if(u & l) printf("1 ");
      else printf("0 ");

    printf("\n");
  }
```

2.
```
#include "stdio.h"
#include "stdlib.h"

void main(int argc, char *argv[])
{
  FILE *in;
  unsigned char ch;

  if(argc!=2) {
    printf("Usage: code <in>");
    exit(1);
  }

  if((in = fopen(argv[1], "rb"))==NULL) {
    printf("cannot open input file");
    exit(1);
  }


  while(!feof(in)) {
    ch = fgetc(in);
    if(!feof(in)) putchar(~ch);
  }

  fclose(in);
}
```

3. Yes, any type of variable can be specified using **register**. However, on some types, it may have no effect.

```
4.  /* A simple computerized telelphone book. */

    #include "stdio.h"
    #include "string.h"
    #include "conio.h"
    #include "stdlib.h"

    #define MAX 100

    struct address {
      char street[40];
      char city[40];
      char state[3];
      char zip[12];
    };

    struct phone_type {
      char name[40];
      int areacode;
      char number[9];
      struct address addr;
    } phone[MAX];

    int loc=0;

    int menu(void);
    void enter(void), load(void), save(void);
    void find(void);

    void main(void)
    {
      register int choice;

      do {
        choice = menu( );
        switch(choice) {
          case 1: enter( );
            break;
          case 2: find( );
            break;
          case 3: save( );
            break;
          case 4: load( );
```

```
    }
  } while(choice!=5);
}


/* Get menu choice. */
menu(void)
{
  register int i;

  printf("1. Enter names and numbers\n");
  printf("2. Find numbers\n");
  printf("3. Save directory to disk\n");
  printf("4. Load directory from disk\n");
  printf("5. Quit\n");

  do {
    printf("Enter your choice: ");
    i = getche( );
    printf("\n");
  } while(i<'1' || i>'5');
  return i-'0';
}



void enter(void)
{
  char temp[80];

  for(;loc<100;) {
    if(loc<100) {
      printf("Enter name: ");
      gets(phone[loc].name);
      if(!*phone[loc].name) break;
      printf("Enter area code: ");
      gets(temp);
      phone[loc].areacode = atoi(temp);
      printf("Enter number: ");
      gets(phone[loc].number);

      /* input address info */
      printf("Enter street address: ");
      gets(phone[loc].addr.street);
      printf("Enter city: ");
```

```
        gets(phone[loc].addr.city);
        printf("Enter State: ");
        gets(phone[loc].addr.state);
        printf("Enter zip code: ");
        gets(phone[loc].addr.zip);
        loc++;
    }
  }
}

void find(void)
{
  char name[80];
  register int i;

  printf("Enter name: ");
  gets(name);
  if(!*name) return;

  for(i=0; i<100; i++)
    if(!strcmp(name, phone[i].name)) {
      printf("%s (%d) %s\n", phone[i].name,
             phone[i].areacode, phone[i].number);
      printf("%s\n%s %s %s\n", phone[i].addr.street,
             phone[i].addr.city, phone[i].addr.state,
             phone[i].addr.zip);
    }
}

void load(void)
{
  FILE *fp;

  if((fp = fopen("phone", "rb"))==NULL) {
    printf("cannot open file");
    exit(1);
  }

  loc = 0;
  while(!feof(fp)) {
```

```
      fread(&phone[loc], sizeof phone[loc], 1, fp);
      loc++;
  }
  fclose(fp);
}

void save(void)
{
  FILE *fp;
  register int i;

  if((fp = fopen("phone", "wb"))==NULL) {
    printf("cannot open file");
    exit(1);
  }

  for(i=0; i<loc; i++) {
    fwrite(&phone[i], sizeof phone[i], 1, fp);
  }
  fclose(fp);
}
```

12 SKILLS CHECK

1. Modifying a variable with **register** causes the compiler to store the variable in such a way that access to it is as fast as possible. For integer and character types, this typically means storing it in a register of the CPU.

2. Because **i** is declared as **const** the function cannot modify any object pointed to by it.

3. **a.** 1100 0100
   b. 1111 1111
   c. 0011 1011

4.
```c
#include "stdio.h"

void main(void)
{
  int i;

  printf("Enter a number: ");
  scanf("%d", &i);

  printf("doubled: %d\n", i << 1);
  printf("halved: %d\n", i >> 1);
}
```

5.
```c
a = b = c = 1;

max = a<b ? 100 : 0;

i *= 2;
```

6. The **extern** modifier is principly used to inform the compiler about global variables declared in one file when they need to be accessed by other files that compose a program. Placing **extern** in front of a variable's declaration simply tells the compiler that the variable is declared elsewhere, but it lets that file reference it.

12.1 EXERCISES

1.
```c
#define RANGE(i, min, max) ((i)<(min)) || ((i)>(max)) ? 1:0
```

2.
```c
#include "stdio.h"

#define ABS(i) (i)<0 ? -(i) : i

void main(void)
{
  printf("%d %d", ABS(-1), ABS(1));
}
```

12.2 EXERCISES

1.
```c
#include "stdio.h"

#define INT 0
#define FLOAT 1
#define PWR_TYPE INT

void main(void)
{
   int e;
#if PWR_TYPE==FLOAT
   double base, result;
#elif PWR_TYPE==INT
   int base, result;
#endif

#if PWR_TYPE==FLOAT
  printf("Enter floating point base: ");
  scanf("%lf", &base);
#elif PWR_TYPE==INT
  printf("Enter integer base: ");
  scanf("%d", &base);
#endif
  printf("Enter integer exponent (greater than 0): ");
  scanf("%d", &e);

  result = 1;
  for(; e; e--)
    result = result * base;

#if PWR_TYPE==FLOAT
  printf("Result: %lf", result);
#elif PWR_TYPE==INT
  printf("Result: %d", result);
#endif
}
```

2. No. You cannot use an expression like **!MIKE** with **#ifdef**. Here is one possible solution.

```
#define MIKE

#ifndef MIKE
  .
  .
  .
#endif
```

12.5 EXERCISES

2. The program displays **one two**.

12.6 EXERCISES

2.
```
#include "stdio.h"
#include "stdlib.h"

int comp(int *i, int *j);

void main(void)
{
  int sort[100], i, key;
  int *p;

  for(i=0; i<100; i++)
    sort[i] = rand( );

  qsort(sort, 100, sizeof(int), comp);

  for(i=0; i<100; i++)
    printf("%d\n", sort[i]);

  printf("Enter number to find: ");
  scanf("%d", &key);
  p = bsearch(&key, sort, 100, sizeof(int), comp);
  if(p) printf("Numbers is in array");
  else printf("Number not found");
}
```

```
comp(int *i, int *j)
{
   return *i - *j;
}
```

3. ```
   #include "stdio.h"

   int sum(int a, int b);
   int subtract(int a, int b);
   int mul(int a, int b);
   int div(int a, int b);
   int modulus(int a, int b);

   /* initialize the pointer array */
   int (*p[5])(int a, int b) = {
      sum, subtract, mul, div, modulus
   } ;

   void main(void)
   {
      int result;
      int i, j, op;

      printf("Enter two numbers: ");
      scanf("%d%d", &i, &j);
      printf("0: add, 1: subtract, 2: multiply, 3: divide, ");
      printf("4: modulus\n");
      do {
         printf("Enter number of operation: ");
         scanf("%d", &op);
      } while(op<0 || op>4);

      result = (*p[op])(i, j);
      printf("%d", result);
   }

   sum(int a, int b)
   {
      return a+b;
   }

   subtract(int a, int b)
```
```

```
{
  return a-b;
}

mul(int a, int b)
{
  return a*b;
}

div(int a, int b)
{
  if(b) return a/b;
  else return 0;
}

modulus(int a, int b)
{
  if(b) return a%b;
  else return 0;
}
```

12.7 EXERCISES

2.
```
#include "stdio.h"
#include "stdlib.h"

void main(void)
{
  int *p, i;

  p = malloc(10*sizeof(int));
  if(!p) {
    printf("Allocation Error");
    exit(1);
  }

  for(i=0; i<10; i++) p[i] = i+1;

  for(i=0; i<10; i++) printf("%d ", *(p+i));
```

```
    free(p);
}
```

3. The statement

```
*p = malloc(10);
```

should be

```
p = malloc(10);
```

Also, the value returned by **malloc( )** is not verified as a valid pointer.

MASTERY SKILLS CHECK

1. When you specify the file name within angle brackets, the compiler searches for the file in an implementation-defined manner. When enclosing the file name within double quotes, the compiler first tries some other implementation-defined manner to find the file. If that fails, it restarts the search as if you had enclosed the file name within angle brackets.

2.
```
#ifdef DEBUG
if(!j%2)) {
   printf("j = %d\n", j);
   j = 0;
}
#endif
```

3.
```
#if DEBUG==1
if(!j%2)) {
   printf("j = %d\n", j);
   j = 0;
}
#endif
```

4. To undefine a macro name use **#undef**.

5. _ _FILE_ _ is a predefined macro that contains the name of the source file currently being compiled.

6. The # operator makes the argument it precedes into a quoted string. The ## operator concatenates two arguments.

7.
```
#include "stdio.h"
#include "stdlib.h"
#include "string.h"

int comp(char *i, char *j);

void main(void)
{
  char str[] = "this is a test of qsort";

  qsort(str, strlen(str), 1, comp);

  printf(str);
}

comp(char *i, char *j)
{
  return *i - *j;
}
```

8.
```
#include "stdio.h"
#include "stdlib.h"

void main(void)
{
  double *p;

  p = malloc(sizeof(double));
  if(!p) {
    printf("Allocation Error");
```

```
      exit(1);
  }

  *p = 99.01;
  printf("%lf", *p);
  free(p);
}
```

INTEGRATING NEW SKILLS CHECK

1.
```
/* An electronic card catalog. */
#include "stdio.h"
#include "conio.h"
#include "string.h"
#include "stdlib.h"

#define MAX 100

int menu(void);
void display(int i);
void author_search(void), title_search(void);
void enter(void), save(void), load(void);

struct catalog {
  char name[80];  /* author name */
  char title[80];  /* title */
  char pub[80];   /* publisher */
  unsigned date; /* date of publication */
  unsigned char ed; /* edition */
} *cat[MAX];

int top = 0;  /* last location used */

void main(void)
{
  int choice;
```

```
  load( ); /* read in catalog */

  do {
    choice = menu( );
    switch(choice) {
      case 1: enter( ); /* enter books */
        break;
      case 2: author_search( ); /* search by author */
        break;
      case 3: title_search( ); /* search by title */
        break;
      case 4: save( );
    }
  } while(choice!=5);
}

/* Return a menu selection. */
menu(void)
{
  int i;

  printf("Card Catalog:\n");
  printf("  1. Enter\n");
  printf("  2. Search by Author\n");
  printf("  3. Search by Title\n");
  printf("  4. Save catalog\n");
  printf("  5. Quit\n");

  do {
    printf("Choose your selection: ");
    i = getche( )-'0';
    printf("\n");
  } while(i<1 || i>5);

  return i;
}

/* Enter books into database. */
void enter(void)
{
  int i;
  char temp[80];
```

```
    for(i=top; i<MAX; i++) {
      /* allocate memory for book info */
      cat[i] = malloc(sizeof (struct catalog));
      if(!cat[i]) {
        printf("Out of memory\n");
        return;
      }

      printf("Enter author name (ENTER to quit): ");
      gets(cat[i]->name);
      if(!*cat[i]->name) break;
      printf("Enter title: ");
      gets(cat[i]->title);
      printf("Enter publisher: ");
      gets(cat[i]->pub);
      printf("Enter date of publication: ");
      gets(temp);
      cat[i]->date = (unsigned) atoi(temp);
      printf("Enter edition: ");
      gets(temp);
      cat[i]->ed = (unsigned char) atoi(temp);
    }
    top = i;
}

/* Search by author. */
void author_search(void)
{
  char name[80];
  int i, found;

  printf("Name: ");
  gets(name);

  found = 0;
  for(i=0; i<top; i++)
    if(!strcmp(name, cat[i]->name)) {
      display(i);
      found = 1;
      printf("\n");
    }

  if(!found) printf("not found\n");
```

```
}

/* Search by title. */
void title_search(void)
{
  char title[80];
  int i, found;

  printf("Title: ");
  gets(title);

  found = 0;
  for(i=0; i<top; i++)
    if(!strcmp(title, cat[i]->title)) {
      display(i);
      found = 1;
      printf("\n");
    }
  if(!found) printf("not found\n");
}

/* Display catalog entry. */
void display(int i)
{
  printf("%s\n", cat[i]->title);
  printf("by %s\n", cat[i]->name);
  printf("Published by %s\n", cat[i]->pub);
  printf("Printed: %u, %u edition\n", cat[i]->date,
          cat[i]->ed);
}

/* Load the catalog file. */
void load(void)
{
  FILE *fp;
  int i;

  if((fp = fopen("catalog", "r"))==NULL) {
    printf("Catalog file not on disk\n");
    return;
  }
```

```
    fread(&top, sizeof top, 1, fp); /* read count */

    for(i=0; i<top; i++) {
      cat[i] = malloc(sizeof (struct catalog));
      if(!cat[i]) {
        printf("Out of memory\n");
        top = i-1;
        break;
      }
      fread(cat[i], sizeof (struct catalog), 1, fp);
    }

    fclose(fp);
  }

/* Save the catalog file. */
void save(void)
{
  FILE *fp;
  int i;

  if((fp = fopen("catalog", "w"))==NULL) {
    printf("Cannot open catalog file\n");
    exit(1);
  }

  fwrite(&top, sizeof top, 1, fp);

  for(i=0; i<top; i++)
    fwrite(cat[i], sizeof (struct catalog), 1, fp);

  fclose(fp);
}
```

2.
```
#include "stdio.h"
#include "conio.h"

#define CODE_IT(ch)   ~ch

void main(void)
{
  int ch;
```

```
    printf("Enter a character: ");
    ch = getche( );
    printf(" coded is %c", ch, CODE_IT(ch));
}
```

• Index •